Author Law A to Z

To Robert Reisman —
whose dedication
and integrity as a
professional is
an example I have
long tried to
emulate myself.
with admiration
and respect,

[signature]

From *Capital Ideas*, practical books that offer expert advice on key personal and professional aspects of life. Other titles include:

A Grammar Book For You and I . . . Oops, Me! All The Grammar You Need to Succeed in Life by C. Edward Good

UPI Stylebook & Guide to Newswriting by Bruce Cook, Harold Martin & The Editors of UPI

Use Your Fingers, Use Your Toes: Quick and Easy Step-by-Step Solutions to Your Everyday Math Problems by Beth Norcross

The Savvy Consumer: How to Avoid Scams and Rip-Offs That Cost You Time and Money by Elisabeth Leamy

Save 25% when you order any of these and other fine Capital titles from our Web site: *www.capital-books.com.*

Author Law
A to Z

A Desktop Guide to Writers' Rights and Responsibilities

Sallie Randolph, Stacy Davis, Anthony Elia, and Karen Dustman

A Capital Ideas Book

CAPITAL
BOOKS, INC.
Sterling, Virginia

Capital Books, Inc.
P.O. Box 605
Herndon, Virginia 20172-0605

ISBN 1-931868-26-3 (alk.paper)

Library of Congress Cataloging-in-Publication Data

Author law A to Z : a desktop guide to writers' rights and responsibilities / Sallie Randolph . . . [et al.].—lst ed.
    p.cm – (A Capital ideas book)
   ISBN 1-931868-26-3 (alk. paper)
   1. Authors and publishers—United States—Popular works. 2. Copyright—United States—Popular works. 3. Press law—United States—Popular works. I. Randolph, Sallie G. II. Title. III. Series.

   KF3084.Z9A938 2004
   343.7309'98—dc22

                                                                        2004006437

Printed in Canada on acid-free paper that meets the American National Standards Institute Z39-48 Standard.

First Edition

10 9 8 7 6 5 4 3 2 1

This book is dedicated to our families and to the worldwide family of writers who regularly face and conquer numerous obstacles on the road to publication. It is also dedicated by Karen Dustman, "to Claire, who taught me my ABCs and then the meaning beyond," and by Sallie Randolph, "to John McElwee Randolph, who demonstrated a remarkable ability in early infancy to rip pages off a yellow legal pad, wad them up, and throw them on the floor, thereby indicating future potential in writing or law."

Contents

Table of Cases   ix

Acknowledgments   xi

How to Use This Book   xiii

A   Abridgement *to* Authorship Credit   1

B   Back Matter *to* Bundle of Rights   67

C   Cable Act of 1984 *to* Cybersquatting   113

D   Damages *to* Due Diligence   158

E   Earn Out *to* Exhibit   179

F   Failure of Consideration *to* Future Technologies   186

G   Galley Proofs *to* Group Registration   205

H   Hardcover *to* Hyperlink   212

I   Imprint *to* ISBN   214

J   Joint Accounting *to* Juvenile Books   220

K   Kill Fee   223

L   Laws *to* Lyrics   224

M   Magazine *to* Musical Works   232

N   National Association of Science Writers *to* Notice and Takedown   238

O   Obscenity *to* Over the Transom   245

P   Packager *to* Punitive Damages   251

Q   Query   269

R   Recitals *to* Royalty-Free Sales   270

S   Sampling *to* Syndication   278

Contents

T Takedown *to* Trespass for Reporters   296

U U.S. Government Publications *to* Uruguay Round   311

V VARA *to* Volunteer Lawyers for the Arts   316

W Waiver *to* Writers Guild of America   322

X X-Rated *to* X-Ray   344

Y Young Adult Books   346

Z Zapruder Film   347

About the Authors   349

Table of Cases

A & M Records, Inc. v. Napster, Inc., 239 F.3d 1004 (9th Cir. 2001)　　144

Alfred Bell & Co. v. Catalda Fine Arts, Inc., 191 F.2d 99 (2d Cir. 1951)　　54

Alva Studios, Inc. v. Winninger, 177 F. Supp. 265 (S.D. N.Y. 1959)　　55

Amana Refrigeration, Inc. v. Consumers Union of United States, Inc., 431 F. Supp. 324 (N.D. Iowa 1977)　　188

American Geophysical Union et al. v. Texaco, Inc., 60 F.3d 913 (2d Cir. 1994)　　53

Ashcroft v. The Free Speech Coalition, 535 U.S. 234 (2002)　　246

Atari Games Corp. v. Nintendo of America Inc., 975 F.2d 832 (Fed. Cir. 1992)　　192

Atari Games Corp. v. Oman, 888 F.2d 878 (D.C. Cir. 1989)　　319

Basic Books, Inc. v. Kinko's Graphics Corp., 758 F.Supp. 1522 (S.D.N.Y. 1991)　　150

Bourne Co. v. Tower Records, Inc., 976 F.2d 99 (2d Cir. 1992)　　215

Brookfield Communications, Inc. v. West Coast Entertainment Corp., 174 F.3d 1036 (9th Cir. 1999)　　235

Campbell v. Acuff-Rose Music, Inc., 510 U.S. 569 (1994)　　252

Castle Rock Entertainment v. Carol Publishing Group, Inc., 150 F.3d 132 (2d Cir. 1998)　　291

Chavez v. Arte Publico Press, 204 F.3d 601 (5th Cir. 2000)　　289

Cohen v. Cowles Media Co., 501 U.S. 663 (1991)　　198

Community for Creative Non-Violence v. Reid, 490 U.S. 730 (U.S. 1989)　　333

Costello Publishing Co. v. Rotelle, 670 F.2d 1035 (D.C.Cir. 1981)　　109

Davis v. The Gap, Inc. 246 F.3d 152 (2d Cir. 2001)　　21

Durham Industries v. Tomy Corp., 630 F.2d 905 (2d Cir. 1980)　　54

Eldred v. Reno, 537 U.S. 186 (2003)　　196, 288

Faulkner v. National Geographic Society, 294 F.Supp.2d 523 (S.D.N.Y. Dec. 11, 2003)　　48

FCC v. Pacifica Foundation, 438 U.S. 726 (1978)　　196

Feist Publications, Inc. v. Rural Telephone Service Co., 499 U.S. 340 (1991)　　249

Food Lion, Inc. v. Capital Cities/ABC, Inc., 194 F.3d 505 (4th Cir. 1999)　　309

Greater New Orleans Broadcasting Association, Inc. v. United States, 527 U.S. 173 (U.S. 1999)　　127

Greenberg v. National Geographic Society, 244 F.3d 1267 (11th Cir. 2001) ... 47

Hard Rock Cafe Intern. (USA) Inc. v. Morton, 97 Civ. 9483 (RPP), 1999 WL 717995 (S.D.N.Y. 1999) ... 201

Harper & Row Publishers, Inc. v. Nation Enterprises, 471 U.S. 539 (1985) ... 190

In re Literary Works in Electronic Databases Copyright Litigation, MDL No. 1379 (S.D.N.Y. March 31, 2005) (preliminary settlement) ... 148, 183, 341

Joseph Burstyn, Inc. v. Wilson, 343 U.S. 495 (1952) ... 203

L. Batlin & Son, Inc. v. Snyder, 536 F.2d 486 (2d Cir. 1976) ... 54

Leggett v. United States, 535 U.S. 1011 (2002) ... 261

Miller v. California, 413 U.S. 15 (1973) ... 245

Morris v. Business Concepts, Inc., 259 F.3d 65 (2d Cir. 2001) ... 50

New York Times v. Sullivan, 376 U.S. 254 (1964) ... 228

New York Times Co. v. Tasini, 533 U.S. 483 (2001) ... 48, 149, 183, 341

Playboy Enterprises, Inc. v. Dumas, 53 F.3d 549 (2d Cir. 1995) ... 335

Princeton University Press v. Michigan Document Services, Inc., 99 F.3d 1381 (6th Cir. 1996) ... 151

Random House, Inc. v. Rosetta Books LLC, 150 F.Supp.2d 613 (S.D.N.Y. 2001), *aff'd*, 283 F.3d 490 (2d Cir. 2002) ... 181

Reno v. American Civil Liberties Union, 521 U.S. 844 (1997) ... 195

Rey v. Lafferty, 990 F.2d 1379 (1st Cir. 1993) ... 204

Ryan v. CARL Corporation, 23 F.Supp.2d 1146 (N.D. Cal. 1998) ... 178

Salinger v. Random House, Inc., 811 F.2d 90 (2d Cir.), *reh'g denied*, 818 F.2d 252 (2d Cir.), *cert. denied*, 484 U.S. 890 (1987) ... 192

Sony Corp. v. Universal Studios, Inc., 464 U.S. 417 (1984) ... 191

Storm Impact v. Software of Month Club, 13 F.Supp.2d 782 (N.D.Ill. 1998) ... 193

Suntrust Bank v. Houghton Mifflin Company, 268 F.3d 1257 (11th Cir. 2001) ... 253

Ticketmaster Corp. v. Tickets.Com, Inc., 2003 WL 21406289 (C.D.Cal. March 7, 2003) ... 163

Time, Inc. v. Bernard Geis Associates, 293 F. Supp. 130 (S.D.N.Y. 1968) ... 189, 346

Time Inc. v. Hill, 385 U.S. 374 (1967) ... 218

Trust Co. Bank v. MGM/UA Entertainment Co., 593 F. Supp. 580, *aff'd*, 772 F.2d 740 (11th Cir. 1985) ... 282

Tufenkian Import/Export Ventures, Inc. v. Einstein Moomjy, Inc., 338 F.3d 127 (2d Cir. 2003) ... 169

Turner Broadcasting System, Inc. v. FCC, 520 U.S. 180 (1997) ... 197

United States v. American Library Association, 539 U.S. 104, 123 S.Ct. 2297 (June 23, 2003) ... 247

Virtual Works, Inc. v. Volkswagen of America, Inc., 238 F.3d 264 (4th Cir. 2001) ... 157

Warner Bros. Inc. v. American Broadcasting Companies, Inc., 720 F.2d 231 (2d Cir. 1983) ... 294

Acknowledgments

The authors are grateful to their many colleagues, clients, students, writers, and friends who contributed information and insight to this work and to the outstanding professionals who helped it into print. There are so many that to list them is an invitation to inadvertently leave someone out. Nevertheless, we are grateful to them all. They have shared their wisdom generously, but any errors are the responsibility of the authors.

We are especially grateful to the following individuals, who are listed in no particular order: Laurie Harper, Noemi Arthur, Kathleen Hughes, John Randolph, Bob Weiland, Alice Ennis Glazier, Anita Bartholomew, Jonathan Landsman, Mike Rosenzweig, Terry McCormack, Tony Kloc, Nils Olsen, Gail Gross, Jennifer Basy Sander, Toni Goldfarb, Susan Lambert, Leah Ingram, Melanie Lefkowitz, Brett Harvey, Jan Vine, Dave Zeigler, Jim Morrison, Kathy Seal, Marvin Wolf, Tim Harper, Lisa Collier Cool, Sheree Bykofsky, Robyn Pharr, Lori Perkins, Gini Graham Scott, Alice Rosenthal, Carol Milano, Dan Carlinsky, Karen Chesnutt, Dodi Shultz, Tina Tessina, Susan Gordon, Florence Isaacs, Leslie Taylor, Janine Latus Musick, Marisa D'Vari, Kay Murray, Ginger Maiman, Kathryn Lance, Alexandra Cantor Owens, Tim Perrin, Barbara DeMarco Barrett, Julian Block, Joe Anthony, Rose Melisz, Fred Gebhart, Shubha Ghosh, Carol Curtis, Lisa Mueller, Beverly Maloney, Christine Johnson, Diana Gleasner, Margery Facklam, Anne Downey, Marybeth Priore, Susan Lankeneau, and Stephanie Cole.

How to Use This Book

Author Law A to Z is intended to be as informative and useful as possible to literary professionals—from authors to editors, agents to attorneys, publishers to packagers. Those who work with words confront an astonishing variety of legal puzzles and perils. We hope this guide to writers' rights and responsibilities will help authors at every stage of their careers navigate safely through the legal maze.

We've tried to make this book as useful as possible to authors and their lawyers by presenting information that can be located in a variety of ways. The resulting format is part dictionary, part almanac, and part encyclopedia. The content ranges from sophisticated legal theory to simple tips. Readers can find answers to specific questions, get help with a particular problem, gain insight into a complicated concept, or simply browse.

Information is organized into alphabetical entries supplemented by various boxes with additional important information. The basic entries cover legal issues related to the business of writing and publishing, from *Abridgement* to *Zapruder*. Some entries are succinct definitions of legal terms; others are extended essays. Entries also have cross references in **boldface** to make it easy to locate additional information.

Boxes add suggestions, opinions, examples, and advice. "Tools and Tips" sidebars have practical suggestions. Cases interpreting such key author law concepts as copyright and electronic rights are discussed in "The Courts Say" sections. In "Ask Author Law" sections, attorneys respond to specific questions. "Tales From the Trenches" include war stories from authors and attorneys. Authors, attorneys, publishing professionals, and other experts share information and advice in "Voice of Experience" interviews and essays.

Sample documents straight from the files of attorneys are included. Although they have been modified to protect the privacy of the parties, they are actual samples. Some are short and self-explanatory, while others are extensively annotated. A strong word of caution here: These documents are intended as illustrative examples—*not* as models, templates or fill-in-the-blanks forms. In the world of author law, there are no "standard" agreements and there isn't boilerplate language for every situation. This isn't to say that writers are not capable of understanding, negotiating, modifying, and drafting their own legal paperwork. But they should proceed with a clear understanding and much caution. Use of forms and templates can lead to disaster. The examples in this book should be used only as a means to understand how you can help yourself; recognize when you need a lawyer; and, most important, find the wisdom to know the difference.

Remember that no book can be a substitute for the advice of a good lawyer. But this book and others like it can—and should—help you better recognize the need to get good legal advice and help you better understand the advice you get. It can help make you a better consumer of legal services and a savvier provider of writing services. But it can't—and shouldn't be expected to—replace solid professional advice.

A

Abridgement—A condensed or shortened version of a longer work. The right to license an abridged edition of a book is a **subsidiary right** often granted in a publishing contract. *Readers Digest,* for example, is a major publisher of abridged articles in its monthly magazine and also publishes a popular line of condensed books. Textbooks and other educational publications are also frequent users of abridged works. Under U.S. copyright law, abridgments are considered to be **derivative works**, which may be separately copyrighted. An abridgement or other derivative work, however, may only be created with the consent of the original copyright holder.

Academic Authors and Publishers—Publishers of textbooks and scholarly journals often pay less and offer poorer terms than general publishers do. That's probably because their authors can be more concerned about recognition of their scholarship than about the rights of writers and favorable contract terms. Although **university presses** occasionally publish trade-style books, they tend to pay less and offer less favorable contract terms than many trade publishers. Many academic writers are victims of a "publish or perish" policy of colleges and universities. Because academic writers sometimes can be less vigilant about their rights, the contracts of university presses and textbook publishers tend to be less adventurous.

Some publishers of peer-reviewed academic journals find their traditional role as printers and distributors of small-circulation (and therefore expensive) publications growing obsolete in the age of the Internet and desktop publishing. A few enterprising editors of such publications are managing to keep standards high and subscription prices low by publishing on the World Wide Web.

Tales from the Trenches: Academic Author Stands Up to Publishing Giant

Dr. Michael Rosenzweig, a professor at the University of Arizona, was the founder and the longtime editor of a prestigious, peer-reviewed scientific journal, *Evolutionary Ecology*. The journal was originally published by a distinguished British firm, Chapman and Hall, under a typical academic publishing arrangement: the publisher provided a modest annual stipend to cover journal expenses and, in return, arranged for the printing and distribution of the printed publication to subscribers and libraries.

The arrangement with Chapman and Hall was mostly typical, but Mike Rosenzweig had negotiated some informal concessions. He convinced Chapman and Hall to keep subscription prices as low as possible in order to facilitate distribution as broadly as possible. He also convinced the firm to publish the journal with a distinctive pink cover that would be easy to locate on library shelves.

Things went well until the takeover of Chapman and Hall by International Thomson and its subsequent acquisition by international publishing giant Wolters Kluwer. According to Mike, such commercial publishers "have so emphasized the maximization of profit that they have restricted the flow of knowledge. In so doing, they have exiled themselves from the academic enterprise. If they actually produced that knowledge, maybe we could forgive them. But library clients actually produce it, and taxpayers pay for almost all of it."

Acting one after the other, Thomson and Kluwer doubled library subscription prices to more than $800 per year, and Kluwer planned

2

to eliminate low-priced individual subscriptions altogether. So Mike Rosenzweig decided to revolt. "I had had enough. My editors had had enough," he said. "We pleaded: Sell us to a university press. Please sell us. But Kluwer refused. So, guided through the uncharted desert by our fiery attorney—a pillar of the community—we girded our loins, put sandals on our feet, took up our staffs and set out for the Sea of Red Ink."

He and his entire editorial board resigned. After researching copyright law, which says that copyright ownership is vested with the author at the moment a work is fixed in a tangible medium of expression, Mike returned all article manuscripts to their authors instead of forwarding them to Kluwer. Kluwer would have asked all authors to assign copyright ownership to it. The authors hadn't yet signed any contracts and Mike felt he had an ethical duty to return their work to the owners after the change in ownership and editors.

Mike and his wife, Carole, then founded a new journal, *Evolutionary Ecology Research,* which they publish from their home office. All the other former members of the *Evolutionary Ecology* editorial board joined in. "At first we planned to be print only," Mike says. "Then a number of things happened to change my mind. For only a little extra, our typesetter could give us PDF files for an Internet version. The state of Arizona's tax office looked favorably on us if we had an Internet service, allowing us to reduce the journal's price by another 5 percent. And librarians were using the Internet to help battle costs; some would be happiest if they could subscribe to an Internet version and forgo the printed copies entirely. So, we took the plunge."

Once the new journal was in the works, Mike invited authors to submit their articles. This brought an immediate response from Kluwer, whose attorneys tried to claim that the manuscripts returned to their authors had been the property of their journal and demanded that they be turned over. "I have advised Kluwer that, if he [Dr. Rosenzweig] does not take steps correct this situation, Kluwer will have no way of protecting itself against unfair competition except by suing," wrote a Kluwer lawyer.

Mike Rosenzweig chose to stand firm. He enlisted the support of the Scholarly Publishing and Academic Resources Coalition (SPARC), an organization formed to encourage scientific societies and rebels like

Rosenzweig to create journals that maintain scientific standards of excellence yet compete with the high-priced commercial publications. He lined up academic librarians, lawyers, and journalists to support his venture. His editors and authors stood with him and his new journal attracted international attention, even becoming the subject of the lead article in the *New York Times* Science Section titled, "Soaring Prices Spur a Revolt in Scientific Publishing."

The result: Kluwer backed down and the new journal is flourishing. Visit its Web site at www.evolutionary-ecology.com. Subscriptions are available at reasonable rates.

Tools and Tips: Tips for Academic Authors

Look in your institution's employment or faculty handbook for its copyright policy.

Your institution's handbook will likely include statements about copyright ownership, assignment, or other matters relating to intellectual property created by faculty and staff. Many universities have adopted policies to formalize the extent to which they will claim the ownership of the copyrighted works. There is some question about the enforceability of blanket provisions that attempt to obtain all copyrighted subject matter produced by employees, but an author should nevertheless be aware of the existence of such sweeping provisions.

The vast majority of works produced at universities by academics are likely to belong to the authors themselves because they not produced within the scope of the employment. Unfortunately, there is no simple way to tell if a work is made within the scope of employment since the legal test applied in these situations requires consideration of the facts surrounding the creation of the work on a case-by-case basis. The main factor in analyzing if the work was created within the scope of employment is whether the institution had the right to control the manner and means of the work's production. Other factors include (1) the work was of the type the employee was hired to perform, (2) the creation of the work occurred substantially within the time and space limits of the employee's job, and (3) the employee was actuated, at least in part, by a purpose of serving the employer's purposes. To illustrate the subtlety of the application of the **work-made-for-hire** doctrine, a professor who elects to write down her lecture notes probably owns the copyright in the notes because note making is not within the scope of the professor's employment, while teaching is.

Don't infringe on others' copyrights.
There is a common myth that educational use of copyrighted materials is a fair use for which no permission is needed. This myth oversimplifies and misstates a complex legal doctrine. Just because a use is for academic purposes does not mean it is a "fair use." Course packets, electronic reserves, and many other classroom uses are probably not "fair uses" of others' copyrighted materials, and require licenses.

Protect your work by registering your copyrights.
Timely copyright registration is critical to fully protecting your work from infringement. The process is easy and inexpensive. In fact, your institution may even be able to offer you some assistance with registering your copyrights. You can't rely on the journal itself for copyright registration, since the journal's copyright only extends to the publication as a whole, not to the individual articles within it.

There is a second good reason to routinely register your unpublished copyright manuscripts: if you are asked to give up your copyright you can reply that the copyright has already been registered and only an exclusive license is available.

Consider joining a rights collective such as the Authors Registry.
If you own the reprint rights to your writings, you may want to consider joining the **Authors Registry** and signing up with the **Copyright Clearance Center (CCC)**. The Authors Registry was founded by a coalition of author groups and modeled on the music licensing agency **ASCAP**. You can get more information from www.authors registry.org. The CCC administers rights and collects royalties on behalf of publishers and authors. The benefit to academic authors is that making works easier to license makes them less likely to be infringed. Individuals as well as publishers can join the CCC. For more information, check out www.authorsregistry.org and www .copyright.com.

Do not give up your copyrights or give overly broad permissions to journals.
Some publications seek overly broad rights. As an academic author you should take care to read the contract and look for ways that the work will be edited and used in the future. Be especially wary of granting electronic rights and such subsidiary rights as reprint and anthology rights.

Establish clear rules for students or others who may be assisting you with research or writing.
If an assistant is contributing copyrightable subject matter to a project by actually composing portions of the work, there should be clear rules about who will own the copyright and whether there will be joint authorship. It is important to keep in mind that joint authorship for copyright ownership purposes is different from authorship credit. "Joint authors" is a legal **term of art** that refers to who owns the copyright. There may be one or more owners (i.e., joint owners) of a work. Those credited with authorship, however, needn't be actual owners of the work. For example, a research assistant can be credited as being an "author" in the byline in a journal, despite the fact that she does not have an ownership interest in the copyright. There should also be clear rules about what uses students and assistants may make of notes and research done in aid of a project.

Acceptable Manuscript—What constitutes an acceptable manuscript can be a major legal concern for authors. Many publishing contracts give the publisher complete control over this question. By giving the publisher the right to reject a manuscript and cancel the contract for reasons unrelated to the quality of the work, the author is effectively giving the publisher an excuse to unilaterally and arbitrarily break the contract.

Tools and Tips: Negotiating an Acceptable Manuscript Clause

An often overlooked and potentially troublesome clause in a book publishing contract is the "acceptable manuscript" clause, which, unfortunately, can result in an "easy out" clause for the publisher. Often the **boilerplate** will give the publisher the right to terminate the contract if the manuscript is not acceptable in form and content. Sadly, such contract language has sometimes permitted the publisher to abandon a book and recover the advance by arbitrarily deeming the manuscript unacceptable. This can happen to a book "orphaned" when an editor leaves and the new editor is not as enthusiastic about the project, or when a competing book appears and the publisher decides to bail out. Here are some tips for authors to protect themselves from being the victim of such arbitrary and unfair decisions.

- Ask for objective standards to determine whether a manuscript is acceptable. For example: "The manuscript shall be deemed acceptable if it conforms in content and style to the proposal."
- Ask for a provision requiring the publisher to provide a written list of reasons for finding the manuscript unacceptable and permitting a reasonable time for the writer to revise and make the manuscript acceptable.
- Ask for a provision that deems acceptance automatic after a certain amount of time has gone by since submission of the complete manuscript to the publisher without a response (thirty to sixty days is reasonable).
- At the very least, ask that the determination of acceptability is the result of the publisher's *"reasonable"* judgment. There are many times when insertion of the word "reasonable" can improve the author's bargaining ability.

Reminder: Contract language can vary widely, so if you have further questions about "acceptable manuscript" issues it's wise to consult an attorney.

Tales from the Trenches: Authors Guild Fights Massive Contract Cancellation

In 1997 HarperCollins was losing money. Publishing pundits blamed everything from huge advances paid to celebrity authors to the influence of mega bookstores to the industry's crippling return policy.

HarperCollins decided to cut some losses and revamp its marketing strategy by canceling outstanding contracts for 107 books in the pipeline.

In axing the books, HarperCollins was able to take advantage of such contract terms as acceptable manuscript clauses and missed delivery deadlines. Some of the affected authors were asked to return their advances. Some were permitted to keep payments to date while forgoing future ones. Others were told they would have to return their advances if they sold their book to another publisher.

When the Authors Guild got wind of the massive cancellations, it went into action, launching a major publicity blitz. Its president at the time, Scott Turow, blasted the tactics being employed against the writers. "It goes without saying that HarperCollins is not the most favored publisher in the eyes of the Authors Guild," he said in a newsletter article for members. "Cancelling contracts wholesale does not speak well for them. I guess that's 107 lives thrown into chaos at best, and misery at worst. I would think twice, three times, and four times and more, before I would wander into the hands of a publisher who was so cavalier."

The guild also sent out more than seven thousand five hundred postcards to members. The postcards warned HarperCollins authors to seek legal advice before signing any waivers in connection with the canceled contracts, accusing HarperCollins of tying strings to the conditions under which writers could keep their advances.

In the face of the public relations black eye inflicted by the Authors Guild, HarperCollins backed down, agreeing to abandon its plans to require authors to pay back any advances. Some authors were even able to negotiate additional payments that had been due.

"I think they realized the importance of good relations with agents and authors and that there were substantial litigation risks," Paul Aiken, an attorney and executive director of the Authors Guild said in the member newsletter. "They had to try to do the best they could to clean things up."

Acceptance—In the field of contracts, "offer" and "acceptance" are two traditional elements of a binding legal contract. *See* **contract**. In the narrower publishing sense, "acceptance" refers to a publisher's approval of a book or magazine manuscript. Acceptance by the publisher is often a trigger point for a scheduled payment.

Accountant—Accountants provide tax and financial advice, perform tax preparation, bookkeeping, and financial tracking for their clients. A certified public accountant (CPA) has met stringent educational standards, has relevant accounting experience, passed a demanding test, and is permitted to represent taxpayers before the Internal Revenue Service. An accounting professional designated as an enrolled agent is also permitted to represent taxpayers before the IRS.

The Voice of Experience: A Certified Public Accountant Does More Than Taxes

Anthony Kloc, CPA
Buffalo, New York

Tony Kloc is a principal with the accounting firm Kloc and Company, LLC, and a longtime certified public accountant.

Q: Why would a writer want to hire a certified public accountant?
A: CPAs can do much more than just prepare tax returns; a CPA can also guide writers on how to set up their books, and advise them what records they should keep and for how long. A CPA can explain which expenses are deductible. And if the writer develops a profitable writing career, the CPA can help them with financial planning. One of the other benefits is that a good CPA will have a network of other people who can help and guide you. So if you decide to incorporate, or if you need estate planning or investment advice, your CPA can often point you to lawyers or other professionals who can help you.

Q: Where do writers typically make mistakes?
A: Many self-employed professionals, not just writers, don't realize they have to pay self-employment tax in addition to income tax. And sometimes writers report their royalty income incorrectly on Schedule

E, as if it were an oil or gas royalty. If a writer is self-employed, he needs to report royalty income on Schedule C, and his net Schedule C income is subject to self-employment tax. That's the other big mistake that writers can make: failing to keep good track of expenses, because you get to deduct them before figuring self-employment tax. So if you make trips to the library that are business related, keep track of your mileage. Similarly, keep receipts for any supplies that you buy, like pencils and toner for your laser printer. If it's used specifically for writing, it's deductible.

Q: How do CPAs differ from other tax professionals?
A: CPAs have to take college training plus two years of auditing experience in the field, and then have to pass an exam to be licensed. If you're a member of the American Institute of CPAs, you also have to have forty hours of continuing education every year. Bookkeepers, by contrast, don't have to be licensed. An enrolled agent (EA) also has to pass a very tough exam to be able to represent you before the IRS, but doesn't have to be a CPA. CPAs can also represent you before the IRS.

Q: And what about writers who would like to do their own taxes?
A: I know sometimes writers don't want to pay a CPA for professional advice, but it's important to remember you're a writer, not a tax accountant. If you're in business to make money, you want to take advantage of every legal deduction. The tax laws change all the time, in both large and small ways, and those are things that people outside the accounting profession are not likely to keep up with. Writers on their own also may not do proper tax and financial planning.

Q: What should a writer look for in choosing a CPA?
A: It's important to make sure they handle the type of work you're doing; not necessarily just writers, but do they prepare returns and offer advice for other self-employed individuals or are they doing strictly big companies or personal returns? Chances are you don't need a large accounting firm; a local CPA is usually the one who would deal with the self-employed client. Look for someone you're very comfortable with and feel you can get along with. And most important of all, once you establish a relationship with a CPA, never be afraid to ask questions.

Accounting, Right to—A party entitled to receive payments based on sales figures, receipts, or royalties may have an implied right to audit the books in order to be sure that proper payments are being sent. Many publishing contracts have an audit clause that recognizes this right and sets forth conditions under which an audit may be conducted. The lack of a formal audit clause, however, doesn't mean there's no right to monitor the accuracy of payments, although the right can be difficult to enforce in some jurisdictions. It's always best to spell out a right of accounting in any publishing contract. An express right is better than an implied right any day.

State and federal statutes may also create a right to an accounting for joint owners of property, including intellectual property such as copyrights. Joint copyright owners, for example, are each entitled by law to enter into nonexclusive license agreements, but they have a concurrent obligation to share information (through an accounting) and any license income they receive with the other owners.

The Voice of Experience: Royalty Review Service Can Help Authors Find Publisher Mistakes

Gail Gross, royalty auditor
New York

Not sure if your publisher's royalty statement accurately reflects what it owes you? A royalty review firm can help. We asked Gail R. Gross, vice president of R & M Royalty Review, LLC, to explain what her company does and how it does it.

Q: How does your royalty review service work?
A: The royalty review process begins with an examination of the pertinent documents (contracts, other agreements, relative correspondence, and the most recent three years' royalty statements). The decision to proceed further, reached jointly by the author and/or agent,

Author Law A to Z

and R & M Royalty Review (R&MRR), is accompanied by a contingent fee agreement between the parties. There is no advance cost, and the fee is determined solely as one-third of the recovery from the publisher. If there is no recovery, there is no fee; the author's only cost would then be the out-of-pocket costs (travel, etc.) in connection with the royalty review. Limits on costs are set in the contract between the parties.

The preliminary review of documents and royalty statements is conducted in total confidence, since there is no need to notify the publisher. Only after an agreement between the author and R&MRR has been signed is the publisher notified by the author that R&MRR has been retained. All negotiations concerning the review are conducted between R&MRR and the publisher, but the author and agent are kept informed of status by periodic reports. Any offers of settlements are reviewed with the author and agent before final action is taken.

Q: Are there many professionals who provide this service for writers?
A: As far as we know, we are the only full-time practitioners of the art of royalty review in publishing.

Q: What kinds of mistakes do you see publishers make most frequently in calculating or paying royalties?
A: There is no consistency in the types of mistakes that occur within a publishing house or even across publishers. Basically, royalty reporting systems were designed to accommodate the boilerplate language in publishers' contracts. Today, authors and agents are generally more sophisticated and are negotiating better royalty terms, some of which the computer systems are not equipped to handle.

In addition, with the escalating number of mergers and acquisitions in the publishing industry, many contract provisions in the acquired contracts are incompatible with the acquirer's royalty reporting systems, and cause some sales information and royalty calculations to fall through the cracks.

Q: What "warning signals" should authors look for that might alert them to potential problems?
A: Here are some caveats we have developed:

- All that is printed is not sold.
- Never assume that there is continuity from one statement to the next.
- Whenever something new or different appears on your statement, reread your contract.
- Never ignore reserve for returns and always track it from statement to statement. If the number is unchanged, challenge the publisher to reduce it or refund it.
- On all subrights deals (and particularly if you've given the publisher world rights), you should ask for copies of and track all contracts, payments, and reports.

Q: If you discover a discrepancy, what should writers expect? Will most publishers willingly fork over any difference, or will you have to threaten to sue to get paid?

A: Once a claim has been filed with the publisher, it is reviewed by its royalty department. After its review, the publisher can submit additional supporting documentation for any item it believes is incorrectly included in our claim. If the review results in agreement with us, the publisher will generally pay the claimed amount. All of our claims include a present value calculation (interest) for monies due from the time the author should have received the funds to the time the funds are actually paid. Most of the time the publisher will agree to pay the interest.

Although the publisher does not "willingly fork over" additional moneys due, it usually does accept the fact that authors have the right to know that they are receiving the correct royalties, that mistakes occur, and that there will be times when additional payments have to paid to the author. We have found the process to be one of mutual respect with no negative ramifications to the author or agent.

Q: Any other tips for writers—perhaps terms they should be sure to include in their publishing contract?

A: Definitely make sure that the contract contains an audit clause, but does not contain a very short (less than three years) "lookback clause" limiting the time in which a request for review must be made or how far back the review period can go. In addition, a sentence should be added to the clause stating that if errors of 5 percent or greater of the total paid by the publisher for the period in review are found, then the publisher is responsible for payment of the audit (review).

R&M Royalty Review, LLC, 845 Third Ave., Suite 1300, New York, NY 10022-6601; Phone: 212-754-1984, Fax: 212-754-3352.

Acknowledgements—Many authors use an acknowledgments section of a book to thank those who helped along the way. This can be a good spot to provide recognition for sources, assistants, researchers, institutions, and individuals whose efforts made a contribution to the author's achievement. Some authors use acknowledgments to lend credibility to their work by providing an exhaustive list of sources (some of them reluctant).

Acquisitions—The acquisitions process includes identifying manuscripts for publication and obtaining the necessary rights. Book publishers typically have at least one (and sometimes several) acquisitions editor charged with finding manuscripts and negotiating contract terms with prospective authors or their agents.

The Voice of Experience: An Editor's Perspective on Negotiating a Book Deal

Jennifer Basy Sander, acquisitions editor
New York

Jennifer Basy Sander has worn many hats over the course of twenty years in the publishing business. In addition to her current position as a senior editor at a major publishing house, she's been a bookseller, publicist, and marketer, as well as author of more than twenty books.

Q: How often do authors handle their own negotiations?
A: From the standpoint of my publisher, we work a lot with authors who don't have agents, so maybe 50 percent.

Q: *Is that a high percentage?*
A: It is a high percentage. We're frequently coming up with the ideas ourselves and finding authors. We also always read our slush pile and have acquired many of our books that way. So authors we acquire in these ways probably don't have agents.

Q: *What is the process of a typical negotiation with an author from start to finish?*
A: It can sometimes be very rapid—or not so rapid. We discuss the project in-house and come up with a dollar figure when we decide we want a book. Then I make the call to the author. We'll discuss the project—how excited we are about the book. I don't start talking about the money but the book itself and the content. I don't flatter someone unjustly, but I talk about the book. Then we talk about the author's schedule, when she could write it. I may ask about a specific date. There are cases when there is a time element with a book. If everything is good, then I say, "We would like to make an offer for X amount. Generally, the advance is paid half on signing and half on acceptance of the manuscript." Then I stop talking. I allow a silence so the negotiating process can begin. The author may make some requests at that point. Then I fill out a form with whatever we decide on and send that down to the contract department, which sends out a contract.

Q: *How should an author request changes to a contract once she gets it?*
A: At the time she gets it, she should call me up and we would talk about it. If it's a fairly minor thing, I can get the author to make the change by hand, a line through this or that paragraph, for example.

Q: *How minor is minor?*
A: Usually omissions are done this way. Like scratching out the "next work" clause. If it's a clean and easy amendment, we can do that over the phone. If there are additions, they should be in writing and then they go to the contract department.

Q: *When would you use a staff attorney in the negotiation?*
A: If the amendment was complicated then it would have to go to the staff attorney.

Q: *What should an author not do in a negotiation?*

A: Here of course is why it's great to have an agent. If things get contentious, the relationship between author and editor can change. I don't want to tell an author to just roll over, because that's not fair, because everyone has a right to fair deal. But I would remind an author that if the negotiations become too contentious then that could set a negative tone for the relationship. It can change the way an editor feels about you.

But I would also say never agree too quickly. There's money to be made in a long pause. Someone will often try to fill that space with something more.

I would also say that an author should be realistic in what she's asking for in terms of money. If it's possible, an author should canvass their author friends or agents. You need to know what the market can bear. Don't ask for two or three times more than you are offered. It will make you seem like you don't know what you're talking about and don't understand the tenor of the book business.

Q: Could you name one thing that authors should ask for in a negotiation but don't?

A: You can always get more free copies of a book. And I would say always try to get rid of a next book (option) clause. The theory with the next book clause is that if you write a book and become a big star, the publisher wants your next book. But my attitude is that by the end of the publishing process, if everyone likes each other then they will want to work together again. If on the other hand, no one is speaking by the end of the process, which sometimes happens, the publisher is not going to want to do another project.

But always ask for more money even it's just a little more. An editor will usually know what she is authorized to pay for a book—say she is authorized to go up to $25,000; she'll offer $22,000. Ask if that's the best she can do. But don't ask for double or you'll look naive.

Acts of God—An exculpatory provision triggered by unanticipated events or conditions outside the parties' control. Due dates for delivery of a completed manuscript or for publication of a work may be extended or excused, for example, if performance according to the original contract terms is hampered by a fire, flood, or another act of God. Though not considered acts of God, other special circumstances typically cited in such a clause include strikes or other labor slowdowns, shortages of labor or materials, mechanical difficulties, and governmental restrictions.

Actual Damages—Actual damages is money awarded by a judge or jury to make up for financial injury done to the plaintiff in a lawsuit. Unlike **punitive** or **statutory damages,** actual damages must be proven to the court before they can be awarded. For example, actual damages in a copyright infringement suit might be awarded for lost profits, demonstrable harm to the economic value of the copyright, or profits of the infringer. Punitive damages are not available in copyright infringements. Statutory damages, so called because they are specifically provided by a statute, are sometimes available in copyright infringement cases, but only if the copyright has been registered prior to infringement or within three months of first publication. *See also* **damages.**

Adaptations—An adaptation is a new work that is based on another work or a work whose format is modified to suit a new purpose. For example, a movie script based on a novel would be an adaptation. Other examples of adaptations include a simplified children's book based on a longer novel, a modern retelling of an ancient folk tale, or a book based on a play. Under **copyright** law, most adaptations are considered **derivative works**, which are protectable by an independent copyright. Of course, creation of a derivative work requires the consent of the owner of the copyright of the work upon which the derivative work is based.

Administrative Law—A vast body of law that flies under the radar screens of most nonlawyers and many lawyers, administrative law is the rules and procedures promulgated by regulatory agencies and administrative bodies that have been given explicit rule-making authority by local, state, and federal legislatures. Many times administrative regulations have the same legal force as a law and the results of many administrative hearings have the force of judicial rulings. The Securities and Exchange Commission, Environmental Protection Agency, Federal Communications Commission, Federal Trade Commission, and Food and Drug Administration are just a few examples of federal agencies whose rules and operating regulations have statutory force.

Advance—An up-front payment by the publisher to the author of a book that is intended to be offset by future royalty payments is called an advance against **royalties**. Authors typically don't receive additional royalties until the book has "earned out" or the advance has been earned back by book sales. Even though an advance is not in addition to the base royalty rate, there are good reasons for writers to secure as large an advance as possible. The advance is generally not required to be paid back, even if the book doesn't earn out, making the advance a guaranteed minimum. A large advance increases the publisher's stake in the book and generates more extensive promotion and a vigorous sales effort. And an advance may be the writer's sole source of support while finishing a book.

That said, authors shouldn't necessarily be discouraged by a small advance or overly impressed with a large one. The advance is merely one term in a complex publishing contract and should be considered in context. How and when an advance is paid, as well as the circumstances under which it must be returned, should be clearly spelled out in the contract. Advances are typically paid in two or more installments keyed to specific events such as signing of a publishing contract, delivery of a complete manuscript, acceptance of the manuscript, or upon publication.

Obviously the more advantageous terms are ones that provide for payment sooner rather than later and do not depend on someone's subjective opinion. For example, an advance payable on acceptance or on publication could mean no advance at all if the manuscript is not deemed acceptable or the book isn't published, even if the reasons had nothing to do with the quality of the author's work.

As important as a good advance can be other payment terms shouldn't be overlooked by writers. The royalty rate and the basis upon which that rate is computed are also crucial factors. Many nonmonetary terms are as important as well.

Tools and Tips: Negotiating an Advance

Getting the best advance means more than negotiating a healthy total amount. Even when the publisher refuses to increase the size of the advance, there are many ways to improve your contract position. Here are some tips for negotiating the terms of an advance:

- Schedule of payments—Try to get more of the advance paid up front, on signing of the contract, and the rest on the delivery of the manuscript. Do your best to avoid or reduce provisions for payments on publication, which might mean never. Propose alternatives to the contract schedule that gets the money in your hands sooner rather than later. If the proffered contract, for example, calls for you to receive half of the advance on acceptance and half on publication, suggest that you receive half on signing the contract and half on acceptance. If the publisher won't go for that you might try for thirds—a third on signing, a third on acceptance, and a third on publication. Be creative in proposing alternatives to the payment percentages and timing. There's usually room to negotiate.
- Return of the advance—Try to establish narrowly defined conditions under which you must return any portion of the advance to the publisher. An author should really only have to return an ad-

vance for complete failure to deliver a manuscript or in the rare event that the manuscript falls substantially below the promises of the proposal or fails to conform to reasonable industry standards. An author shouldn't have to return an advance simply because the publisher fails to get the book out or changes its mind.

- Concessions you can request if you must accept a small advance:

  1. Ask for a better royalty rate. You can explain that you have confidence the book will sell well, so you are willing to defer compensation until the book is making money for both publisher and author.
  2. Ask for a better basis on which the royalty rate will be applied. If the publisher has offered a royalty rate based on "net proceeds," for example, ask that it be based on the list, or cover, price of the book instead. If you already have negotiated a list rate, ask that shipping not be charged against your royalties.
  3. Ask for a royalty escalator clause. Even if the publisher won't budge on the initial rate or the basis, it may agree to an increase after sales have reached a certain level. If your contract already has an escalator clause, ask that the trigger number of books sold be reduced so that the escalator kicks in sooner.
  4. Ask for additional free author copies and/or a higher author discount.

- Reasons to increase the amount—try these arguments to support your request for a larger advance:

  1. I expect to incur research expenses.
  2. I intend to invest some of the advance into a personal publicity campaign to enhance sales.
  3. My track record and credentials justify a larger advance.
  4. I need the money to pay my living expenses while finishing the manuscript.

Adversary Proceeding—Technically, an adversary proceeding is any court action involving opposing parties. In federal bankruptcy court, it is a term of art for any bankruptcy-related lawsuit.

Advertising (art and copy)—Freelance writers and artists are often hired to produce copy and visual art for advertisements. Sometimes the advertising agency or business commissioning such work asks the writer to sign over all rights, but often there is no written assignment of copyright. Advertisers frequently assume, falsely, that they own the copyright to ads for their products, but this is rarely true. Under copyright law, unless there has been a written assignment of copyright, such text and visual art is usually the property of the artist or writer. Agencies and others who commission such work should make sure that they control the necessary rights. Freelancers would be wise to clarify what rights are being acquired by the commissioning party. If the freelancer agrees that the work should belong to the advertiser or ad agency, it would be a professional courtesy to point that out. If the freelancer wants to be paid residuals for additional uses of the work, that should be pointed out early in the relationship as well.

The Courts Say: Unauthorized Use of Copyrighted Material Costs Advertiser Big Bucks

Davis v. The Gap, Inc., 246 F.3d 152 (2d Cir. 2001)

A copyright holder was recently held to be entitled to damages for the infringing use of the work—despite being unable to prove that the infringement caused him lost sales, lost opportunities to license, or in any way diminished the value of his copyright. The copyrighted subject matter was a pair of chic eyeglasses. The infringer, an advertiser, featured a model wearing the glasses in its widely distributed advertisements. Even though the designer was unable to show evidence of actual damages, the court found that the use of the eyeglasses in the photo had a discernable fair market value and the designer was therefore entitled to recover that amount.

Advertorial—This is the name given to copy written in an editorial style but placed in a magazine or newspaper as a paid advertisement. Many special sections in magazines or newspapers are advertorials. Advertorials should be identified as advertising, and reputable publishers are careful to keep their editoral and advertising sections conceptually separate and clearly distinguishable. Some newspapers and magazines, for example, avoid conflicts of interest by requiring advertorials to be entirely prepared by the advertiser or advertising staff and prohibit editorial staffers from writing such material. Publications that use freelance writers sometimes unfairly blacklist those who write advertorial material or do public relations writing.

Tales from the Trenches: Crossing the Line

Advertising-related writing can raise ethical issues for writers. Long-time medical writer Toni Goldfarb discusses the especially difficult issues that arise in writing for medical communications companies, and where she's chosen to draw the line:

> Medical communications agencies work in several ways. A pharmaceutical company might tell an agency, "We need a scientifically oriented training manual for our salespeople to let them know the pharmacology of this particular antibiotic. It will help our sales staff to be more knowledgeable when they talk with a physician or hospital pharmacist." The agency says fine, and they hire an in-house writer or a freelancer to write that training manual. I don't see any ethical dilemmas there.
>
> But now the company says, "We want something that our sales rep can hand to doctors to summarize the recent findings on a particular drug. And just so you know, we won't be mentioning any competitors, even though there is one that has a slight advantage." I say, "I don't do that." Why not? Because now you're trying to sell a doctor on a particular drug; I never do anything involved with sales or advertising. Ethically, it's a problem for me because there might be other drugs that are more effective or cheaper, and I know the material the company is putting out

---

> won't cover that. They might say, "It's the same as writing an ad that will appear in a medical journal." And I'd tell them I don't write those either.
>
> Writers need to pay attention to that tiny voice that tells them what's okay and what's over the line, because often there are no clear-cut rules. What made me draw that line? I view myself as a consumer writer, and I never want anyone who sees my byline to feel I am in any way beholden to any drug company or pushing any particular product.

In addition to the ethical issues, freelancers engaged in straight reporting (nonadvertising work) also need to question their sources of information closely, veteran writers emphasize. Articles and other sources that appear to be disinterested may, in fact, represent placements by public relations firms.

Authors should always remain alert to ethical issues and should be especially cautious when mixing public relations and corporate work with freelance journalism.

Advice of Counsel—This is a recommendation from one's own attorney, recommending that a client act or refrain from acting in a certain manner. Typical advice of counsel may include not answering questions from the media about a pending case or dispute. Sometimes having acted on the advice of counsel constitutes a defense or a mitigating factor when an activity is later held to have been illegal. For example, a taxpayer who has filed an erroneous return based on advice of counsel might be held responsible for payment of the taxes involved but excused from penalties and interest. In most cases, however, an individual is ultimately responsible for his or her own actions, regardless of reliance on various advisers. It's important to pick professional advisers such as lawyers, agents, and accountants carefully and to provide these advisers with accurate and complete information.

Affiliated Companies—Companies are affiliated when they are owned by the same company or own one another. A publishing agreement may give affiliated companies special rights. This should be avoided because of the risk that the deal struck between the affiliated companies would not be "an arm's length transaction" or the best possible deal.

Affirmative Defense—This is the denial of the **plaintiff**'s legal right to make a claim rather than a denial of the truth of the claim itself. **Fair use,** for example, is an affirmative defense to a claim of **copyright infringement**. In making this affirmative defense the defendant doesn't deny copying of the plaintiff's work, but claims that the copying was a fair use permitted by law.

Agents—The job of a literary agent is to approach publishers on the behalf of an author in an effort to sell an author's work, then to negotiate contract terms on behalf of the author. An agent's relationship to a client is fiduciary and includes legal responsibility to account for funds collected on the client's behalf. An agent may also provide editorial advice, advise the author about possible strategies for publication and marketing, negotiate contracts, review royalty statements, and monitor licenses of an author's work. The majority of works that agents represent are book length and agents rarely sell magazine articles for clients.

Although an unpublished author who wishes to be published should think seriously about getting an agent, the conventional wisdom emphasizing the need for an agent may be changing. Some trade authors, particularly already published authors, may be successful by choosing not to be represented and by representing and selling their works to editors and publishers with whom they already have relationships.

The first step toward becoming represented by an agent is to find one to approach. Many agents specialize and represent mainly one type or style of work. Others are generalists. It's usually easier to persuade an agent to represent you if your work is a good fit with other work the agent has placed. Literary agents are listed in many sources, including *Literary Market Place*, a directory of the publishing industry, which is available at most libraries, or the *Writer's Digest Guide to Literary Agents*, a reference that includes agents' specific submission guidelines and marketing areas. A good place to look for established agents is the **Association of Authors' Representatives** (AAR) membership list on the group's Web site at www.aar-online.org. Another resource for finding agents is Jeff Herman's *Guide to Book Editors, Publishers, and Literary Agents 2005*, by Jeff Herman (Writer, Inc., 2004). You should also ask for recommendations from editors, writing instructors, or fellow writers.

The Voice of Experience: How I Found an Agent

The magical writer-agent connection, like a marriage, can materialize by many routes. For some writers, it happens the conventional way: by sending an introductory letter and/or proposal. For others, it's pure serendipity—like bumping into the right person in the supermarket. Here, five writers tell how they found their current literary agent.

Leah Ingram
Author of eight books including Buying and Selling Your Way to a Fabulous Wedding with EBay *(Muska & Lipman, 2004)*

I've had two agents in my professional life. The first, who no longer represents me, came through a recommendation from a writer friend. Getting a personal recommendation from someone you know and then mentioning that recommendation in a cover letter or introductory e-mail or phone call is a great way to get an agent to notice you and seriously consider you, as long as the book you want to write is up his or her alley. But keep in mind who is doing the recommending. If it's a person you don't respect professionally, then his or her choice in an agent may not be up to your standards, which was my case with this first agent I gladly left two years ago.

I found my second agent through my membership in American Society of Journalists and Authors and from polling my book editor at my publishing house. I knew that I wanted to write a book on gift giving and I thought this topic was perfect for a *Complete Idiots* or *Dummies* guide. So I searched the ASJA directory for members who'd written these kinds of books. Then I e-mailed each one to explain my book idea and to find out who had represented them on their deal and to ask if they would recommend their agent to me. As the responses started coming in, three agent names appeared repeatedly. At the same time, I asked my book editor to recommend any agents that she'd had a particularly positive experience working with. Of all the names she sent me, only one matched the three names on my short list.

With three names to consider, I e-mailed each agent to briefly introduce myself, talk about my publishing history, and pitch my book idea. All three were interested, but only one responded quickly and professionally—that is, she sent an e-mail with complete sentences, typed in upper- and lowercase letters (as opposed to sentence fragments all in lowercase, as one agent did), and sent her phone number. The other two seemed too busy to deal with me, and one even admitted she's impossible to reach on the phone and only checks her e-mail occasionally. Since that was not the type of person I wanted to be representing me, I scratched her off my list. The other agent was going out of the country for a few weeks, so I couldn't consider her.

The third gave me good vibes, and I sent her my proposal. She ended up selling my proposal not to *Complete Idiots* or *Dummies* but rather to Contemporary Books, which had originally rejected the idea when I pitched it on my own. My editor later told me that my agent had done such a nice job of packaging me, my platform, and my book idea that they couldn't help but reconsider my idea—and then give me an advance that was way beyond what my agent and I had expected.

Here's an interesting footnote to this story: the second agent, the one who was going out of the country, later spoke on a panel at one of the ASJA conferences and admitted she was "afraid" to approach a certain book editor about an idea. I was thrilled that I hadn't signed with her. The last thing I want is a fearful book agent. I want my agent to be a pit bull on my behalf!

Kathy Seal
Coauthor of Motivated Minds: Raising Children to Love Learning

I found my agent by attending a panel on agents at a writers' conference. Afterward, I contacted two of the agents on the panel by phone

26

who seemed not only competent, experienced, and knowledgeable, but also approachable. They also had indicated that they or their agencies did books on my subject. Eventually I chose the one who things just went better with—who was better about returning my phone calls and seemed more interested and "together." She referred me to another agent in her agency who handles the kind of books I write. And I am still working with that agent. It hasn't been a completely happily-ever-after relationship, but she got me a good advance on my book, which goes a long way.

Marvin Wolf
Author of eight books including Where White Men Fear to Tread

Divine intervention, two counts. I met my first agent at a Christmas-season party thrown by a woman who owned a stock photo agency that sold rights to my images. The agent was there because he represented the husband of the stock agency owner. I drank some eggnog, which had a terrible effect on me. After three passes at the bathroom I had to excuse myself and go home. Because of this, the agent later remembered me from the party and agreed to meet me for coffee. My present agent was the house guest of a screenwriter and novelist who is an old softball pal. When I was in the Bay Area for my niece's bat mitzvah, I paid a call on my friend. The next morning, we all went out to breakfast together in San Francisco. It was the beginning of a lovely relationship.

Tim Harper
Author of ten books, including License to Steal: Moscow Madness and Doing Good

I found my current agent when a friendly editor at a publishing house recommended that this agent contact me. The editor, with whom I'd worked before, suggested I step in as a book doctor on a project that was going badly for one of the agent's clients. The agent and I e-mailed, talked on the phone, met in person, and made a tentative deal. In the end, her client balked at having anyone else work on the book and the project was killed. But the agent and I stayed in touch and began talking about other ideas. I had an agent, but he was easing out of the business in a career switch. So I was looking, but not too hard.

I suppose my reasons for liking this particular agent were the same as any author's: she seemed to like me as a writer. I also was impressed that she had gotten a book contract for the first-time author who had messed up the book I was asked to doctor. I figured if she could get six figures for a first-timer who in the end couldn't put a book together, she must be hot stuff. I should point out this all happened just last year. We have several projects cooking, but so far she hasn't sold anything for me.

Lisa Collier Cool
Author of hundreds of articles and many books, including Beware the Night: A New York City Cop Investigates the Supernatural, *with Ralph Sarchie (St. Martin's Press 2001)*

I didn't find my agent, he found me. He read an article I'd written for *Penthouse,* of all places, and contacted me to see if he could represent me. Later on, he read an article in the *New York Post* about a cop who participated in exorcisms and signed him up too, then teamed us up to write *Beware the Night.*

Back when my late father was an agent, he often got clients the same way. He read a number of newspapers every day, looking for people with interesting stories he could represent, then put the people together with writers from his stable. He also contacted people whose magazine work he admired and got some good clients that way.

Most agents do not accept queries by telephone, fax, or e-mail. To contact an agent, write a brief letter describing your work and listing your prior publications (if any). You may approach several agents at the same time. Submit material only when an agent asks you to do so, and be sure to follow the agent's submission requirements. Because an agent looks at many submissions in a day, you should avoid making unnecessary work by failing to follow the submission guidelines. Tell an agent when you are submitting material to more than one agent simultaneously. Be sure to include a stamped, self-addressed mailer for return of your manuscript. Always retain a copy of your submitted materials.

When searching for an agent beware of those who charge a reading fee or up-front expenses, or refer you to on-demand publishers, "book doctors," or other providers of paid editorial services.

The Voice of Experience: An Agent's Perspective

Sheree Bykofsky, literary agent
New York

Sheree Bykofsky is a literary agent and president of Sheree Bykofsky Associates, Inc. She is also the author of several books including *The Complete Idiot's Guide to Getting Published* and *The Complete Idiot's Guide to Publishing Magazine Articles*.

Q: Do you use a written agency agreement?
A: About 90 percent of the time. My standard agreement is negotiable. It spells out what the author wants and what the arrangement between us is. I want that arrangement to be clear and fair. But sometimes the written agreement scares people away. I don't want them to feel like they have to hire a lawyer to deal with me. I want the relationship to be comfortable. Also, I feel that the relationship is covered by the agency clause that goes in the publishing agreement. The agreement between author and agent should be fine-tuned to fit the relationship.

Q: What should an author look for in the agency agreement?
A: The key points are that I make the best efforts to sell the book and that I will have a certain number of months to sell the book. It should also state the percentages for the agency commission and whether the publisher or I will retain the subsidiary rights. The agreement should also indicate whether the book has been sent out to publishers before I send it out. My agreements also say that I am to be reimbursed for expenses that I incur in selling a client's book, but there is cap on the expenses.

Q: Are there cases when you would keep the sub rights?
A: Yes, then I sell them through my foreign agents or otherwise as the case may be.

Q: Does your agreement use an arbitration clause?
A: Yes. I use several standard clauses. My boilerplate agreement is in *The Complete Idiot's Guide to Getting Published.*

Q: How do you negotiate which rights a publisher gets?
A: It's a matter of whether the publisher feels that I can place the rights. Also, it's about who's in a better position to sell the rights, the publisher or me. And it's about the author's wishes.

Q: How often, if ever, do you intercede in an author-publisher conflict (like missed deadlines, manuscript rejection, etc.)?
A: It's a major part of my work. I'm constantly troubleshooting. It's also very rewarding. I feel like I'm part diplomat and part psychologist. If I can save a project, then I'm really happy—I feel like I'm in the right business. I had this author whose manuscript was rejected and the publisher was about to ask for the advance back. We finally worked out a deal where the publisher hired a freelance editor and paid the editor with the second half of the advance, so the project went forward and everyone was happy.

Q: Do you represent collaborators?
A: Yes.

Q: Have you represented just one party to a collaboration?
A: Yes, in one case where I coagented the work, each collaborator had an agent. We both looked at the book. We both worked to sell the book, then we split the commission.

Q: Have you ever had trouble with an author and a ghostwriter or other collaborators?
A: I work hard to avoid problems by making sure that the collaborators have a collaboration agreement between them. Once that's in place, I'll represent the book, not the authors.

Q: Should writers use lawyers instead of agents?
A: Agents are not lawyers, but they are well versed in publishing contracts. If a writer uses a lawyer instead of an agent, he needs to make sure that the attorney is knowledgeable about publishing. An agent's relationships should not be underestimated. While I can be tough, I can get more flies with honey.

Q: What is something that a writer has done that has impressed you?

A: It impresses me when an author takes the time to learn about my list and read my books. I'm impressed when an author follows the steps of being a professional author. I prefer a query letter with a SASE over an e-mail, and it impresses me when an author takes the time to find that out. I'm impressed when an author respects my time and learns the ropes of the business. Another thing is when they have the credentials to write the book they are proposing to write. When they do a proposal that has the market information, I'm impressed. I also like an author who is willing to do some legwork, for example, by getting her own publicist.

Being turned down a few times should not discourage a writer seeking an agent. Many rejections, however, could mean that some aspect of either your work or your presentation needs to be polished. One remedy can be continued attention to your professional development and further networking. Attending conferences, talking to other writers, and reading up on the industry can help you develop professionally, and it will increase your chances of meeting an agent who is willing to represent your work, or getting a referral to an agent that you can approach. Alternatively, you may decide to market the work to publishers yourself.

Tools and Tips: Ten Things to Ask Your Prospective Agent

- Do you belong to any professional organizations?
- Do you subscribe to a code of ethics?
- Do you have a written agency agreement? If so, can it be fine-tuned through negotiation?
- Do you use subagents to sell any rights in the work?
- Is your agency commission higher when subagents are used?
- What are your commission rates and what are your procedures and time frames for processing and disbursing client funds?

- What are your policies about charging clients for expenses.
- Do you furnish clients with a detailed account of their financial activity?
- How long have you been an agent?
- Will you or someone at your agency be representing my work?

The role of a literary agent is different from that of a literary attorney. An agent's primary function is to represent the author in marketing and selling the author's work. An agent will know a great deal about the nuts and bolts of publishing industry agreements, mainly book contracts. An attorney's primary function is to advise the client on the legal effect and significance of agreements, or to represent a client in a dispute. An attorney's role is not to market an author's work. An attorney can review and negotiate publishing contracts, but may be less adept at obtaining the contract in the first place. Both roles can be important, and an agent may wish to have an attorney review changes to publishing agreements, agency contracts, or other agreements. A useful analogy may come from the field of real estate sales: the real estate agent markets and sells the product, while the attorney attends to the legal details. Both have a role to play, but the transaction can often take place with the help of only one.

Agency Agreement—An agency agreement is the understanding between an author and a literary agent for the representation of the author's work. The agreement may be oral, but many agents prefer a written agency agreement. There are several essential points to consider when reviewing an agency agreement.

The first crucial issue is the scope of the agent's representation: is the agent representing all your work or just a single work? Will the agent be selling the rights to your work globally or just in the United States? The agency agreement should also spell out the term of the representation, how representation can be terminated, and what commissions will be due to the agent after termination. The agreement should specify that termination of the representation must be in writing. The issue of what happens if the relationship is ended while the agent is shopping the manuscript around is important. What if an offer is being negotiated? These questions should be answered by the agreement.

The agent's commission should also be spelled out in the agency agreement. Frequently, the agreement will provide for one commission rate for work sold by the agent in the United States and another, higher rate for work sold abroad. The reason for this is that agents frequently use foreign subagents in other countries to sell foreign rights to the work. The foreign subagent is paid out of the agent's commission. When this rate applies should be spelled out. Another significant "money issue" is the payment of expenses. The agent will incur expenses in representing an author's work for things such as copying, phone bills, and postage. The author and the agent should discuss (and put into writing if they chose to use a written agreement) which expenses the author is expected to reimburse the agent for.

Sample Agency Agreement

This sample agency agreement contains the elements discussed above. It's basically fair to both author and agent. It is important for writers to remember that sample agreements are not perfect, nor right for every occasion. Any written contract should reflect the terms agreed to by the parties. There is no such thing as a one-size-fits-all contract and samples should be used with extreme caution. Fill-in-the-blanks form agreements are downright dangerous and should be avoided.

AGENCY AGREEMENT

This is an agreement between Arthur Author of Street Address, City, NY 10000 ("Author") and Literary Agency of Street Address, City, NY 10000 ("Agent"). Author and Agent agree to the following terms and conditions:

This is the preamble that identifies the parties and indicates that the terms of agreement are to follow. If either of the parties is a corporation or other business entity, make sure that its status is clearly and accurately identified. Many times the preamble also includes the effective date of the agreement. In this particular agreement the effective date is designated in Paragraph 1.

1. As of the date of execution below, Author designates Agent as his sole and exclusive representative in connection with any book-length writing projects that Author specifically submits to Agent on a project-by-project basis. Such specific submission will be considered to have taken place when Author gives Agent either a written book proposal, outline, or manuscript for marketing to publishers, or a letter of intent describing a particular idea or project for which Author desires representation by Agent. Any rights of representation not specifically granted by Author to Agent in the above manner are reserved by the Author. Agent retains the right to render services to other authors, including those whose works may be in the same subject area, as long as such works do not directly compete with a work of the Author being represented under this agreement. Author retains the right to enter into agreements for different projects with other agents, as long as those projects do not directly compete with a work represented by Agent under this agreement.

This paragraph describes the nature of the author-agent relationship. Note the use of the term "exclusive," which means that this agent is the only one authorized to represent the designated book. Once the author has signed this agreement and offered a particular project to the agent, she is precluded from making any manuscript submissions herself.

2. Agent agrees to make every reasonable effort to market and license all possible rights to each book project represented on behalf of Author under this agreement, including, but not limited to, serialization, translation, book club, reprint, condensation, electronic reproduction, commercial exploitation, and dramatic and performance rights. Agent will present to Author all offers received regarding the work and will

subsequently negotiate and review all contracts for Author's signature, subject to approval by Author and, if Author desires, Author's counsel.

> *Paragraph 2 spells out the duties of the agent to make "every reasonable effort" to market the author's book. This language is not very specific. Authors may want to describe the agent's obligations in more detail, such as "agent will submit each book project to at least ten editors in a timely manner and keep author informed of where the book has been submitted and what response has been received." The agent, however, may prefer not to be so tightly pinned down. It is difficult to regulate the exact conduct of the parties. Eventually, agent and author must decide to trust each other.*

3.a. Author agrees to pay Agent a commission of fifteen percent (15%) on any and all moneys payable to Author as a result of exploitation of works represented by Agent under this agreement for print and subsidiary rights in the English language in the United States and Canada and for exploitation of motion picture, television, radio, dramatic and all other nonprint subsidiary rights in the represented works, including but not limited to electronic/multimedia rights in the United States and Canada; and twenty percent (20%) of any and all moneys payable to Author as a result of exploitation of works represented by Agent under this agreement from British, foreign language, and translation publication rights including but not limited to all print and nonprint subsidiary rights outside the United States and Canada.

> *Agents typically charge a commission of 10 to 15 percent. You should consider a different agent if the charge is higher, although the higher rate for foreign sales is justified. Avoid signing any agency agreement if you are expected to pay an up-front fee for any reason!*

b. The obligation of Author to pay the above commissions shall survive termination of this agreement. Author shall reimburse Agent's expenses represented by Agent's actual expenditures of money on Author's behalf. Agent will obtain Author's prior approval to incur expenses exceeding a total of $100 per book represented. No commissions shall be due on agreements for exploitation rejected by the Author or for which the Author does not receive payment.

> *Subparagraph 3b covers two separate things. It first says that a commission is due for any book represented by the agent at the time the book is placed with a publisher, even if the agency agreement is terminated. It also makes the author responsible for expenses, but gives the author the right to notice and approval for expenses over a particular threshold. These are reasonable and standard terms.*

c. The Agent shall make all payments due to Author within thirty days of receipt of Author's moneys, except that Agent may deduct his commission and allowable expenses before forwarding balance of payment to the Author. Author's moneys received by the Agent shall be deemed trust funds and shall not be commingled with funds belonging to the Agent. Late payments shall be accompanied by interest calculated at the rate of one and one half percent (1½%) per month thereafter. The Agent shall send copies of statements of account received by the Agent to the Author when rendered. If requested, the Agent shall also provide the Author with semiannual accountings showing all income for the period, along with the names and addresses of all licensees, fees paid, dates of payment, amounts on which Agent's commissions are calculated, and sums due less those amounts already paid. The Agent shall keep the books and records with respect to payments due each party at his place of business and, upon reasonable notice, permit Author or his representative to inspect these books and records during normal business hours.

> *The agent's fiduciary responsibilities to the author are detailed in this subparagraph. Although it is good for the agent's duties to be clearly defined in this way, the author still has the right to an accounting and timely payment even if it's not spelled out in the contract. The level of clarity here protects both parties, but it's not strictly necessary and some agents will object to such specificity.*

4. This contract may be terminated by either party or by mutual consent with a thirty-day written notice. The contract shall remain in force

until terminated by either party. Literary Agency will remain the agent of record, with full payment of commission due, for any contracts from publisher(s) considering a book project(s) at the time of termination, for any projects in negotiation at the time of termination, or for any contract negotiated and in place prior to termination. If either party is indebted to the other according to the terms of this agreement at the time of termination, such debt will remain in force until paid.

> *This paragraph covers how and under what circumstances the agreement may be terminated. It is important for any contract to have clear termination provisions. Note that this particular contract requires a one-month written notice and that the financial obligations of the parties to one another survive the termination.*

5. This agreement shall not be assigned by either Author or Agent. It cannot be altered or amended except in writing. It shall be binding on the heirs, executors, administrators, and assigns of both parties. Both parties agree that the Agent is acting as an independent contractor and that this agreement is not an employment contract, nor does it constitute a joint venture or partnership between the Author and Agent.

> *These standard terms are all reasonable. Neither agent nor author can assign the contract, meaning that the agent (or agency) relationship is personal and cannot be transferred by the agent in the event, for example, the agency is sold.*

6. Any disputes arising under this agreement shall be settled by arbitration under the rules of the American Arbitration Association in a mutually convenient location, except that the parties shall have the right to litigate claims of $5,000.00 or less. This agreement shall be governed by the laws of any state where jurisdiction is obtained or arbitration takes place.

> *This arbitration clause is well crafted because it provides for arbitration following the rules of the AAA, but does not necessarily require the parties to have the arbitration conducted under the auspices of the AAA.*

> *There is also language permitting the litigation of smaller disputes which can be less expensive than arbitration.*
>
> IT IS HEREBY AGREED, by and between the undersigned, that this agency agreement shall go into effect on the date when both parties have signed below.
>
> _____ _____
> Author   Agent
>
> _____ _____
> Date   Date
>
> *The signature block should clearly identify the parties and their authority to sign. This one would be better if it had each party's name and title clearly printed below the signature line. The date is important here because the contract becomes effective on the date the last party signs. Signing of a contract is called execution. Enough duplicates should be prepared for each party to retain a fully executed original and signatures should be in blue ink when possible.*

Agency Clause—If an author is represented by an agent, the agent will ensure that the publishing agreement includes an agency clause recognizing the agent's involvement and entitlement to a commission. This is true even with agents who do not use a written agency agreement with the author. If an author does not have a written agency agreement the agency clause is the sole written reflection of the relationship. If you do have a written agency agreement, the agency clause should be consistent with it.

The function of the agency clause is to specify the agent's rights and duties in the contract between the author and the publisher. The agency clause will generally direct the publisher to make payments of money due to the author to the author's agent.

Agency Coupled with an Interest—Some agency agreements specify that they are creating an "agency coupled with an interest." This rather benign-sounding legal **term of art** is intended to provide additional protection for the agent by giving the agent not just the right to a commission if the work is sold, but also (ostensibly) a financial or ownership interest in the underlying literary work. It also is intended to make the agency agreement more difficult for the author to terminate because, unlike a traditional agency agreement that can be canceled at will by the principal, an "agency coupled with an interest" cannot be unilaterally set aside by the writer.

Merely calling the relationship an agency coupled with an interest in an agreement may not in fact create such a relationship—and may not prevent the author from canceling. For the agency to be accurately described as coupled with an interest, the agent must have taken an interest in the underlying work (such as a share in the copyright), and not simply be entitled to a commission.

Nevertheless, from the perspective of the author, such a clause is a red flag. The agent is overreaching when the contract purports to grant the agent rights extending beyond the normal right to a commission. While this language alone may not accomplish the agent's intended result, it's not wise to rely on a contract provision being unenforceable. Rather, an author should insist on having any "agency coupled with an interest" language stricken from the contract. If an agent won't negotiate on this point, it might be wise to consider someone else.

Agreement—An agreement is an understanding between parties; the term is also used as a synonym for **contract**. Common agreements in the writing business are publishing agreements, agency agreements, and collaboration agreements. Both written and oral agreements may constitute legally binding contracts under certain conditions (*see* **contract**), and their terms can be enforceable by the courts. It is easier, of course, to prove the terms of a written agreement, and most lawyers emphasize the importance of "getting it in writing."

Agreement on Trade-Related Aspects of Intellectual Property (TRIPS)—TRIPS is an international agreement that mandates the substantive standards for intellectual property protection and requires mechanisms for the enforcement of those rights around the world. The TRIPS agreement incorporates the minimum standards of protection of the **Berne Convention** as the General Agreement on Tariffs and Trade (GATT) intellectual property rights standards. The TRIPS agreement also brings the protection of global intellectual property rights within the scope of the World Trade Organization (WTO). As a result, the WTO is empowered to hear intellectual property disputes and resolve conflicts between member nations arising out of the TRIPS Agreement.

All-in Artist Royalty—A royalty structure in the music business in which the royalty the music label pays to the artist has the producer's royalty included. The amount of the producer's royalty over and above the artist's royalty is usually between 3 and 5 percent.

All Rights—A contract that transfers all the rights in a copyrighted work is an "all rights" contract. What *are* "all the rights" in a copyrighted work? A list in the Copyright Act itself includes the right to reproduce the work; the right to display the work; the right to create the work in another form, a **derivative work**; the right to distribute the work by selling it or lending it; the right to perform the work in public; and the right to display the work in public.

An all rights contract is not the equivalent of a copyright assignment, however. All rights agreements may be made subject to various restrictions, such as a time limit, if the parties so agree. For example, the copyright owner may sign an all-rights contract allowing use of those rights for just one year. There are many ways to transfer just a portion of the copyright's "bundle of rights" (in other words, *less* than all rights); for example, by limiting the geographic location (e.g., North America), or by the medium (e.g., "print rights only" or "serial rights only"). *See* **bundle of rights, First North American Serial Rights, grant of rights.**

All Rights Reserved—The phrase All Rights Reserved often appears on the copyright page of books, under magazine articles, and on Web pages. It is a form of legal notice that tells users of the copyrighted work that the author has reserved the right to further distribute, copy, or reproduce the work, and that others are not free to do so. Does this mean if the phrase all rights reserved is not present, that the work is in the public domain or that the author has given permission to further copy the work? No. Failure to place the notice does not imply permission to copy.

The all rights reserved phrase is required for protection under the Buenos Aires Convention, so simply as a matter of caution it's very often included as part of a copyright notice. It is legally required only for maintaining copyright protection in countries that subscribe only to the **Buenos Aires Convention**. Since virtually all countries subscribe to at least one other copyright treaty that does not require this language, such as the **Berne Convention** or the **Universal Copyright Convention**, the phrase is not a necessary part of a copyright notice in most cases. Since the United States didn't join the Berne Convention until the late 1980s, the phrase used to be more important than it is now.

Alternative Dispute Resolution—A catch-all term that includes **arbitration**, **mediation**, "rent-a-judge," and other methods for resolving a controversy without traditional courtroom litigation.

The best-known forum for alternative dispute resolution is the **American Arbitration Association**.

Tools and Tips: Is an Arbitration Clause a Good Thing to Have in a Contract?

Well-intentioned parties often include an arbitration provision in their publishing contract, but leave important terms unspecified, making the clause difficult or impossible to apply in practice. Among questions that should be answered: Is arbitration mandatory, or may parties pursue their remedies in court instead? Where and under what rules will the proceeding be conducted? Who will pay for arbitration services? How many arbitrators will be appointed? Will the final arbitration award be binding, or can the losing party appeal the decision? The **American Arbitration Association** has published a list helpful tips at its Website: www.adr.org.

Amendments—Amendments are changes to an agreement. For example, if a publishing contract provides for a delivery date for the manuscript, the parties can later agree that the manuscript may be delivered at a later date. It is prudent to make amendments in writing. Sometimes the primary contract will specify that any amendments must be made in writing, signed by both parties.

American Arbitration Association—The AAA is a nonprofit organization that helps settle disputes between parties by providing out-of-court dispute resolution procedures. If engaged to resolve a dispute, the organization provides a set of rules, a forum, and an impartial party to help the parties resolve their differences. There are several different procedures available through the AAA, from procedures that resemble court proceedings to informal discussions. Despite the name, AAA can provide both mediation and arbitration services.

A freelance writer is most likely to run into AAA in the context of a publishing or freelance contract that contains an arbitration clause. Staff writers may have arbitration clauses in their employment contracts. Common arbitration clauses require either that the parties resolve their differences by going to the AAA or by applying AAA rules. Because the AAA is one of the best-known groups, its name is often included in agreements. But other arbitrating bodies do exist. Although the AAA is a nonprofit organization, it does charge substantial fees for providing arbitrators and the forum for an arbitration. You can find more information about the AAA at its Web site, www.adr.org, or by telephone at 800-778-7879.

American Library Association—The American Library Association is a nonprofit group dedicated to advocating and promoting libraries and librarians. The ALA's activities run the gamut from assisting local libraries with public relations through a prepackaged promotional campaign, to weighing in on significant legal cases with amicus briefs, to monitoring legislation affecting libraries and information and lobbying. ALA's electronic newsline regular updates on legislative and policy issues that concern libraries. You can find the ALA on the Web at www.ala.org.

American Society of Indexers—A professional organization dedicated to indexing, abstracting, and database building, ASI's membership is open to any interested individual or group. The ASI Web site (www.asindexing.org) is a good resource for anyone interested in learning more about indexing or how to become a professional indexer. Naturally, the site boasts a thorough index.

The index is an important part of a nonfiction book, and its presence and quality can affect sales. Libraries in particular are less likely to purchase a trade book lacking a good index. Traditional trade book contracts often place the burden of indexing on the author, although most authors do not actually index their own work. Rather, publishers will often charge the cost of an index to the author. For authors who choose to prepare the index themselves, indexing software can make this once-tedious job considerably faster and easier. Indexing involves art and judgment, however. It's not a task authors should undertake lightly.

The American Society of Indexers can be contacted at 10200 W. 44th Ave., Suite 304, Wheat Ridge, CO 80033. Phone: 303-463-2887, Fax: 303-422-8894, e-mail: info@asindexing.org.

American Society of Journalists and Authors—Founded in 1948, ASJA is the nation's leading organization of independent non-fiction writers with a membership of almost twelve hundred free-lance writers of magazine articles, trade books, and other forms of nonfiction writing. The society was established to advance professional development of its members by providing them with regular confidential market information, a network of professional colleagues, an exclusive referral service, seminars and workshops, and the opportunity to explore professional issues and concerns with fellow freelancers. Since its inception more than fifty years ago, ASJA has become a leading voice in efforts to protect freelancers' interests and the rights of writers to control and profit from all uses of their work.

ASJA can be contacted at 1501 Broadway, Suite 302, New York, NY 10036. Phone: 212-997-0947, Fax: 212-768-7414, e-mail: execdir@asja.org, Web site: www.asja.org.

The Voice of Experience: Why I Belong to ASJA

Writers' organizations can be an important legal and professional resource for writers. Here, members of the American Society of Journalists and Authors explain the benefits they derive from membership.

Gini Graham Scott
Owner of Changemakers/Creative Communications Research and author of numerous books

One reason I value ASJA is the great assistance I got in dealing with an irrational editor a few years ago. Also, I find the help from the Writers Referral Service has been great in getting a few good projects to work on. A third benefit has been the associations in the San Francisco Bay Area with a great group of people.

Carol Milano
Freelance journalist

I actually joined ASJA because I think it's important to be part of a professional association in one's field (especially when working alone).

Aside from the confidential pay information, the responsiveness and genuine helpful attitude of other members of ASJA's online discussion group is invaluable. I'm an infrequent participant, but whenever I post questions, I always get prompt and useful responses.

I also cherish the local ASJA lunch group in my own community. A bunch of us have been meeting once a month for years now, and I really feel these people are a support group, "watercooler," and vital element to offset the isolation of being a writer working alone in a home office.

Tina B. Tessina, PhD
Author of numerous books including The REAL 13th Step *(Career Press, 2001) and* The Ten Smartest Decisions a Woman Can Make After Forty *(Renaissance, 2001)*

I've been an ASJA member so long, I can't remember why I joined. It seemed like a good idea at the time, and it was. This organization has taught me so much, provided so much support and information, it's priceless! I directed two ASJA West Coast Writers Conferences, which were amazing learning experiences for me. It was through ASJA that I found two coauthors and my agent.

Susan J. Gordon
Freelance journalist

Writing, by nature, is a solitary profession. The network of writers I've met in ASJA has been inspiring, comforting, and always beneficial.

Paycheck reports about magazine rates have enabled me to ask for more money; this alone is worth the price of my membership.

Janine Latus Musick
Freelance journalist

ASJA gives me daily support, encouragement, and a reminder that I am a professional writer, not just an unemployed person who is lucky enough to see her name in print at the grocery store. ASJA takes away my isolation. The online discussion group connects me immediately with other professionals who help with everything from which kind of software really works to how to approach top-level editors. The annual conference introduces me to editors and issues I wouldn't even consider on my own. I've had the contract committee go over a contract for me and suggest changes, I've used Paycheck reports and the advice of fellow members to negotiate higher pay from magazines. ASJA has earned me well more than it costs.

Marisa D'Vari
Script writer, writing coach, freelance writer, and publicity consultant

To writers looking at ASJA from the outside, it's a prestigious organization requiring serious credentials for entry. Once an ASJA insider, it's a network of friends and colleagues helping one another achieve greater levels of success through seminars and content-rich online discussion groups.

Florence Isaacs
Freelance journalist

I joined ASJA because my freelance career was floundering and I was starved for contact with other writers. I remain in ASJA because it's a lifeline—to inside information, support, and camaraderie that just doesn't exist anywhere else. It's a tremendous comfort to know that colleagues are always available to provide advice, tips, and TLC.

American Society of Media Photographers (ASMP)—The ASMP is a trade organization of five thousand members that promotes photographers' rights, educates photographers in better business practices, and produces business publications for photographers. General membership requires photographers to have published photographs for three or more consecutive years and earn more than 50 percent of their income from publication photography. There are, however, other, less demanding membership levels, and members at all levels are entitled to numerous benefits including a newsletter, travel and rental discounts, and life and health insurance plans. If you are looking for a photographer, ASMP has a membership roster and a searchable database on its Web site. Contact the American Society of Media Photographers at 150 North Second Street, Philadelphia, PA 19106. Phone: 215-451-2767, Fax: 215-451-0880, Web site: www.asmp.org.

The Courts Say: Compilation of Back Issues on a CD ROM by Magazine Is Unauthorized Use

Greenberg v. National Geographic Society, 244 F.3d 1267 (11th Cir. 2001)

Jerry Greenberg's photographs had been published by *National Geographic Magazine* with permission. Afterward, the rights reverted to the photographer. Years later, the National Geographic Society created a compact disc that included all its published magazines, along with an animated clip that automatically ran one of the plaintiffs' photographs every time the CD was used. In a lawsuit supported by the American Society of Media Photographers and other creator groups, Greenberg asserted that this CD constituted a new use of his photograph and an infringement of his copyright.

National Geographic had originally used the photographs with permission, and consequently had the right under the Sec. 201c of the Copyright Act to later reproduce and distribute the plaintiffs' photographs "as part of any revision of that collective work, and any later collective work in the same series." But was a CD of the complete works of *National Geographic* merely a "revision" of the original magazine?

In a decision favorable to copyright holders, the Court of Appeals found infringement. The decision, however, relied on reasoning very different than that applied in a factually similar case decided only months later by the Supreme Court in *New York Times v. Tasini* (see page 181). How much of *Greenberg* stands after *Tasini* is unclear, although shortly after deciding Tasini, the Supreme Court declined to hear an appeal of *Greenberg*. At least one district court has followed *Tasini* to reach a different result. *Faulkner v. National Geographic Society*, 294 F.Supp.2d 523 (S.D.N.Y. Dec. 11, 2003). The precise scope of the publisher's rights to repackage old works is likely to be the subject of future litigation.

American Medical Writers Association (AMWA)—With more than five thousand members around the globe, AMWA bills itself as the "leading professional organization for biomedical communicators." Members include not only pharmaceutical writers and journal editors, but also researchers, administrators, public relations specialists, publishers, college professors, translators, and other professionals with an interest in the biomedical communication field. Student memberships are also available. For more information, contact: AMWA, 40 West Gude Drive, Suite 101, Rockville, MD 20850-1192. Phone: 301-294-5303, Web site: www.amwa.org.

Ancillary Rights—In addition to the primary right to publish a work, publishing contracts may also grant a publisher additional **subsidiary** or related rights such as the exclusive right to distribute and/or license electronic versions of the work; the right to license publication of excerpts or abridgements in newspapers, magazines, digests, and compilations; or the right to license foreign-language editions of the work. The control and the profit splits from these ancillary rights are a matter of negotiation between the parties. When publishers offer low advance or royalty rates, for example, authors may seek to retain foreign and other ancillary rights.

Animation—Animated or "cartoon story" versions of a work are generally a created under a license for television, video, movie, film, or performance rights, and are considered **derivative** works.

Anonymous Works—Anonymous works are those published without an author's name attributed. An author will sometimes deliberately seek to keep his or her identity a secret; in other instances, the correct author attribution may have been lost over time. Both anonymous and **pseudonymous** works *are* covered by copyright, though the length of their copyright protection is different from the term that applies to attributed works. For anonymous or pseudonymous works, the copyright term is ninety-five years from the date the work is first published, or one hundred twenty years from the date the work was created, whichever is shorter. Since these dates can be difficult for an outsider to pinpoint, the copying of anonymous works (such as an anonymous poem) should be approached with caution.

Anthologies—An anthology is a collection of articles, stories, or other short individual works, often selected to revolve around a central theme (for example, *Best Short Stories of 2003*, or *Heartwarming Animal Stories from XYZ Magazine*). It is important for authors to understand that the registration of the copyright in an anthology covers only the overall compilation, not the individual articles or stories. Authors retaining these rights should regularly register their copyrights in contributions to magazines, newspapers, periodicals, compilations, and anthologies in order to qualify for attorneys' fees and statutory damages in case of infringement.

The Courts Say: Copyright Registration of a Publication Does Not Entitle Authors of Individual Articles to Statutory Damages and Attorneys' Fees

Morris v. Business Concepts, Inc., 259 F.3d 65 (2d Cir. 2001)

Timely registration of copyrights is critical to obtain the full protection provided by the Copyright Act, including attorneys' fees and statutory damages. Unfortunately, the magazine's registration of the entire periodical as a collective work *does not* protect the author of an individual contribution in which the author retains the copyright. In the Morris case, a journalist wrote a series of articles for a magazine, but did not register the individual articles. The magazine publisher registered its copyright in the magazine as a whole as a collective work. The author claimed that as a contributor to the collective work he was entitled to the benefits of the magazine's copyright protection. The court disagreed and held that the author was not entitled to the benefits of the publisher's registration. It is not enough, therefore, for a freelance author to rely on the publisher's registration of the periodical to protect her individual contribution against infringement.

Anticybersquatting Consumer Protection Act—An addition to the existing federal trademark law, the ACPA exposes cybersquatters to civil liability. **Cybersquatting** is defined as faith registration, use or attempt to sell a domain name that contains another's trademark. In order to hold a defendant liable for cybersquatting, the plaintiff must be able to claim valid trademark rights in the name, although the plaintiff doesn't need to have a registered trademark to sue successfully. Second, the person registering the domain name containing the trademark must have done so in bad faith—basically defined by the statute to mean as a form of unfair competition or with the intent to sell the domain name back to its rightful owner. Under the statute, the cybersquatter may be held liable for **actual** or **statutory damages** and possible attorney's fees.

Appeal—Appeal is the process of review of a trial court's decision by an upper-level court, or of an administrative agency's determination by a trial court. Several levels of appeal may be possible; for example, a federal district court's decision may be appealable to the United States Circuit Court of Appeals, and that court's decision in turn may be appealed to the U.S. Supreme Court. Certain decisions are appealable as a matter of right; other matters will be accepted for appeal only at the discretion of the upper-level court. The United States Supreme Court, for example, decides which cases it will take for review by ruling on a request for certiorari. Generally, cases may be appealed only on the basis of the law, not on the basis of the facts. For example, an appellate court is unlikely to hear a case in which a jury has decided, as a matter of fact, that an individual committed a particular crime. But it may review the same case if a matter of law, such as the admissibility of certain evidence or the behavior of the police, is disputed.

Applicable Law—Typically found in a contract's boilerplate provisions, applicable law or choice of law paragraphs designate a particular state as the jurisdiction whose laws will govern interpretation and enforcement of a contract. As a practical matter, variations in state law on matters of contract interpretation or enforcement are generally slight. Of much greater significance to both parties, however, are **choice of venue** clauses that often appear in or near applicable law provisions. Choice of venue agreements are significant because they may force a party to litigate a dispute in a faraway jurisdiction.

Approval Rights—Both authors and publishers often desire certain approval rights. For example, a publisher will typically retain the right to approve a manuscript before final payment is made. An author might negotiate for the right to approve a book's cover design, or for rights to approve the actor selected to play the lead role in a screenplay based on an autobiography. Unless the contract expressly states that approval is solely within a party's discretion, the unstated assumption (enforced by most courts) is that approval rights should be exercised *reasonably*.

Arbitration—Arbitration is a method for resolving disputes in which a decision is rendered by one or more neutral arbitrators, rather than by a court of law. Parties may agree to submit either current or future disputes to arbitration, and may agree to arbitrate all or only certain matters. While arbitration is frequently touted as a means to avoid lengthy, expensive litigation, its benefits may come with a downside. In exchange for an expedited proceeding, parties typically give up certain rights such as trial by jury or right of appeal. In the case of binding arbitration, arbitrators' award can be set aside on only a few, limited grounds; a party unhappy with the arbitrator's decision will often find it difficult or impossible to obtain relief. And while arbitration proceedings *do* often advance more quickly than in civil court, the process may still be time consuming and expensive. Well-drafted clauses should provide that an arbitrator's decision may be enforced by the appropriate court. For helpful drafting tips, see the **American Arbitration Association** Web site, www.adr.org. *See also* **alternative dispute resolution, mediation**.

Architectural Designs—Architectural works, "the design of a building, architectural plans, or drawings," were added to the list of subject matter entitled to copyright protection by a 1990 amendment to the Copyright Act. Because this change applies only to architectural structures built after the act's effective date, December 1, 1990, different and convoluted copyright rules still apply to earlier buildings and plans.

Archives—Libraries or other repositories for historical or research purposes are called archives. Archival intent may defeat a claim of fair use for the photocopying of articles. Writers should watch out for magazine contracts that give publishers the right to archive an article indefinitely, especially on a Web site or an electronic database.

The Courts Say: It's Not Fair for a Company to Maintain a Scientific Research Archive by Photocopying

American Geophysical Union et al. v. Texaco, Inc., 60 F.3d 913 (2d Cir. 1994)

American Geophysical and eighty-two other publishers of scientific and technical journals brought a class action suit against Texaco, alleging that photocopying of the journals by in-house research scientists at Texaco violated the plaintiffs' copyrights. The parties agreed to use the photocopying practices of one scientist named Chickering, chosen at random, as representative of the copying patterns by the approximately four hundred to five hundred research scientists employed by Texaco. A Texaco scientist, selected as representative of the group, copied eight scientific articles and placed them in his personal research files for possible future use in his research. Texaco claimed that such archival copying was protected under the fair use copyright exception.

The federal appellate court found that the institutional, systematic copying by four hundred to five hundred scientists (of which Chickering was just one example) *did* infringe the plaintiffs' copyrights, and was not protected by the fair use doctrine. The court noted that the burden of proof is on the party claiming the fair use exception. In a lengthy decision considering in detail each of the statutory factors for fair use under Section 107 of the Copyright Act, the court seemed particularly swayed by the fact that the copying was widespread and that Texaco could easily have avoided infringement by purchasing additional subscriptions or paying a license fee through the Copyright Clearance Center. The court emphasized that its decision was not intended to apply to photocopying by private individuals for personal use.

Arm's-length—An arm's-length transaction is one entered into freely by the parties, based solely on each participant's perceived self-interest and free from preexisting business or personal entanglements that could create conflicting loyalties. Examples of a *non*-arm's-length publishing transaction might include a publisher's agreement to promote his brother's book or a sweetheart license deal offered to a subsidiary corporation.

Art Reproductions—An art reproduction (such as a print of a fine art painting) is a **derivative work** of the original, and as such, may be separately copyrighted if the reproducer has added enough of his own distinctive creative stamp to make it more than a mere out-and-out copy. Exactly how much originality must be added to produce a sufficiently "different" work to be copyrightable, however, has been a subject of much dispute, and court decisions have attempted to split some rather fine hairs. One fairly early case, *Alfred Bell & Co. v. Catalda Fine Arts, Inc.*, 191 F.2d 99 (2d Cir. 1951), held that an engraver's choice of colors and skill in the engraving process added sufficient originality to engraved reproductions of public domain paintings to make the reproductions themselves copyrightable.

Later cases, however, have emphasized that trivial differences will not be enough. See *L. Batlin & Son, Inc. v. Snyder*, 536 F.2d 486 (2d Cir. 1976), denying copyright for plastic reproductions of old cast-iron Uncle Sam banks, and *Durham Industries v. Tomy Corp.*, 630 F.2d 905 (2d Cir. 1980) disallowing copyright to three-dimensional toy reproductions of Walt Disney's two-dimensional cartoon characters like Mickey Mouse. On the other hand, an exact scaled-down reproduction a famous Rodin sculpture was held to be copyrightable in *Alva Studios, Inc., v. Winninger,* 177 F. Supp. 265 (S.D. N.Y. 1959) because of the high degree of skill necessary to accurately reproduce the scale version).

Even reproductions entitled to their own copyright must be careful not to infringe on the copyright of the original work, however. The producer of an art reproduction must either base her reproduction on artwork that is already in the public domain or obtain permission of the original's copyright owner.

Artworks—A wide variety of artworks are protected under Section 102(a)(5) of the Copyright Act, which recognizes "two-dimensional and three-dimensional works of fine, graphic, and applied art, photographs, prints and art reproductions, . . . technical drawings, diagrams, and models." In part because this definition is so broad, it has sometimes been difficult to distinguish between the purely aesthetic aspects of a work (which can be copyrighted) and utilitarian features (which cannot).

ASCAP—Acronym for the American Society of Composers, Authors, and Publishers. The first and still the largest performing rights society in the United States, ASCAP was formed in 1914 by a group of prominent songwriters (including Victor Herbert, John Philip Sousa, and Irving Berlin) who were tired of not receiving royalties when their copyrighted musical works were performed in public. Recognizing the practical difficulties inherent in collecting and distributing payment every time a particular musical work is performed, this pioneering group established ASCAP to simplify licensing and royalty payment procedures.

Today, ASCAP represents 200,000 music composers, songwriters, lyricists, and music publishers, and each year adds many thousands of new titles to its clearinghouse of more than 3 million musical works. ASCAP licenses the **performance rights** for its members' work to users in a wide variety of public performance venues, including television, radio, live concerts, bands and symphonies, bars, and shopping malls. ASCAP has also developed a program for use of music on the Web.

Users pay ASCAP an annual blanket license fee that allows them to use any work in the ASCAP registry. (Note that only *non-*dramatic public performances are included in ASCAP's licensing arrangements. ASCAP does not license music for use in dramatic performances, although its licenses will cover tunes from a theatrical show played on the radio, for example.) ASCAP's blanket license means that radio stations and other users don't need to obtain a separate, individual license for each song they play. Fees are based on a sliding scale, based on the type and size of the music user (licensee).

ASCAP apportions the royalties it receives among its publisher and writer members, based on the number of performances of a work (performance data are obtained through a combination of statistical sampling, self-reporting of information by television and radio stations, digital tracking, and expert analysis of taped broadcasts). While ASCAP is the largest performing rights clearinghouse, there are others such as **BMI** and **SESAC**.

Contact ASCAP at: ASCAP Building, One Lincoln Plaza, New York, NY 10023. Phone: 800-95-ASCAP; Fax: 212-595-3276, Web site: www.ascap.com.

Associated Press—The Associated Press is a cooperative news organization that provides content to member newspapers and other publishers and distributors of news. AP has staffers and freelancers around the world. Member newspapers and news distributors often make their content available to other AP members via a content-sharing arrangement. The AP also publishes a well-regarded *Style Book and Libel Manual* that should be on every writer's bookshelf.

Association of American Publishers—A major trade association of the book publishing industry, the AAP maintains offices in

New York City and Washington, DC. Its mission includes not only expanding the American book market but also protecting copyright and intellectual property rights and supporting other issues of interest to publishers. Contact AAP at 71 Fifth Avenue, New York, NY 10003-3004. Phone 212-255-0200, or 50 F Street NW, Washington, DC, 20001-1530. Phone: 202-347-3375, Web site: www.publishers.org.

Association of Authors' Representatives (AAR)—A professional association of literary and dramatic agents. To qualify for membership, agents must have sold ten works in the preceding year and a half. Members are also required to agree in writing to follow the AAR's strict Canon of Ethics, which among other things forbids the charging of reading fees to prospective clients. Reach AAR at 676A 9th Ave. #312, New York, NY 10036. Web site: www.aar-online.org.

Assignment Letter—A preliminary letter or memorandum from a magazine editor assigning a story to a writer. Because an assignment letter typically serves to confirm an oral agreement about what the publisher will pay for what rights under what conditions (such as timely submission of an acceptable manuscript covering designated topics), the assignment letter itself may be an enforceable **contract** (or, more accurately, may be enforceable as a memorandum of an oral contract). It is in both the writer's and publisher's best interest to specify as clearly as possible the scope of the assignment and important terms such as the due date, the rights being acquired, et cetera.

As a practical matter, however, an assignment letter is typically followed by a more formal publishing contract stating that the formal contract's terms will supersede any prior oral and written agreements between the parties. Again both parties should make sure (*before* signing) that the formal contract is consistent with and accurately reproduces the terms described in the initial assignment letter. Any inconsistencies should be addressed and resolved promptly.

Assignment of Contract—An assignment transfers both a party's rights and his obligations under a contract to another party. Publishing contracts typically provide that the writer may *not* assign his writing duties considered to be personal to the agreement. The publisher's rights and obligations, however, may typically be assigned (at a minimum) to its successors if the business is sold or merged.

Assignment of Rights—Both authors and publishers may be able to transfer (assign) certain specific rights, whether those rights were created by contract or by copyright. A writer, for example, may transfer any or all of the **bundle of rights** in a copyrighted work. The Copyright Act requires, however, that any transfer of copyright be in writing. Whether or not certain contractual rights are assignable will depend upon the terms of the agreement. Certain types of personal performance may not be assignable, for example. The right to receive royalties or other revenue stream under a contract, however, typically can be assigned by an author who wishes the funds be paid to someone else such as a dependant or charity.

As Told To—An "as told" to byline acknowledges the writer of an article, typically for stories reciting an unusual personal experience by the primary author (who often does little of the actual writing). Writers asked to create "as told to" works with expert collaborators should have a carefully crafted **collaboration agreement** that clearly spells such details as copyright ownership, the duties of each collaborator, payment terms, and what happens if the work isn't completed or published.

Attorneys—You wouldn't go to an ear, nose, and throat doctor for a skin disorder, or to a heart specialist for a broken bone. Yet many folks don't realize that attorneys aren't one-size-fits-all legal-problem solvers either. For contract and other general matters involving publishing law, look for a lawyer who practices primarily in intellectual property or publishing law. Litigation is its own specialty, however; so if your matter will involve arbitration or courtroom proceedings, a litigator familiar with publishing disputes or who will find experienced publishing co-counsel is probably your best bet.

How can you find a good attorney? Word of mouth is the tried-and-true (and often best) source; begin by asking friends in the writing or publishing business, or contact writers' or other professional organizations you belong to. Other referral sources may include local or state bar association hot lines. Local telephone yellow pages are not generally a good source for publishing attorneys.

When you retain an attorney, get a written agreement outlining the matters he or she will be handling for you and the firm's fees and billing policy. It's also reasonable to ask the attorney up front how quickly you can expect phone calls to be returned, how often you'll receive written or verbal updates, and the overall time frame you can expect for the legal work to be performed or the case to proceed.

You and your attorney aren't getting along? Lay your cards on the table as soon as possible. Simple communication problems can often be resolved just by talking about them. If you decide it's necessary to terminate the relationship with your attorney entirely, be sure to document your decision in writing, and ask for a copy of your complete case file. Local bar associations often provide mediation assistance in resolving fee and other attorney-related disputes.

Attorney-Client Privilege—Communications between attorney and client are privileged. This means that the attorney is not permitted, and cannot be compelled, to testify about the communications, unless the client consents. The purpose for the protection is the notion that a client can receive effective representation only when the client's attorney is fully informed as to the facts of the case. The privilege therefore seeks to promote frank communication between client and attorney. What this means in practical terms is that you can and should tell your attorney anything and everything related to your legal matter. In certain extremely rare circumstances, however, attorneys may have an ethical duty at odds with their duty of confidentiality. An attorney who learns that a client is about to commit a crime of violence may have a duty to warn the intended victim, for example.

Attorneys' Fees Clause—Buried in the boilerplate of many common contracts is an innocuous-sounding clause that reads something like, "In the event of an action to enforce or interpret this agreement, the prevailing party shall be entitled to recovery of court costs and reasonable attorneys' fees." For David battling Goliath, that's a good thing—it means David's attorney can expect to get Goliath to pay the bill if David wins (a point not lost on attorneys who may be deciding whether or not to take David's case).

Not surprisingly, the Goliaths of the publishing world feel just the opposite. An attorneys' fees clause means they stand to pay David's litigation costs if Goliath loses the dispute. And even if Goliath should win, collecting its attorneys' fees from David's puny pockets may be difficult or impossible. The upshot has been that attorneys' fees clauses are most notable for their absence in publishing contracts today. And while writers might be tempted to negotiate to have such a clause inserted, they should realize that—at least for writers with assets—such a clause can be a double-edged sword.

Auctions—Agents will occasionally hold auctions for proposals they believe will make exceptionally popular—and profitable—

books. In a book auction, publishing houses are asked to submit bids for the manuscript by a particular date and time. A publisher that is extremely anxious to obtain a book may halt the bidding process by paying a premium price, called a **preempt**.

Audio Books—These are recorded versions of a book in which the text is read aloud by the author or a professional actor and made available for purchase on CD or audiocassette. Audio books have become especially popular among commuters, as well as the visually impaired. Royalty splits for **audio rights** are usually separately specified in a publishing contract.

Audio Home Recording Act of 1992—This law added Chapter Ten, "Digital Audio Recording Devices and Media," to Title 17 of the *United States Code*, the **Copyright Act.** This addition to the copyright law exempts consumers who record music for private use from liability for copyright infringement, simplifies access to advanced digital audio recording technologies, provides for the payment of modest royalties to music creators and copyright owners financed through a fee on blank media, and requires technology in consumer recording equipment to limit making copies of copies.

Audio Rights—Contracts sometimes refer to audio rights as meaning the right to distribute a work as a book on tape or audio book. Despite the word audio, the phrase typically does not include radio rights or sound recording rights. Because this contract term could have different interpretations, it is best to specify exactly what rights are included when licensing audio rights.

Audiovisual Works—Works that combine an audio sound track with still or moving images are audiovisual works. This term is often used in an educational context to denote filmstrips, slide shows, audio materials, and films typically handled by audiovisual departments at educational institutions. Like **audio rights,** this is another imprecise term that should be further clarified when it appears in contracts and license agreements.

Audit Clause—This contract provision allows an author to inspect (often at a designated time and place, and after proper notice) the financial records of the publisher pertaining to payments due under the publishing agreement. Whenever an author is entitled to payment of royalties or license fees, she has a concurrent right to an **accounting,** regardless of whether there is an formal audit clause included in the contract. It is usually best, however, to have a good audit clause in the contract.

Sample Audit Clause

The author or author's duly appointed representative shall have the right to examine the publisher's books and records relating to the work upon reasonable notice and during normal business hours at the publisher's regular place of business. The cost of such an audit, which shall be limited to no more than once per royalty period, shall be the author's sole responsibility, unless the audit reveals a discrepancy in the author's favor of 5 percent or more, in which case the publisher shall be responsible for the cost of the audit and for prompt payment of any additional royalties due.

This audit clause is specific, clear, and reasonable. A fair audit clause will not specify particular qualifications of the author's representative and will not prescribe payment arrangements between the author and representative. A few publishers have tried to limit fees and impose burdensome qualifications to discourage author audits.

Author—Generally, an author is the creator of a book or other written work. In the case of **work made for hire,** however, the legal author for copyright purposes may be the employer or hiring party.

Author's Likeness—A photograph or other visual representation of an author is a likeness. Many publishing contracts allow the publisher to use the author's likeness in connection with marketing or promotion of his work. Examples of such use might include a photo on a book jacket, or inclusion of publicity photos in press kits or media releases. Obtaining the author's consent to this commercial use of his likeness protects the publisher against claims that the author's **right of publicity** has been violated. Authors may want to ask for approval rights or limit use in certain ways.

Authority to Sign—The legal ability of a person to bind a party to an agreement stems from his authority to sign. While an individual can usually make legal commitments on his own behalf, not every employee or official of a corporation, partnership, or other business entity is authorized to sign contracts and enter into deals for the business. In order to confirm that a person signing a particular agreement is acting with the proper authority to do so, signature lines on a contract typically require the person signing to specify his or her corporate or other title. Some contracts go even further, requiring that the parties represent and warrant to each other that they are authorized to enter into the contract and that no preexisting contract precludes them from entering into the contract at hand.

Tools and Tips:

Just received a contract? Be sure to review it carefully for appropriate authority statements before you sign.

- Signature lines should clearly specify both the name *and title* of any person who will be signing on behalf of a business.

- A business's full legal name and the kind of entity it is (a California corporation, an Ohio LLC, a Michigan general partnership, etc.) should be spelled out in two places: where the parties are first identified in the body of the agreement, and above the appropriate signature line.
- Don't exceed your own authority to sign. Are you a coauthor on the work? Both authors' names typically should be specified and both of you should sign. Have you entered into a previous contract that might conflict, either for timing reasons or because the topics are too similar? Don't sign the new agreement until you've had a chance to seek legal advice.

Authors Guild—The Authors Guild, Inc., is a national association of almost ten thousand published writers of periodical stories, articles, and books of all genres. Members include novelists, children's book authors and illustrators, journalists, historians, biographers, and other writers of fiction and nonfiction. Founded in 1912, it is the oldest and largest organization of published writers in the United States. The Authors Guild's principal purposes include expressing its members' views in cases involving the interpretation of the Copyright Act and protecting the invaluable copyright rights of authors. The organization works to promote the professional interests of authors in various areas, primarily copyright, publishing contracts, and freedom of expression. It has fought to procure satisfactory domestic and international copyright protection and to secure fair payment of royalties, license fees, and nonmonetary compensation for member authors' work. It also actively promotes fairness in publishing contracts. Since as early as 1947, the Authors Guild has published a Recommended Trade Book Contract and Guide. This model contract, well known throughout the publishing industry, is intended to be used by authors as an aid in negotiating their publishers' standard-form contracts. Since the early 1990s the guild has employed a staff of attorneys to help negotiate and enforce their publishing contracts. Contact the Authors Guild at 31 E. 28th St., 10th Floor, New York, NY 10016. Phone: 212-563-5904, Fax: 212-564-5363, e-mail: staff@authorsguild.org, Web site: www.authorsguild.org.

Authors Registry—Modeled on **ASCAP**'s royalty collection and distribution model, the Authors Registry is a rights clearinghouse for writers founded by **ASJA** and the **Authors Guild** in cooperation with virtually every important writers' organization, and more than a hundred literary agencies. It is a nonprofit organization formed to help expedite the flow of royalty payments and small reuse fees to authors, particularly for new-media uses. Individual writers may sign up independently, but many writers are automatically covered by their membership in organizations. Billing itself as "the largest coming-together of authors ever," the Authors Registry maintains an extensive database of author contract and payment information. It also collects payments for certain overseas photocopy fees and forwards those payments to eligible authors, acts as a nonexclusive licensor of certain rights controlled by authors, and helps prospective reusers of author-controlled works contact the authors. Contact information: 31 E. 28th Street, 10th Floor, New York, NY 10016. Phone: 212-563-6920, Fax: 212-564-5363, e-mail: staff@authorsregistry.org, Web site: www.authorsregistry.org.

Authorship Credit—The **byline** or other words attributing a manuscript to one or more authors is the authorship credit. The order in which author names appear on a book jacket and the precise word used to describe an author's affiliation with the project are sometimes topics of intense negotiation. In order of diminishing desirability, linking terms include: "and," "with," and "as told to." In many popular books ostensibly written by a celebrity author, medical doctor, or other expert, a ghostwriter (*see* **collaborator**) actually writes the lion's share of the book but gets no authorship credit beyond a veiled "thanks for the assistance" note in a prologue. In such cases, however, the ghostwriter will typically expect higher compensation than if his or her name appeared on the cover. It is very important for writers who collaborate with expert authors to have a well-crafted **collaboration agreement** in place that spells out such details as authorship credit, duties of each party, copyright ownership, and terms of payment.

B

Back Matter—Material collected at the end of a book, such as an **index**, epilogue, or appendix, is called back matter. *See also* **front matter**.

Bad Debt—A bad debt is just what it sounds like, a debt owed to you by someone who can't or won't pay it.

**Tools and Tips: Prying Payments Loose
When Publishers Don't Pay**

Finished an article and sent an invoice weeks ago and still no payment? A publisher for whom you write regularly has been paying more and more slowly and the amount due to you is building up steadily? You work well with a wonderful editor but the accounting department is the pits? Here are some tips on extracting payment.

- Keep good records and submit requests for payments promptly and regularly. "You'd be surprised at the number of writers who don't get paid because they fail to ask," says one magazine editor. "At my publication, payment is not automatic. Our accounting department uses a purchase order and invoice system. Once I've sent the purchase order to the accounting people when the article is first assigned, my involvement in the payment process is essen-

---

tially over unless a writer asks for help. I try to remind writers to send invoices, but sometimes payment issues slip through the cracks. So if a writer is expecting payment that doesn't come through, the first thing to do is ask about the publisher's payment processing practice and make sure you're following it."

- Ask for payment in a polite and businesslike way and follow up with a second polite reminder. Do this in writing. "I always send an invoice to an editor with a pleasant note asking her to please approve it for payment and pass it on to the accounting department," says one writer.

- Don't let payments become overdue by more than thirty days. Send a second invoice, marked "past due," along with a polite cover letter asking that payment be expedited.

- If your second invoice fails to get results, send a formal "demand" letter via certified mail, return receipt requested, saying that you are owed payment for a specific service and/or invoice, that your requests for payments have been ignored and that you expect payment to be forthcoming within a firm deadline or you will need to take action. If you have a working relationship with an attorney, you may want to use her name in a carbon copy (CC) line. Don't, however, use an attorney's name without checking first.

- Report problem publications to writers' organizations and seek their assistance in obtaining payment. Many such organizations have committees or staff to help with collection. Some report delinquent publishers in their newsletters or online discussion groups.

- Enlist a lawyer or a collection agency to collect on your behalf. A lawyer might be willing to write a collection letter for a modest fee. A collection agency will expect a hefty commission, often as much as half of the fee owed.

- Sue. If the amount owed is large enough or there is an important principle at stake, consider filing suit to get your money. You might be able to use a small claims court or represent yourself **pro se** in a regular state or federal court. You might also be able to find a lawyer to represent you on a **contingency fee** basis.

- Let go and move on. If your methodical efforts fail, you might be

> better off learning a lesson and moving on. Some publishers get
> into financial trouble and can't pay. Others won't. Sometimes it
> just isn't worth it to invest time, money, and serenity to get blood
> out of a stone and it's best to move on.

Bankruptcy—Bankruptcy is when an individual or business has more liabilities than assets and is unable to generate enough income to cover the liabilities. From a legal perspective, filing for bankruptcy is an honorable way to get a fresh start. Bankruptcy has biblical roots and was important enough to the founders of the United States that they provided for it in Article I of the Constitution. This makes sense from a practical and historical perspective. Some of the early American colonists were escaping from crushing debt in England. They were sharply aware of harsh punishment and debtors' prisons. Other colonists recognized that economic growth would be essential if the new republic was to survive. They knew such growth would require taking risks. The founders used the safety valve of bankruptcy to ensure the growth of a new nation by creating an entrepreneurial society, while at the same time protecting the poor and unlucky from a lifetime of hopeless debt. Various forms of relief are available to businesses and individual debtors under the Bankruptcy Code (Title 11 of the *United States Code*). Chapter 7 is a straight liquidation bankruptcy for individuals or businesses. This is a true bankruptcy in which the debtor turns over all nonexempt assets to a trustee for liquidation and most debt is completely discharged. Chapter 13 bankruptcy is for individuals with regular income who may be in a position to partially repay some debts and may have assets they can keep under Chapter 13 that would have to be surrendered under Chapter 7. Chapter 11 is a business reorganization bankruptcy in which the business seeks the protection of the court while it attempts to restructure its debt and get itself back onto a profitable footing.

Ask Author Law: Can Bankruptcy Solve My Financial Problems?

Q: For the past two years I've been working on a book for an academic press. I received a modest advance and also a foundation grant for some of the research. During this period I've had very little other income and have been living off the grant, the advance, and, unfortunately, my credit cards. Now the publisher has rejected my book on the grounds that the manuscript is not acceptable. I think it's really because my book is no longer "politically correct." I'm now in a complete financial hole because I was counting on the book to produce some royalty income while I got my other writing back up to speed. I'm afraid I'm going to have to get a home equity loan just to survive for a little while longer.

A: Bankruptcy filing is an option for you to consider. The federal bankruptcy law was created in order to give people like you a fresh start. If you have significant debt and no realistic way to repay it, some of it can probably be discharged through bankruptcy. The specifics will depend on your individual situation and location, but you can usually keep your personal belongings, a reasonable equity in your home, a car, and the tools of your trade. Bankruptcy sounds like a dirty word to most people, but I hope you'll give it serious consideration before incurring further debt. It's an honorable and legal way to resolve a financial crisis. If you're going to consider it, you should consult an attorney right away, because recent reforms will make filing for bankruptcy more expensive and difficult. Please remember that when you don't have enough money to meet all of your obligations, the sane thing to do is to meet your own needs before meeting the needs of your creditors. An alternative to bankruptcy might be some form of consumer credit counseling, but if you don't have a steady income, there might not be much that can be done to help you.

Whatever you do, please don't take out a home equity loan. These loans are dangerously seductive. Such a loan is easy to get because it's secured by your property and if you can't pay it back you won't be able to discharge that secured debt in bankruptcy. You may find yourself in a house that is not worth what you owe on it. If you can't make the payments, you won't be able to sell it for enough to pay off the loan and you'll end up losing your house to foreclosure. This is a recipe for disaster.

Bankruptcy Clause—Many publishers have a contract clause that basically says that if the publisher becomes insolvent or files for bankruptcy all rights revert to the author. This sounds good to many authors, but, unfortunately, such clauses are usually invalid or unenforceable. That's because of their **preemption** by the Bankruptcy Code (title 11 of the *United States Code*), which applies at the moment a company files for bankruptcy protection. Under bankruptcy law, all assets of the filing company are frozen by an automatic stay and all rights held by that company, such as the rights in a book, become part of the bankruptcy estate to be dealt with by the court.

Tips and Tools: What to Do When Your Publisher Files for Bankruptcy

If your publisher files for either Chapter 7 (liquidation) or Chapter 11 (reorganization) bankruptcy, the rights to your book will come under the control of the court (unless they had fully reverted to you well prior to the bankruptcy filing).

Depending on a set of highly complex circumstances, the rights could be:

- Reverted to you
- Sold to another party to pay off creditors of the publisher
- Transferred to another party who will have to honor the contract with you.

Depending on the circumstances, you could become:

- A creditor of the bankrupt publisher with the right to notice and standing to participate in the proceedings to come.
- The holder of an executory contract that the publisher can either

reject (in which case the rights will probably come back to you) or accept, in which case the publisher may continue to publish or, possibly, sell the right to publish (together with all corresponding obligations) to someone else.

You might or might not receive a notice of the filing from a court. And there may or may not be anything you can do. But you need to be aware that you are stayed from taking any direct action against the bankrupt publisher once the filing has taken place. If you knew or should have known about the filing, even if you didn't receive notice, and you attempt to collect any money or get your rights reverted, you could be held in contempt of court for violating the automatic stay.

You may need to file a claim with the court. If your rights have significant value it might be a good idea to consult with a bankruptcy attorney to see what, if anything, you can do to protect your rights. If your rights have a modest monetary value, you should probably wait and see what happens.

Bench Trial—When a case is heard by a judge without a **jury**, it's called a bench trial. Because there is a constitutional right to a trial by jury, bench trials are conducted when the parties consent.

Berne Convention—The Convention for the Protection of Literary and Artistic Works, commonly known as the Berne Convention, is an international copyright treaty that was signed at Berne, Switzerland, on September 9, 1886. The United States, however, did not become a signatory to the treaty until 1988. Its provisions became effective in the United States on March 1, 1989.

The Berne Convention is one of the oldest international copyright treaties in existence, and has been amended several times throughout the twentieth century, most recently in 1979. It establishes uniform guidelines for copyright protection for all member countries, and provides for the reciprocal protection of published and unpublished works by authors of one country in other member countries. The works of authors of nonparticipating countries are also provided protection under the Berne Convention if the work is first published in a member country or is simultaneously published in a member country and a nonmember country. The treaty provides that copyright protection in member countries is not subject to registration or notice requirements. It also establishes, with some exceptions, a minimum copyright term of the life of the author plus ninety years.

The Berne Convention also recognizes certain **moral rights** of authors, including the rights of integrity and attribution. Although the treaty permits these moral rights to endure after the death of the author for the duration of the copyright's economic right, it recognizes the authority of individual member countries to determine whether moral rights should terminate at the time of the author's death.

Other rights conferred on authors by the Berne Convention include the rights of translation, reproduction, adaptation, and the right to authorize the broadcast or other wireless communication of their work. Authors of dramatic or musical works have the right to authorize the performance of their work. The treaty also establishes certain rights pertaining to cinematographic works.

While the United States has incorporated many of the provisions of the Berne Convention into the federal copyright law and even exceeds the minimum standards set by the treaty in some instances, the convention is significant in terms of what rights and benefits are provided to U.S. authors who wish to protect their copyrights in foreign countries, and for foreign authors who wish to protect their works in the United States.

Berne Convention Implementation Act of 1988—The BCIA was enacted by the United States to bring federal copyright law into compliance with the provisions of the **Berne Convention**. The law became effective on March 1, 1989, the same day the Berne

Convention entered into force in the United States. The legislation specified that a lawsuit alleging a violation of the Berne Convention in the United States could only be brought under U.S. law and not under the treaty itself because it was not a self-executing treaty. The legislation clarified that the Berne Convention did not create any **moral rights** for United States authors. The Visual Artists Rights Act (**VARA**), however, would later establish limited moral rights for visual artists.

Bestseller Clause—Many publishing contracts include language providing for a bonus payment if a book makes the official bestseller list of a publication such as the *New York Times*. The language and terms of a bestseller clause can vary in amount, definition of a bestseller, particular list or lists necessary for bestseller status, and length of time on the list.

Blackline—When negotiating a deal, one party will typically offer the other a proposed contract containing various **deal points** and **boilerplate**. The last step before execution of the contract is to mark it up so that it accurately reflects what the parties have agreed to. The **markup** can be done by hand or a contract can be redlined or blacklined by drawing a line through proposed deletions and underlining proposed insertions. Most word processing programs have a change/tracking feature that can be used to blackline or **redline** a contract. Once the blacklined version has been agreed to by all parties, the changes can be rejected or accepted and a clean copy of the contract printed for execution. It is not necessary, however, to reprint a blacklined or marked-up contract. Many final contracts are extensively marked up. When a contract is marked up by hand, rather than redlined or blacklined, the changes should be initialed and dated by both parties in the margins. This is not necessary when the blacklining has been done by computer.

BMI—Acronym for Broadcast Music, Inc. Established in 1939, BMI is a nonprofit performing rights organization that represents American and foreign songwriters, composers, and publishers in all genres of music. Other performing rights clearinghouses include **ASCAP** and **SESAC**. BMI was formed to provide an alternative to existing performing rights organizations, offering licensing services to popular types of music, including rhythm and blues and country, that were previously unrepresented. The organization now maintains a catalog of approximately 4.5 million compositions. BMI acquires nondramatic **performance rights** from its members and then licenses those rights to entities that wish to use a work in a public performance context, including radio, television, the **Internet**, and other live and recorded performances. BMI offers a "blanket license" that allows use of its extensive catalog through a variety of flexible contract plans. BMI then distributes the collected fees to its members in the form of royalty payments. Web site: www.bmi.com.

Bogus Agents—Anyone can call himself a literary agent. Unfortunately some purported literary **agents** make the money by charging **reading fees** rather than earning commissions. Such charges as reading fees and up-front expense payments are banned by the premier agents' organization, the **Association of Author's Representatives**. Any agent who asks for an up-front payment from a client should be avoided. There are also bogus publishers, book doctors, packagers, and others who make money by exploiting gullible would-be authors. Investigate thoroughly before dealing with any purported publishing professional asking for payment.

Boilerplate—Standard language contained in a contract or other legal document is frequently referred to as boilerplate. When reviewing a publishing contract, it is very important to make sure that the all the terms of the contract, not only the major **deal points**, are carefully evaluated. Boilerplate provisions that do not

meet the requirements of your specific situation should be negotiated and modified. A publisher's standard boilerplate clauses
usually can contain some negotiable items. It is wise to have an
attorney review your publishing contract to ensure that it adequately protects your work and your rights.

Book Club—Books have long been marketed to groups of readers with common interests through specialty clubs that acquire
book club rights from publishers and distribute "book club editions" (often smaller and cheaper) at attractive prices to club
members. Book club rights are traditionally a **subsidiary** right
with the usual fifty-fifty split of payment between author and publisher. Book club distribution can be a significant source of income for the author and the primary publisher.

Book Doctors—Book doctors are publishing consultants or freelance editors who offer, for a fee, to assist would-be writers with
polishing, revising, or shaping up a manuscript in order to make
it suitable for submission to publishers. While there are many
such consultants who are reputable and who do good work, there
are at least as many with highly questionable credentials and
techniques. Before paying anyone for editorial services, it's best
to check thoroughly. If significant sums are involved, consult an
attorney. Always check with a Better Business Bureau, or a writers' organization such as the **Authors Guild** or **AJSA**'s Writers
Referral Service *before* making any commitments or payments.

Book Fair—Book fairs and festivals are gatherings organized in
schools and communities to celebrate writing and reading.
Sometimes they are organized by nonprofit organizations; sometimes they are put on by a single publisher, or a for-profit company to sell books. School book fairs are often put on by
companies that pay a commission to the sponsoring school
group.

Book Packager—A packager typically takes a core idea for a book and lines up everything necessary to deliver a ready-to-publish product to a larger publisher for distribution. Some packagers contract with sponsoring organizations to prepare a book for publication with a major house. Others dream up interesting book ideas and then find the people to make the book happen. Usually a packager will contract with a publisher on one side and with writers, illustrators, and designers on the other side. Packagers are often former editors. See **Tools and Tips: Book Packaging,** page 108 and **Packager,** page 251.

Book Publishing Contract—Most of the time books are published only after the author and publisher have entered into a **contract.** Publishing contracts can vary from simple, single-page letter agreements to long, complex legal documents filled with wherefores and whereases. There is tremendous variety in publishing contracts and they can be difficult for authors to understand and negotiate. It's not wise to sign a publishing agreement without having it reviewed by a competent attorney or agent or both. The **Authors Guild** provides legal reviews of publishing contracts as a member service and also puts on contract seminars.

Tools and Tips: What Do You Say When the Editor Calls?

There is no such thing as a standard publishing agreement and an author shouldn't rush into signing one. A contract offer from a reputable publisher will not evaporate because an author wants to review it and negotiate some of its terms. What should you do when offered a contract?

- Take a deep breath and pause before saying anything.
- Don't make any firm commitments at this stage other than to express delight and say you look forward to receiving the contract.

- If the editor offers specific terms or presses you to agree to something try to respond carefully.
- Here are a few things you might say:

"That sounds good, although I'll have to look over the contract before making a firm commitment."

"Those terms sound fine to me, but I'll have to run them past my _____ (lawyer, best friend, mother, financial advisor, priest, spouse)."

"I am absolutely thrilled that you've called and I'll get back to you right after I've had a chance to absorb this great news and go over the contract."

Robin Davis Miller, counsel to the Authors Guild, has often said that if the publisher is making you an offer, they've already invested time and money in your work and the offer won't go away just because you want to think it over.

Sample Book Publishing Contract

While there is no such thing as a standard contract, the following example from a traditional trade publisher is fairly typical. This one is in the process of being negotiated partially or redlined. (This particular redlining is accomplished with deletions in strikeout and additions in boldface. Oftentimes additions are underlined, but that is not the case here. To read the original boilerplate, include the strikeout and ignore the boldface.)

Note that the royalty rate is half of the traditional rate. This is because this contract is for a children's picture book in which the royalties are split with an illustrator. If it were an adult trade hardcover, the royalties would be doubled. This particular contract was a version typically offered to agented authors or experienced authors. Publishers also have "sucker" versions of their contracts for less experienced authors.

CREATIVE PUBLISHING COMPANY, INC.

AGREEMENT made as of this **10th** day of **April, 2004,** between Creative Publishing Company, Inc, 100 Fifth Avenue, New York, N.Y. 10000 ("Publisher") and

Name of Author
123 Street Address
City, ST 00000

("Author") with respect to the text (the "Text") of a book tentatively entitled

TITLE OF BOOK (the "Work")

This preamble identifies the parties, the date of the agreement, and the subject of the contract, and the text of a tentatively titled children's picture book. It also indicates how the parties and the book will be referred to throughout the rest of the contract (i.e., Publisher and the Text).

1. GRANT OF RIGHTS

Author grants to Publisher the exclusive right to print, publish, distribute and sell the Work incorporating the Text and to exercise the subsidiary rights listed in paragraph 5 below throughout the world (the "Territory"). Except as otherwise provided herein, Publisher may exercise the rights granted for the full term of copyright (including any renewals and extensions) provided by law in each country included within the Territory, under any copyright laws now or hereafter in force.

The grant of rights is covered in more than one place in many book contracts. This grant of rights is quite broad in that it covers virtually all book rights around the world. It also refers to subsidiary rights to be covered later in the contract. Although these worldwide rights are typical in children's picture book contracts, they are usually more limited in trade book contracts and often broader in academic contracts. Ways to limit the grant of rights might include restricting the lan-

guage or territory. Note that this grant of rights does not include the copyright and does not grant "all rights." Writers should be wary of overly broad grants of rights and should think especially hard about giving up the copyright. When attempting to negotiate a grant of rights with a publisher whose starting offer is unfairly broad, a good strategy is to hit the ball back into the publisher's court by asking it to identify the rights it realistically needs to control. There is very rarely any justification for grabbing the copyright or all rights.

2. THE WORK

a) The Text of the Work shall be a description of text. Illustrations will be furnished by Publisher, at Publisher's expense, pursuant to a separate agreement between Publisher and the Illustrator.

This redlined contract is still being marked up. The description remains to be filled in. It should include the subject, the approximate length, and an indication of the target audience and style. This description usually comes from the publisher and should be carefully checked by the author for accuracy.

b) ~~Except as otherwise disclosed by Author in writing to Publisher prior to the execution of this Agreement, Author agrees that the Work will be Author's next work. Author will deliver to Publisher on or before _____ ("Due Date"), time being of the essence, two clean, typed, numbered, double spaced text copies of the manuscript, and one copy on computer disk, in form and content satisfactory to Publisher and complete and ready for the copy editor. Author will submit with the manuscript, on or before the Due Date, all necessary permissions, releases, licenses and consents.~~ Publisher acknowledges receipt of an unedited draft of the Text.

Subparagraph 2 (b) has been crossed out because this writer has already delivered an acceptable manuscript. If this were a contract being offered on the basis of a proposal and including this boilerplate, the writer should try for modifications to several onerous provisions. First, it says that this will be the author's next work, meaning that the author must finish this project before working on another. If the author is uncomfortable with this restriction, she should negotiate to strike it. The manuscript deadline is established here as well. The author should make sure she won't have a problem meeting the deadline and attempt to negotiate additional time, if necessary. Beware of language that says "time is of the essence," a legal term of art that means the contract can be terminated by the publisher if the deadline isn't met. An author should try to negotiate this out. If she can't, she should get any deadline extensions in writing. Note also that permissions, licenses, and consents for outside material are the responsibility of the author and must be obtained by the deadline. It's a good idea for an author to ask the publisher to provide the model consent forms or to ask for guidance in the development of an acceptable form. Make sure the consent form grants permission for all editions of the work.

c) (i) ~~If Author does not deliver the complete manuscript to Publisher within thirty (30) days after the Due Date, or at another date as may have been agreed to by Publisher in writing, then upon Publisher's written notification thereof Author immediately will repay to Publisher all amounts paid to Author under this Agreement.~~ If the text of the Work is ~~delivered but~~ deemed unsatisfactory, Publisher shall notify Author in writing and shall list in reasonable detail why said manuscript is not satisfactory and Author shall be given a reasonable period of time to revise the manuscript. If Publisher determines in good faith that Author's revision of the manuscript has not resulted in a satisfactory manuscript, Publisher may terminate this Agreement, then upon Publisher's written notification thereof Author immediately will repay to Publisher all amounts paid to Author under this Agreement. Upon re-payment in full, Publisher will return to Author all rights in the text granted herein.

This subparagraph deals with the consequences of fail-ure to deliver an acceptable manuscript. While this ver-sion has been redlined to reflect the fact that a manuscript has already been delivered, the boilerplate seems to provide a thirty-day grace period. This is in-consistent with the time of the essence language of the previous subparagraph, and would probably (but not absolutely) be interpreted in favor of the author if the manuscript were to be delivered late, but fewer than thirty days late. It wouldn't be a good idea to rely on this, though. Notice that this author has managed to add a provision that the publisher will provide written reasons and an opportunity to revise in the event that the publisher finds a manuscript unacceptable. This is far preferable to the boilerplate that gives the publisher the right to declare the manuscript unacceptable, ter-minate the contract, and require the author to repay the advance, terms very unfair to the author.

(ii)   If Author fails to repay Publisher in full, all sums paid to or for the benefit of Author under this Agreement, then Publisher may, in addition to its other remedies, retain for its own account monies due Author under the terms of this agreement ~~or any other agreements between Author and Publisher~~ until the amounts so retained equal the amount owing to Publisher.

This author has managed to strike the cross-collateral-ization provision. Cross-collateralization (sometimes called joint accounting or bucket accounting) means that if the author owes the publisher any money it could collect from royalties due under other contracts. Cross-collateralization is an unfair provision that can pop up in a variety of places.

d) If Publisher decides to submit Author's manuscript for legal, medical or other professional review then the Work shall not be deemed complete and satisfactory unless all changes which may be requested by Publisher as the result of such review have been made by Author, regardless of whether or not any advance payment otherwise due to Author on delivery and acceptance of the manuscript has been made. Nothing contained in this paragraph will alter or vary any of the parties' rights under paragraph 15 of this Agreement.

This is a fairly standard clause giving the publisher the right to have the manuscript reviewed for legal reasons. The boilerplate of this particular version is less fair than some because it makes acceptability contingent on legal review. The author could have redlined it to make it a requirement to edit out objectionable parts rather than make the manuscript unacceptable, but in this case it wasn't important because the contract is for an innocuous picture book that presents no legal or medical information.

3. ADVANCE

Publisher shall pay to Author as an advance against all monies accruing to Author under this Agreement the sum of Number of Dollars ($00,000) which shall be paid as follows:

$00,250 upon execution of this Agreement; and
$00,250 upon Publisher's acceptance of a complete and satisfactory manuscript in conformity with paragraph 2 herein.

The actual figures have not been included here. Advances for children's picture books are often modest. This author did better than average because she has a track record with this particular publisher. Note that the advance is payable in two parts, half on signing and half on acceptance. The schedule for advance payments can vary widely, however. Advance payments can come later in the process. It is to the advantage of the author to negotiate more money up front and the earliest possible payment benchmarks.

4. BOOK ROYALTIES

Note that there is no escalator clause that would pay higher royalties when sales have reached a particular level. This author has not attempted to negotiate an escalator clause because she was unsuccessful in doing so in previous contracts. She did, however, successfully negotiate a royalty based on list rather than net, as was offered in earlier contracts, so she compromised here. She intends to seek an escalator clause with her next contract with this publisher. Her negotiating strategy to date has been to get one or two major concessions with each new contract.

Publisher will pay to Author the following amounts:

a) **Domestic**

   (i)   **Hardcover**

On all copies, less returns, of a regular trade hardcover edition (and revisions thereof) sold by Publisher in the United States through normal trade channels (except as hereinafter set forth), the following royalties: 5% of Publisher's list price on all copies of the Work sold; provided, however, that where the discount to booksellers is 55% or more from the suggested list price, the royalty shall be 5% of net receipts.

The provision that the royalty will be reduced in the event of a discount of 55 percent or more is called a "deep discount" clause. This calls for changing the royalty rate from list to net, which usually means an effective royalty rate of about half of list. This author has not tried to negotiate any changes here because this publisher rarely deep discounts. Deep discount terms would be far more important to an author whose pub-

B

lisher sells through outlets such as Wal-Mart and whole-sale clubs.

(ii) **Paperback**

On all copies, less returns, of a paperback edition, sold by Publisher in the United States through normal trade channels (except as hereinafter set forth), a royalty of: 3% of Publisher's list price on all copies of the Work sold; provided, however, that where the discount price to booksellers is 55% or more from the suggested list price, the royalty shall be 5% of net receipts.

(iii) **Board Books**

On all copies, less returns, of a board book edition sold by Publisher in the United States through normal trade channels (except as hereinafter set forth), 3% of Publisher's list price on all copies of the Work sold; provided, however, that where the discount to booksellers is 55% or more from the suggested list price, the royalty shall be 5% of net receipts.

(iv) **Unbound Sheets**

On sales of sheets of the Work, 5% of the amounts actually received by Publisher from such sales.

(iv) **Special Sales**

On all copies, less returns, of a regular hardcover or paperback edition sold by Publisher outside normal wholesale and retail trade channels in the United States, 5% of the amounts actually received.

b) **Export**

On all copies, less returns, of a regular trade hardcover edition or paperback edition of the Work sold by Publisher outside the United States, an amount equal to 5% of the amounts actually received by Publisher.

The rest of these royalty provisions are fairly standard. Again, note that those based on list or cover price are worth about twice as much as those based on net or actual receipts. Also keep in mind that these rates are half the normal rate because of the fact that this is a picture book contract where royalties are traditionally split fifty-fifty with the illustrator. For a standard trade contract the rates would probably be doubled. One other concern about royalties—authors should double-check to make sure that a specific royalty rate is included for all rights granted to the publisher. If there is any doubt, insist on a catch-all rate that sets the royalties on sales not specified elsewhere in the agreement a negotiated percentage of the amounts actually received by the publisher.

c) **Electronic**

On all copies of the Work sold as an "Electronic Book" as defined herein, the royalty shall be based on the prevailing rate, as set forth in Paragraph 4(a)(i), (ii) and (iii), applicable to the most recently published print edition of the Work and calculated on the retail price of the Electronic Book. On all copies of the Work sold as an "Electronic Version" as defined herein, the royalty shall be 7.5% of the amounts actually received by Publisher subject to good-faith negotiation between Author and Publisher in the event publication of an Electronic Version of the Work is contemplated. As used in this Agreement, Electronic Book means the text of the Work in complete, condensed, adapted or abridged versions (including, but not limited to, electronic anthologies and other electronic compilations) by any means of distribution or transmission, whether now or hereafter known or developed, intended to make the text and any illustrations or photographs contained in the Work available in visual form for reading. Electronic Versions means the text of the Work in complete, condensed, adapted or abridged versions, whether sequentially or non-sequentially, together with added sounds, images, and/or graphics which are more than incidental to the text, and distributed in electronic formats (provided, however, that if Movie and Television Rights are not also granted to Publisher by this Agreement, Electronic Ver-

sions shall not include dramatic versions of the Work in electronic media).

This author wisely struck the electronic rights clause altogether because she wants only print rights licensed under this contract. The publisher probably gave in so easily because it has no plans to publish an electronic picture book. Otherwise this might have been a tougher negotiation. Electronic rights clauses should be carefully negotiated and clearly understood. One possible solution might be to agree to negotiate in the future for such rights.

d) **Premium**

On all copies of the Work sold by Publisher for premium use, and on all copies sold of an edition specifically manufactured for another party, Publisher shall pay 2.5% of the amounts actually received by Publisher.

e) **Direct Marketing**

On all copies, less returns, of the Work sold by Publisher directly to consumers as distinct from sales made to bookstores or wholesalers, 2.5% of the amounts actually received by Publisher.

f) **Promotions**

On all copies of the Work given away or sold at or below Publisher's cost to promote the sale of the Work, no royalty shall be paid.

g) **Special Printings**

Six (6) months or more after publication date, if in order to maintain the Work in print Publisher arranges for a printing of two thousand (2,000) **one thousand (1,000)** copies or less, then the royalties on all copies sold which were produced from such printing shall be one-half ($1/2$) of the royalty rates set forth in subparagraphs 4(a)(i) and 4(a)(ii).

This provision is designed to keep the book in print for as long as possible by allowing for smaller, and there-

fore more expensive, printings with a lower royalty rate. Note that this author has reduced the size of small printings to make sure they are truly small. Small printings might not be a good thing for the author of an evergreen book, one that might sell to another publisher if it went out of print and the rights were to revert. On the other hand, this could be a useful provision for a midlist novel or other book that would otherwise not be reprinted.

h) **Reduced Sales**

~~If after the first two royalty accounting periods, sales during any accounting period fall below five hundred (500) copies, the royalties on all copies sold during such accounting period shall be one-half (½) the royalty rates set forth in subparagraphs 4(a)(i) and 4(a)(ii).~~

i) **Freight Pass Through**

It is understood and agreed that if Publisher uses a freight pass-through system while this Agreement is in effect, all royalties calculated on the basis of a suggested list price shall be calculated on Publisher's Invoice Price. "Publisher's Invoice Price" shall mean the suggested list price less the freight pass-through increment. The freight pass-through (or jacket price) will not exceed Publishers Invoice Price by more than five percent (5%).

This freight pass-through system means that the publisher passes though the cost of shipping by deducting shipping from the list price upon which the royalty is calculated prior to calculating the royalty. Don't confuse this with income pass-through provisions that benefit the author by passing income from subsidiary rights sales directly to the author rather than holding it in a royalty account.

5. **SUBSIDIARY RIGHTS**

This author didn't use a literary agent, so she is willing to let the publisher license subsidiary rights on her behalf. She feels that the publisher is in a better position to exploit the sub rights and that she will ultimately benefit. She also knows from previous experience that the publisher is unwilling to change the rights split, so she is saving that fight for a future contract.

a) The exclusive subsidiary rights referred to in paragraph 1 include all of the rights enumerated below. The net amounts actually received by Publisher in the United States from the sales or license of such rights within the Territory are to be shared by Author* and Publisher in the percentages indicated below.

Note that these subsidiary rights are exclusive, meaning that only the publisher can exploit them on behalf of the author and the author must not license any sub rights on her own. She may want to make some of the sub rights nonexclusive.

~~"Author's Share" of all subsidiary rights income derived from the sale or licensing of rights in and to the Work shall be shared equally between Author and Illustrator, except in those situations where only the Text is used, in which case Author shall be entitled to the full "Author's Share" of income. If only the Illustrations are used, Illustrator shall be entitled to the full "Author's Share" of income.~~

This provision would apply only if the illustrator was a party to this contract or if the author and illustrator were the same person. As this contract applies only to the text, the publisher has agreed to delete it.

		Author's	Publisher's
(i)	**First Serial**	80%	20%

To license portions of the Work for publication in periodicals or newspapers, in one or more installments, before publication in book form.

| (ii) | **Second Serial** | 50% | 50% |

To license portions of the Work for publication in periodicals or newspapers, in one or more installments, after publication in book form.

(iii) **English Language** 75% 25%

To license English-language rights in and to the Work in book or serial form in full-length, condensed, or abridged versions for publication in countries outside the United States.

(iv) **Translation** 50% 50%

To license translation rights in and to the Work in book or serial form in full-length, condensed, or abridged versions.

(v) **Reprints** 50% 50%

To license the Work to one or more publishers for reproduction in full-length, condensed, or abridged versions in hardcover or paperbound reprint editions, including mass market, trade paperback, or large-print editions.

(vi) **Permissions** 50% 50%

To license excerpts from the Work for publication.

(vii) **Anthologies, Abridged Versions, Collections** 50% 50%

To license for publication adaptations or abridgements of all or part of the Work. In addition, if Publisher publishes the complete Work in a collection or anthology with one or more other works, Author shall be entitled to receive that proportion of the royalty payable under paragraph 4 which the Work bears to the total number of works contained in such collection.

(viii) **Book Club** 50% 50%

To license the right to print, publish, and sell an edition of the Work to a book club or any organization which purchases book club rights.

(ix) **Electronic Reproduction See Division of Income Below**

To license non-dramatic reproduction of the Work or parts of it by electronic, mechanical, digital, optical, laser-based or any other forms of copying, recording, storage, retrieval, or transmission recording in any electronic form now or hereafter known or devised, including, with-

~~out limitation, microfilm, microfiche, digital media and/ or other electronic text format, or any other human or machine-readable medium, whether interactive or not, but excluding all uses included in Subparagraph 5(a)(xi).~~

~~**Electronic Book** 50% 50%~~

~~Verbatim reproduction of the Work (i.e., the Text and Illustrations) in complete, condensed or abridged form.~~

Exploitation of all Electronic Rights are subject to Author's approval (which approval shall not be unreasonably withheld or delayed) and the good-faith negotiation of a division of income.

Authors should be sure that rights they wish to retain are covered in both the main grant of rights and the subsidiary rights sections of the contract. Here the author has done her best to keep control of electronic rights by getting an approval right and agreeing not to withhold her approval unfairly. She also agrees to negotiate the split of income in good faith. This would probably be interpreted as following the industry standards at the time of negotiation.

(x) **Audio Recording** 50% 50%

To license sound reproduction rights for any nondramatic audio recording developed from the Work in whole or in part (including condensed, adapted, and abridged versions)

(xi) **Motion Picture, Performance, Dramatization Rights** 75% 25%

To license motion picture rights, radio rights, television rights, video cassette rights, or dramatic stage rights with or without music and public reading rights in, and in connection with, the Work.

(xii) **Merchandising and Commercial Rights** 50% 50%

To license merchandising and/or commercial rights in and to Author's name and the Work, subject to Author's approval, which approval shall not be unreasonably withheld or delayed. Merchandising and commercial rights shall include, without limitation, the exploitation of the Work and of Author's name in connection therewith; and use of all material in the Work, including the characters contained therein, through the use of the characters' names or images and the simulation or graphic exploitation thereof on or in connection with the rights specified in subparagraph 5(a)(xi), then the royalties payable hereunder shall be paid in the same proportion as subparagraph 5(a)(xi). In addition, Publisher may exercise any of the aforementioned rights and pay Author a royalty of 5% of the net amount received from such exercise. Nothing herein shall be construed to limit Publisher's rights pursuant to paragraph 7.

b) **Promotional and Free Copies**

Publisher may publish or permit others to publish or broadcast without charge and without royalty such selections from the Work for publicity purposes as may, in its opinion, benefit the sale of the Work. Publisher shall also be authorized to license publication of the Work without charge and without royalty in Braille or by any other method primarily designed for the physically or mentally handicapped.

6. PUBLICATION

The terms of Paragraph 6 are quite fair to the author in that they require prompt publication with the date pegged to the acceptance of the manuscript. In the event that the publisher ultimately fails to publish, the author gets to keep the advance and all rights revert. Note, though, that the author is required to make a demand upon the publisher and allow some additional time before reversion.

a) Within eighteen (18) months of its acceptance of the complete Work (i.e., the final text and a complete set of illustrations) and delivery of any other materials required pursuant to subparagraph 2(b), Publisher will publish the Work at its own expense, in hardcover and/or in paperback, in a style, manner, and at a price it deems best suited to the sale of the Work. It is understood that advertising, number and destination of free copies, and all details of design, manufacture, distribution, marketing, and promotion shall be at the discretion of Publisher. Publisher's failure to publish within such period shall not be deemed a breach of the Agreement if the delay is caused by any circumstances beyond its reasonable control.

b) In the event Publisher shall fail to publish the Work within eighteen (18) months after Publisher's acceptance of the Work, Author may as his/her sole remedy at any time thereafter serve a written demand upon Publisher by registered mail, return receipt requested, requiring Publisher to publish the Work within ninety (90) days after receipt of such written demand, and if Publisher shall fail to comply with such demand within such ninety (90) day period, then this Agreement shall terminate without further notice at the end of such period, and all right, title and interest in and to the Text shall revert to Author for his/her sole use and disposition. In the event of termination by Author pursuant to this paragraph, such payments as shall have been made to Author hereunder as advances shall be deemed in full discharge of all Publisher's obligations to Author pursuant to this Agreement and no other damages, claims, actions or proceedings, either legal equitable for breach of contract, default, failure to publish, or otherwise, may be claimed, instituted, or maintained by Author against Publisher.

7. PROMOTION AND PUBLICITY

This author is guarding her reputation by inserting approval language into this promotion and publicity language. Publishers are sometimes reluctant to grant such approval rights, but may be more likely to do so if approval is changed to consultation or if approval is not to be unreasonably withheld.

a) Publisher and its licensees may use Author's name, preapproved photograph and pre-approved likeness in the Work and in all revisions, editions, and versions thereof and in connection with the advertising and promotion of the Work and the exercise of all rights in the Work granted to Publisher hereunder.

b) Author shall cooperate with Publisher in promoting the Work, and upon Publisher's request, shall make himself/herself available to Publisher for such promotional activities as Publisher shall require in connection with the publication of the Work. Publisher will pay for Author's reasonable travel expenses in accordance with its standard practices for authors' tours and will consult closely with Author concerning the scheduling of any such promotional activities.

Note that nothing in this promotion paragraph requires the publisher to promote the book by arranging for a tour. This is a mildly misleading way for a publisher to make the author happy without committing to anything specific while hinting at promotional glory to come. All writers should be aware that book tours and extensive publisher promotion are the exception rather than the rule. This author knows and accepts that much of the promotional burden will fall on her. All writers should plan on actively promoting their own books, even with good publisher support.

8. COPYRIGHT

The boilerplate copyright language in this contract is outdated. This author secured the publisher's agreement to register the copyright to the text in her name within sixty days of publication, which ensures that the copyright gets registered with time to spare (within ninety days) in order to qualify for statutory damages and attorney fees in the event of infringement. The publisher normally handles copyright registration formalities on behalf of an author, but all authors should follow up on registration to make sure it has been taken care of. Authors should also request copies of both the registration application and certificate. If there is any doubt about whether the publisher has taken care of this properly, the author should consider registering the copyright herself.

Within sixty (60) days of first publication, Publisher shall register the Text of the Work for copyright in the United States in the name of the Author. ~~If any part of the Work has been published and registered for copyright prior to January 1, 1978, Author: (i) agrees to timely apply for the renewal of the copyright prior to the expiration of the first term thereof, (ii) authorizes Publisher to make such application in the name of Author, and (iii) if this Agreement has not been terminated previously, hereby assigns to Publisher the sole and exclusive right to print, publish and sell the Work, and exercise the other rights referred to herein, during the full term of renewal and extensions of copyright, on the same terms and conditions as for the original copyright term.~~

Note that the boilerplate leaves open the name of the registered party. Authors should be especially careful to make sure that the registration is in their name. There is rarely a justifiable reason for the publisher of a normal trade book to own the copyright. The author can grant all the rights the publisher needs in an exclusive license. Publishers don't need to own copyrights. This core principle was recognized by Congress when it passed new copyright legislation in 1976.

9. REPORTS AND PAYMENTS

Statements of sales and earnings shall be made up semiannually to June 30th and December 31st, and statements and settlement thereof in cash shall be made the following October 25th and April 25th, respectively. Whenever the semiannual earnings fall below Twenty-five Dollars ($25) no accounting or payment shall be made until the next settlement date after the earnings have aggregated Twenty-five Dollars ($25). Where any such statement indicates that Author has received an overpayment of royalties or is otherwise indebted to Publisher (individually and collectively, "Overpayment"), Publisher may deduct the amount of such Overpayment from any sums then or thereafter due Author from Publisher under this ~~or any other~~ [Another cross-collateralization provision that the author caught and deleted] agreement, it being understood and agreed that the term "Overpayment" excludes unearned advances. If in Publisher's judgment there is risk of booksellers returning unsold copies of the Work for credit, it may withhold a reasonable portion of Author's earned royalties for the purpose of adjusting Author's royalty account to make copies of the Work reported as sold represent firm sales.

Note that the publisher has provided for a reserve for returns. This language is, however, a bit vague. It would be better to set clear limits on the percentage of royalties that may be held in reserve (perhaps 15 percent) and a length of time the reserve may stay in place (perhaps one or two royalty periods). A provision that the author didn't request but maybe should have is an audit clause giving her the right to examine the publisher's books in order to verify the accuracy of the royalty accounting. In some states such an audit right is implied, but it's far better to get the right into the contract. It is also better to specify that the books may be audited by the author or a representative, but not necessarily a certified public accountant.

10. AUTHOR'S CHANGES

Author shall read, revise, correct and return to Publisher first proof sheets of the Work within fourteen (14) days of receipt of such proof sheets by Author. Any expenses incurred by Publisher for Author's changes (other than corrections of printer's errors) which exceed ten percent (10%) of the total cost of composition shall be paid by Author.

11. AUTHOR'S COPIES

Publisher shall furnish to Author, free of charge, ~~twenty (20)~~ *thirty (30)* copies of the Work, and should Author desire more copies for personal use, Publisher shall supply such copies at one-half (½) the suggested retail price. No royalties shall be paid on copies purchased by Author. Author will be billed for such copies and payment shall be made within thirty (30) days of receipt of bill.

The number of author copies can often be negotiated upward. This is an area where editors seem to have some discretion. The discount rate can also be changed. Authors are often successful asking for "the best available trade discount." Try to get restrictions on resale limited, if possible. This clause says free copies are for personal use but does not specifically prohibit resale. If faced with a restriction on resale, try for a restriction on directly competitive sales or through the publisher's channels of distribution instead. It's also worth trying to delete the ban on royalty payments, especially if royalties are paid on net or if the discount is below 50 percent.

12. AUTHOR'S MATERIALS

Publisher shall be responsible for only the same care of any of Author's materials in its custody as it takes of its own. However, except in the case of Publisher's gross negligence, Publisher shall not be responsible for loss or damage to any materials furnished by Author while in Publisher's custody or in the custody of anyone to whom delivery of such materials is necessary in connection with the production of the Work or is otherwise made with Author's consent. Author shall retain copies of any such materials and, in the case of photographs, the negative or duplicate positive of each photo furnished.

In this era of digital manuscripts this clause isn't nearly as important as in the days when a manuscript had to be typed and copies were made as carbons. In those days the loss of a manuscript was a disaster. Today, this is only a concern for original art and photos.

13. EXCESS INVENTORY

a) If at any time after one (1) year from publication of the Work, Publisher has copies on hand which, in its judgment, cannot be sold through usual marketing channels, Publisher may sell such copies at a "Remainder Price," that is, at a special discount of sixty percent (60%) or more from the retail list or freight pass-through price. All copies sold at a Remainder Price shall be accounted for separately and not included in sales totals, and the royalty on each copy sold shall be ten percent (10%) of the net amount received by Publisher reduced by the manufacturing cost. Publisher will not pay any royalties on copies sold at or below manufacturing cost.

b) If the sale at a Remainder Price involves the entire inventory, Publisher will notify Author in advance of the planned sale and provide Author the opportunity to purchase all or part of the inventory at the manufacturing cost. Author must notify Publisher within thirty (30) days of the date of Publisher's notification as to whether or not Author wishes to make such purchase.

Sometimes an author is able to get language that says if a book is remaindered it is deemed out of print and the rights revert. Other times, publishers insist on being free to reduce inventory even while the book remains available for sale. Authors should try to set limits on remaindering whenever possible.

14. WARRANTY AND INDEMNITY

a) **Warranty**

Author warrants and represents that:

(i) Author is the sole author and proprietor of the text of the Work.

(ii) Author has full power and authority to make and perform this Agreement and to grant the rights granted hereunder, and Author has not previously assigned, transferred or otherwise encumbered the same;

(iii) the text of the Work is not in the public domain and has not previously been published;

(iv) the text of the Work does not infringe upon any statutory or common law copyright, or any trademark or service mark, or any literary property right;

(v)   the text of the Work, to the best of Author's knowledge, does not invade the right of privacy or publicity of any person, nor contain any matter libelous or otherwise in contravention of the rights of any third party; and, if the Work is not a work of fiction, all statements in the Work asserted as facts are true and accurate;

(vi)   the text of the Work, to the best of Author's knowledge, contains no matter which violates any federal or state statute or regulation thereunder, nor is it in any other manner unlawful; and.

(vii)   the text of the Work, to the best of Author's knowledge, contains no recipe, formula or instruction which if reasonably followed would be injurious to the user.

Sometimes the author can get the publisher to agree to insert "to the best of Author's knowledge" into the warranties that are vulnerable to subjective interpretation. Publishers are usually reluctant to modify warranty requirements and these provisions can be the subject of tough negotiations.

b) **Indemnity**

Author hereby indemnifies and agrees to hold Publisher, any seller of the Work and Publisher's licensees harmless from any claims, suits, action, losses, or damages, including reasonable attorneys' fees and disbursements, incurred or sustained by any of them, in connection with or resulting from any claim, suit, action, or proceeding arising out of, or relating to, a breach of any of Author's warranties, representations, or agreements herein contained. In defending any such claim, action, or proceeding, Publisher shall control the defense and will use counsel of its own selection. Publisher shall promptly notify Author of any such claim, action, or proceeding. Publisher shall have the right to withhold its reasonable estimate of the total damages and expenses from sums otherwise payable to Author pursuant to this Agreement ~~or any other agreement between Author and Publisher~~ and to apply such sums to payment of such estimated damages and expenses. In the event such claim, suit, action, or proceeding is discontinued or dismissed without liability to Publisher, Author shall be liable for and shall pay to Publisher fifty percent (50%) of the amount of Publisher's counsel fees and other expenses. No settlement shall be made by Publisher without consultation with Author.

Indemnification is the way the publisher protects itself in the event of the breach of warranty. This indemnification clause is quite broad in that it indemnifies against frivolous claims as well as actual damages "finally sustained." It's not bad, however, in that the author only has to pay half of the publisher's legal fees and expenses. It's also quite fair in that it's only triggered in the event of a breach of the warranty not merely a claimed breach (although this could well be a distinction without a difference.) If there was no actual breach, there would be no indemnification. Note, too, that the author was successful in crossing out yet another cross-collateralization, so she is protected against deduction from sums owing her under other contracts. This dilutes her risks somewhat. Another way to soften warranty and indemnification costs is to ask to be covered under the publisher's insurance, as this author is below.

c) **Survival of Warranties and Indemnities**

Any warranties, representations, agreements, or indemnities contained in this paragraph shall survive the termination of or any reversion of rights under this Agreement.

d) **Insurance**

Subject to the other terms and conditions of this Agreement, if Publisher has in effect a media perils policy of insurance that covers Author, and applies to occurrences which are the subject of any claim or claims relating to the Work, Publisher will use best efforts to assure that such policy is applied for the benefit of Author in accordance with the terms and conditions of the policy; provided, however, that Author's obligation to indemnify and hold Publisher harmless in accordance with paragraph 14(b) shall continue in effect with respect to all losses not recovered by Publisher under the policy, and provided further that, upon Publisher's request, Author promptly furnishes to Publisher, at Author's sole expense, any requested documents or information Publisher's counsel deems necessary or helpful to the defense of such claims, and otherwise fully cooperates, at Author's sole expense, with the defense.

This insurance coverage might help the author in the event of a lawsuit, but it might not help much. A careful reading reveals a lot of "ifs and howevers." One good thing about insurance, though, is that even if a policy does not protect against actual damages, the insurance company is probably required to provide a defense and thus must pay legal fees to defend frivolous cases.

15. OUT OF PRINT

a) The Work shall be considered in print if it is on sale by Publisher in any edition or if it is subject to an option or an outstanding license under this Agreement. If the Work is not in print, Author may request in writing that Publisher keep the Work in print. Publisher will have six (6) months in which to comply. If Publisher fails to comply, or does not wish to keep the Work in print either by Publisher or any licensee, then at the end of such six-month period this Agreement shall terminate and all of the rights in the text of the Work granted to Publisher shall revert to Author upon and subject to the payment by Author to Publisher of any outstanding indebtedness, it being understood that an unearned advance hereunder shall not be deemed an indebtedness. The Work shall be deemed out of print if orders for copies of the Work are filled only by copies produced on an on-demand basis (i.e., neither Publisher nor any licensee maintains an inventory of the Work) and for each of two (2) consecutive accounting periods fewer than 125 copies of the Work are sold by Publisher and its licensees.

This out-of-print clause has been modified to deal with the impact of print-on-demand technology. Note that reversion of the rights is not automatic, but requires the author to make a demand in writing and then to wait for an additional six months. This author should monitor the sales of the book and, if sales are dwindling, consider negotiating to get the rights back. Sometimes a publisher will remainder the book to the author and revert the rights. It doesn't hurt to ask. Don't forget that a contract term like this can be modified through negotiation, so if it looks like the publisher has given up on the title an author can always try to expedite the return of rights. Many publishers are willing to discuss such modifications when sales have declined to minimal levels.

b) In the event of termination under this paragraph 16 Author shall have the right to purchase the film or plates, if available, of the Work at one-third ($^1/_3$) of the manufacturing cost, including composition, and any remaining copies or sheets of the Work at the manufacturing cost. It is understood that nothing herein shall be construed to convey to Author any rights in the Illustrations contained in the Work. If Author does not elect to make this purchase within thirty (30) days, then Publisher may dispose of such materials as it sees fit.

16. PUBLISHER'S TRADEMARKS

Author acknowledges that Publisher has sole and exclusive ownership of the trademark, trade name, logo, imprints, and any other identification now or hereafter used by Publisher. Nothing in this Agreement (including, but not limited to, the right of Author to purchase books and film on termination) shall permit Author to use Publisher's identification during the term of this Agreement or thereafter, without first obtaining Publisher's consent in writing.

17. ~~OPTION~~

~~Author agrees to offer to Publisher his/her next work before submitting the same to any other publisher. Publisher shall have a period of thirty (30) days after receipt of a manuscript to make an~~

offer for Author's next work. Thereafter, Author shall negotiate exclusively with Publisher for a period of thirty (30) days. If at the end of such period, the parties are unable in good faith to reach a mutually satisfactory agreement, then Author may submit the proposal elsewhere, provided, however, that (i) Author shall not enter into a contract for publication of the work proposed upon terms less favorable than those offered by Publisher, (ii) Author shall provide Publisher with the details of any terms offered prior to entering into any agreement with another publisher and (iii) Publisher shall have the right to acquire rights in the work proposed by matching all the material terms of the best bona fide offer for the work that Author receives from another publisher. Publisher shall not be required to consider Author's next work until publication of the Work which is the subject of this Agreement.

Option clauses are almost never an advantage for the author, and publishers are generally willing to delete them, as this publisher did. As option clauses go, this one is relatively benign where it limits the publisher to thirty days to negotiate and doesn't require the next book to be subject to the same terms. One unfair term is the right to match any other offer, which effectively destroys the author's opportunity to negotiate with other publishers in good faith. It's also unreasonably limiting to require the author to wait until the publication of this contract's book before being free to submit an option book. Authors should be wary of provisions that tie them up for too long, bind them prematurely to particular terms, or give publisher an unreasonable marketplace advantage by including the right to match or top any offer.

18. ADDITIONAL DOCUMENTS

a) Each party agrees to execute such documents as may be reasonably necessary to confirm the rights of the other party in respect to the Work.

b) If the Work has been previously published and the rights have reverted to Author, Author shall provide Publisher with the documentation relating to the reversion of the rights and certified copies of the original copyright registration certificate.

19. FORCE MAJEURE

Neither Author nor Publisher shall be liable because of delays in its performance caused by wars, civil riots, strikes, fires, acts of God, governmental restrictions, or because of other circumstances beyond either party's control, provided such delay does not exceed three (3) months. If a party's performance is delayed for a period in excess of three (3) months, then the other party shall have the right to terminate this Agreement.

20. OTHER PUBLICATIONS OR LICENSES

a) Should first publication of the Work in any language occur outside of the U.S., Author shall furnish Publisher with one (1) copy of the first printing of such edition, as soon as it is available, together with the exact date of publication of such edition, so that Publisher may be assured that Publisher's U.S. edition is protected according to the requirements of the U.S. copyright law.

b) In the event that foreign rights and/or first serial rights are retained by Author, Author shall notify Publisher promptly of any arrangement made for publication of the Work in whole or in part in any language, including English, which would precede book publication in the United States. Author further agrees to consult with Publisher before licensing first serial rights.

c) It is understood and agreed that audio and/or electronic version rights, if such rights have been retained by Author, shall not be exercised until Publisher's initial publication of the Work.

d) During the term of this Agreement, Author shall not publish or authorize publication of another work which would be competitive with the Work and likely to detract from, impair or frustrate Publisher's sales of the Work or Publisher's ability to exercise in full its rights in and to the Work.

This noncompete clause is buried in a batch of otherwise benign boilerplate. It extends for the entire life of the book and has relatively subjective standards of what would constitute unfair competition. Although overly broad noncompete clauses are rarely enforceable, it would be best to try to limit them in terms of time (perhaps to two years from publication) and insert language making it certain to detract from sales (rather than "likely") and "directly" competitive rather than just simply competitive.

21. **AGENT**

   ~~All statements and sums of money due and payable to Author under this Agreement shall be rendered and paid to _____ ("Agent"), which is authorized to collect and receive such monies and Author declares that the receipt by Agent shall be a valid discharge of Publisher's obligations under this Agreement. Agent is empowered to act in Author's behalf in all matters arising out of this Agreement. Agent's Federal I.D. Number: _____; Incorporated? Yes / No (circle one)~~

   This agency clause has been crossed out because the author didn't use an agent. An agented author should review the agency clause carefully. This one makes no provision for termination of the author-agent relationship. An agented writer should be protected by adding that future funds will be paid directly to the author upon written notice of the termination of the agency agreement from the author. Even with such language, though, publishers will be reluctant to send funds to the author without consent of the agent.

22. **MISCELLANEOUS PROVISIONS**

   a) This Agreement constitutes the complete understanding of the parties. No modification, waiver, or extension of any provision hereof shall be valid unless in writing and signed by both parties and no waiver shall be deemed a continuing one.

This means that any changes to one term don't affect the other terms and that the author must get any changes in writing.

b) This Agreement shall be binding upon and shall inure to the benefit of the heirs and personal representatives of Author and the successors and assigns of Publisher. Author shall not assign his/her rights under this Agreement without the prior written consent of Publisher, except that without such consent Author may assign any net sums due him hereunder. Publisher may assign any right hereby granted to it, but may not, without the prior written consent of Author, assign this Agreement as an entirety except to a parent affiliate, or wholly owned subsidiary or in connection with the sale or transfer of substantially all its business or any division or department thereof.

The author may not assign this contract to someone else to write the book, but she can assign payments to someone else, a family member or charity perhaps. The publisher can assign rights to another publisher, but only with the permission of the author. That's fair because it bars the publisher from making a sweetheart deal with someone else.

c) Paragraph headings and captions have been inserted as a matter of convenience and do not define, alter, vary or serve to interpret any provision of this Agreement.

d) If there are multiple authors under this Agreement, the obligations of all the authors will be joint and several unless otherwise expressly provided in this Agreement, and Publisher may exercise any or all of its remedies with respect to the authors individually or collectively. For the purposes of this Agreement, all authors are to be collectively referred to as "Author."

e) This Agreement shall be deemed to have been entered into in the State of New York and shall be interpreted and construed in accordance with the laws of the State of New York applicable to agreements executed and to be performed therein by each party. Each party hereby agrees to submit to the sole and exclusive in personam jurisdiction of the courts of the State of New York, New York County, for the resolution of all disputes between them or, if jurisdictional prerequisites exist at the time, to the sole and exclusive in personam jurisdiction of the Federal Courts of New York, with venue to be in the Southern District of New York.

This choice of law and venue clause means that the author agrees that the contract will be interpreted according to New York law and that any suits must be brought in New York. Publishers are usually reluctant to change such provisions, but in this case that's not a problem. New York has a large body of publishing law and courts experienced in publishing law issues. New York is also where you can most easily find experienced lawyers to help you resolve any disputes that might arise. If the venue provisions seem really unfair, for example, limiting the author to seeking redress in Podunk, Iowa, it doesn't hurt to ask for a change or to have the clause deleted. Note also that there is no arbitration clause in this contract. This author preferred not to have an arbitration clause, so didn't ask for one. Some publishers will consider including arbitration provisions on request and others routinely include it in boilerplate. Again, such clauses covering venue, jurisdiction, choice of law, and arbitration can sometimes be added, subtracted, or modified.

IN WITNESS WHEREOF, the parties hereto have duly executed this Agreement the day and year first above-written.

AUTHOR

CREATIVE PUBLISHING COMPANY, INC.

By: _____
Name of Author

By: _____
Name of Officer
President

Social Security No.: 000-00-0000
Citizenship: U.S.A.

The requirements to provide the social security number and citizenship are necessary for income reporting and copyright registration.

Tools and Tips: Book Packaging

While many packagers are excellent, a few use questionable practices. It can be difficult to know the difference, so package deals should be approached with caution.

PREVENTING PACKAGING PITFALLS

- Check out the reputation of any packager you are thinking of working with. It's especially useful to look at other books produced by the same packager and check with the writers of those books.
- It's not always necessary to give up your copyright to work with a packager, but there is sometimes a legitimate reason for the packager to need it. This might be true, for example, of a corporate history or a publication of a nonprofit organization. If you are asked to assign the copyright, ask the reason and try to get a license agreement that meets the publisher's needs.
- If the packager insists on owning the copyright, make very sure the project is worth it in terms of compensation and credit. Protect yourself by using contract language that says transfer of the copyright is not effective until you are paid in full. See **book packager**, page 77; **packager**, page 251.

Breach—A breach is the violation of a promise, guarantee, or agreement by the commission or omission of a specific act.

Breach of Contract—A contract is breached when a party fails to perform a duty as agreed in the contract.

Tools and Tips:
What Is a Material Breach of Contract?

A material breach occurs when one party's violation of a contract is significant and substantial and the nonbreaching party is excused from further performance under the contract and/or may sue for damages.

A partial breach is a less significant violation that could result in the nonbreaching party becoming entitled to damages, but not excusing performance of other terms.

A publishing contract usually contains a clause, often referred to as a termination clause, that requires the author to indemnify the publisher from damages, liability, and expenses, including attorneys' fees, arising out of a breach of the contract on the part of the author. Overly broad clauses might not specify that the breach needs to be a material one, and could subject the author to liability for insignificant and unintentional breaches that would not normally affect overall performance. Contract language should clearly limit early termination to material breaches. The author should make certain that he also has the right to terminate in the event of a material breach on the part of the publisher.

The Courts Say: Material Breach of a Copyright Licensing Agreement Can Also Constitute Copyright Infringement

Costello Publishing Co. v. Rotelle, 670 F.2d 1035 (D.C. Cir. 1981)

In an antitrust action involving a copyright licensing agreement the Court of Appeals for the District of Columbia Circuit concluded that the breach of a copyright licensing agreement might also constitute copyright infringement if the breach is a material breach or if it results in the failure to satisfy a condition to the license. The court noted that the allegedly infringing activities of a book distributor were performed in compliance with a licensing agreement with the publisher. The court determined, however, that if the publisher materially breached its contract with the copyright holder, any use by the book distributor, as a licensee of the publisher, would amount to copyright infringement. The court stated that an action for copyright infringement would exist, regardless of whether the contract contained an express reversion clause, if the publisher's breach of contract was so material that it would create a right of rescission in the copyright holder. The court remanded the case to the district court for a determination as to whether the publisher materially breached its contract with the copyright owner.

Break Points—Some publishing contracts call for royalty rates to escalate as sales increase beyond certain levels, called break points. A typical **escalator clause** might call for royalty rates at 10 percent for the first five thousand copies, 12.5 percent for the next five thousand, copies, and 15 percent for anything above ten thousand copies.

Broadcasting—Broadcasting is the transmission of data over the radio or television. Broadcasting also encompasses **Webcasting**, which is broadcasting over the Internet. Broadcasts are entitled to copyright protection in the United States, and even live broadcasts that are recorded as they are transmitted to the public qualify for copyright protection since they are considered to be fixed under federal copyright law.

Broadcasts can infringe the copyright of the underlying work if the transmission has not been authorized by the copyright owner. **Performing rights societies** such as **ASCAP**, **BMI**, and **SESAC** have been established to facilitate the licensing of musical works to radio stations and others that wish to broadcast these works.

Bucket Accounting—Bucket accounting, also called **cross-collateralization**, or **joint accounting**, is unfair to writers because it authorizes a publisher to make deductions from the income of one work for sums owing on another work. Such sums can be charges for the cost of alterations, permission fees, fees for revisions, overpayments, or an unearned advance. It's unfair because it gives the publisher de facto insurance against an unsuccessful project by permitting recovery from funds due on author's other projects.

Tips and Tools: Is Bucket Accounting Buried in Your Contract?

- A bucket accounting or cross-collateralization clause is not likely to be labeled as such. It may be referred to as "Overpayments," "Deduction of Sums Owing Under Other Contracts," or "Joint Accounting."
- Look for any language in the contract that authorizes the publisher to deduct money owed to the author for other works.
- If the publisher refuses to delete the provision entirely, try a compromise position:

  (1) that no deductions for sums owed under other contracts be made from an advance owed to the author, but rather, any deductions be made from the future income stream;
  (2) that unearned advances not count as sums owed to the publisher.

Buenos Aires Convention—The Convention of Buenos Aires on the Protection of Literary and Artistic Copyright was signed on August 11, 1910, and revised in 1928. Adopted by the United States in 1914, the treaty establishes reciprocal copyright protection between the United States and sixteen Central and South American countries. The treaty also required the use of the phrase "**all rights reserved**" in the copyright notice of a protected work. All of the signatories of the Buenos Aires Convention are now members of either the **Berne Convention** or the **Universal Copyright Convention**.

Bundle of Rights—The exclusive rights enjoyed by the copyright owner of a work are often referred to as a bundle of rights because they can be divided and be exploited by the author in a variety of ways. For example the author of an article on the grooming of horses might license **first North American serial rights** to a horse magazine, reprint rights to the newsletter of an equestrian organization, and anthology rights to include the piece as a chapter in a book for horse lovers. Writers should try to license the rights legitimately needed by a publisher and retain the rest. A **grant of rights** can be very broad or quite limited. Thinking of the rights as a bundle that can be divided and licensed in various ways is a helpful concept for freelancers.

C

Cable Act of 1984—The Cable Communications Policy Act of 1984 was signed into law in October 1984 to establish a policy for the regulation of cable television. Among its provisions, the law permitted a person to own a cable telecommunications system even if the person owns other media interests. The act required cable systems to set aside a certain percentage of channels for public, educational, or governmental programming. Government regulation of the provision of or nature of cable services was restricted, and the law also deregulated cable subscription rates. The law also established standards governing the privacy rights of cable subscribers. The provisions of the law were further amended by the Cable Television Consumer Protection and Competition Act of 1992.

Camera Ready—A camera-ready manuscript is one that is edited, typeset, proofed, and otherwise prepared to go to press. It will include all necessary text, **front matter**, blank pages, appendices, and indices as well as charts, graphs, or pictures positioned on a page just as they will appear in print.

Cancellation of Contract—A contract can be canceled, rescinded, or terminated in a variety of ways. Sometimes the contract itself will have a provision for an automatic cancellation, such as a requirement for one party or the other to do something specific within a certain period of time or the contract is automatically canceled. If both parties agree, they can cancel a contract between them. Verbal agreement to cancel is sometimes sufficient, but a prudent author will verify a contract cancellation in writing. Sometimes the material **breach** of a contract is enough to cause automatic cancellation. Cancellation of a major contract, such as a book publishing agreement, is usually accomplished by formal rescission where the parties cross out and initial all of the clauses to clearly indicate that it is no longer in force. At the very least, when a contract is rescinded, there should be a clearly written and superceeding cancellation agreement signed by both parties. When a contract is unilaterally canceled by one side, there should always be written notification to that effect signed by the canceling party. Such a cancellation isn't always legally effective, but unilateral notification with the reasons for cancellation clearly spelled out is better than leaving the situation ambiguous. Such notification should be sent by some sort of traceable communication, such as certified mail, a confirmed fax, or e-mail with a delivery receipt.

Caption—Headings or captions on a contract are not usually considered an enforceable part of the agreement. It is important to read an entire contract clearly and look for agreement between the caption and the text of each contract section. If there is an inconsistency between the caption and the text, the text will probably control. A caption is also the text describing photos or illustrations in a published work.

Caribbean Basin Economic Recovery Act—The United States enacted the CBERA in 1984 to promote trade between itself and certain Caribbean countries. The law established a series of eligibility requirements that, among other things, denies participation to any country that supports or engages in the broadcast of copyrighted material belonging to U.S. copyright owners without express consent.

Case Law—Every court decision and written opinion becomes part of the body of case law for its **jurisdiction**. Case law illustrates a court's interpretation of constitutions, statutes, and regulations and establishes precedent for later cases that present similar issues. *See* **common law**.

Cease and Desist Letter—An author whose work is being published without her consent should clearly inform the infringer in writing. She or her lawyer will typically write a cease and desist letter that puts the infringing party on formal notice of the illegal activity. Such a letter should be straightforward, concise, and clear. It should be sent by certified mail or some other method in which delivery can be confirmed. Such a letter is often the first step in an effort to stop a violation of an author's rights and start laying a paper trail as proof of efforts to enforcing those rights.

Cessation of Publication—Many publishing contracts provide for what happens to the author's rights when the book is **remaindered** or goes **out of print**. A fair publishing contract should include a reasonable procedure for a **reversion or rights** to the author in the event publication ceases.

Characters—Characters are the people who populate fiction and are usually thought to be the product of an author's imagination. But even a fictional character can be the basis of a libel suit if readers might recognize that character, even mistakenly, as based on someone else. Writers who base their characters on real people should disguise identifying information by changing as many details of name, physical description, location, and occupation as possible, by using an appropriate disclaimer, and, in some cases, having a potentially inflammatory manuscript vetted for libel prior to publication. Characters based on **public figures**, however, are fair game.

Cheap Edition—This is an older publishing term for a inexpensive version of a traditional hardcover book.

Choice of Law—Choice of law refers to which jurisdiction's laws will be interpreted or applied in a **lawsuit** or contract dispute. Sometimes parties can specify that the law of a particular jurisdiction will apply and other times it will become a matter of legal strategy or a problem for the courts. For instance, a court may have to determine whether to apply state or federal law, or procedural or substantive law depending on the issues involved, the residence of the parties, and the place where the cause of action arose.

Choice of Venue—Choice of venue refers to the forum, or place, where a **lawsuit** will be brought. A choice of venue clause in a contract indicates where and in what court a dispute will be settled.

Choreography—Copyright protects more than literary works. Choreography, or plans for a dance routine, is an example of **copyrightable subject matter** protected by copyright law.

Citation—A reference to a specific case, legal authority, or precedent is called a citation, or cite for short. Cites are used in court documents and **legal research** to provide support for a particular proposition or argument, and to substantiate facts. *The Bluebook: A Uniform System of Citation,* published and distributed by the Harvard Law Review Association, is the definitive source for the rules and principles of legal citation. More information about the *Bluebook* can be found on its Web site at: www.legalbluebook.com.

Citizenship—Citizenship can be important in the context of copyright law because the work of a U.S. citizen, for example, is entitled to copyright protection under U.S. law even if it was first published in a country that is not a member country of the international treaties adhered to by the United States.

In the context of litigation, diversity of citizenship occurs when the parties to a lawsuit are from different states or countries. In cases of diversity of citizenship it may be possible to bring a lawsuit in federal court. This is called **diversity jurisdiction**, and is one way to get what would otherwise be a state law case into federal court.

Claim—In a general legal context, a claim is a cause of action. When commencing a lawsuit, the plaintiff must file a **complaint** in which she states a claim upon which relief can be granted.

The person or entity being sued, the **defendant**, may raise a counterclaim against the **plaintiff** by stating a cause of action against the plaintiff and demanding damages or other relief. The defendant may also file a cross-claim to bring a person or entity who was not named by the plaintiff into the suit.

A patent claim is the portion of an inventor's application filed with the U.S. Patent and Trademark Office that contains a formal and very specific description of the invention to be patented and that in essence defines the boundaries of the patent to be granted.

Class Action—A group of people sharing a specific legal interest or having suffered a common injury may bring a class action **lawsuit** in court. A small group or a single person is identified as the "representative" of the class in the action. Class representatives are named in the action and their claims, similar to those of the other class members, provide the basis for the lawsuit. If successful, a class action can result in a single award of damages to be divided among the class members. See **settlement**.

Clause—A clause is a subsection of a contract. It is often a single paragraph, but can also be a sentence or even a portion of a sentence. Clauses are often identified by letter or number within a single section of a contract. Many lawyers refer to the clauses of a contract in other ways, such as provision, paragraph, subparagraph, letter, or number.

Click-Wrap Agreement—This term has evolved from the earlier **shrink-wrap agreement** developed by licensors of consumer software products. In order to make it clear to consumers that the software was protected by copyright, software companies started putting a prominent notice or seal on the outside of the box indicating the copyright status of the software and the terms of license. The consumer was informed that if he didn't agree with the terms he could return the package unopened for a refund, but that by breaking the seal or opening the shrink wrap he was indicating acceptance of the terms and agreement with the license. Courts have generally upheld clear shrink-wrap agreements. When software started to be distributed over the **Internet**, terms of the license would be displayed to the consumer, who would be required to mouse-click on a button indicating acceptance of the license terms. Such click-wrap agreements have also been generally upheld.

Coauthor—When one or more people collaborate on a work, they are often called coauthors or **joint authors.** The identification and intention of all the contributors to a copyrighted work are legally significant because copyright ownership vests in the authors at the time the work is **fixed** in a **tangible medium of expression**. Under copyright law, coauthors must have intended to create a joint work before its creation. Authorship status is something that **collaborators**, coauthors, **contributors**, and joint authors should be clear about when they decide to work together.

Collaboration—When two or more individuals work together on the creation of a book or other literary work, they are collaborators and the work is called a collaboration. Collaborations can be highly successful, but can also break down in catastrophic ways if the collaborators have unrealistic or unclear expectations about who will do what and how each will be compensated.

Tools and Tips: Collaborations and Collaborators

Collaborations and collaborators come in an almost infinite variety of combinations. Here are just a few:

- Two or more fiction writers who produce on a single book or short story. One example is *Double*, in which mystery writers Bill Pronzini and Marcia Mueller (husband and wife) paired up their series characters the "nameless detective" and PI Sharon McCone for a joint adventure.
- Two or more nonfiction writers who work together on a book or article.
- An expert, such as a doctor or therapist, who seeks and teams up with a professional writer.
- Two or more fiction writers commissioned to write novels about a series character under a common pen name.
- A professional writer who seeks out and teams up with an expert.
- A celebrity who gets the help of a professional writer to pen an autobiography, memoir, or advice book.
- A writer who does an "authorized" biography of a celebrity with that celebrity's cooperation.
- Two writers who collaborate on an unauthorized biography of a celebrity.
- A group of experts who collaborate on a book project and hire a writer/editor to pull the work together.
- A writer who surveys or solicits a number of individuals about a particular topic to put into a book or article. Such a project is often called a **roundup** or anthology.

- A writer and expert who are brought together by a publisher, packager, or agent to work on a special project or series title.

Authorship credit in collaborations is also handled in a variety of ways:

- A ghostwriter may be completely anonymous or perhaps given credit in the acknowledgments.
- "As told to" is a credit sometimes used for personal-experience stories written in the first person by a professional writer who interviews a nonwriter about a dramatic experience.
- "With" is sometimes used for a collaboration between a celebrity and a professional writer. Often the writer's name is in a smaller typeface than the celebrity's.
- "And" can link the names of two collaborators. Sometimes the names appear as a full, joint byline with the names in equal size and prominence. Other times, one name will precede the other and/or be larger or more prominent.

The Voice of Experience: What to Look for in a Collaborator

KATHRYN LANCE, author and collaborator
Tucson, Arizona

Kathryn Lance has been a full-time writer since 1976. She is the author or coauthor of more than 50 books of nonfiction and fiction. She has collaborated with experts on diet, health, and medical topics. She currently lives with her husband and two cats.

Q: What should an expert look for in a writer–collaborator?
A: If you are the expert looking for a writer to turn your expertise into a book you should look for a well-qualified professional writer, one who has experience and a track record. Nobody expects you to be good at two things; it's the rare expert who can also write. Even when an expert can also write, the professional writer can make the

expert sound even better. An expert should look for a collaborator with:

- Publishing connections—it's helpful if the writer already has an agent.
- Experience—ask to see previous books.
- Writing skills—check the writer's previous work and presentation.
- Knowledge in your area, especially for technical topics. However, beware of technical writers who may be too close to the subject to write well for a popular audience.
- Internet savvy—this is much more important than geographical closeness.

Q: What should a writer look for in an expert collaborator?
A: In today's publishing climate you often need an expert's name on your book. Even if you have extensive credentials as a writer or reporter, you are likely to need someone with credentials in the subject area of the book.

- Find an expert with a "high platform"—media or lecture credentials for a built-in audience.
- Find someone who understands the contribution made by the writer, respects you as a writer, and understands that writing is hard work.
- Be wary of experts who use lawyers with no publishing experience.
- Avoid an expert who refuses to sign a collaboration agreement.
- Make sure you discuss the terms of your collaboration carefully with the expert and then make sure to get a written collaboration agreement that reflects the terms of your deal. Use an experienced attorney or agent if you can.
- Don't work for anyone you get bad vibes from—a collaboration is like a marriage, and it's better not to enter into it than have to dissolve it later.

Collaboration Agreement—The most potentially problematic contracts in the field of publishing today, according to many publishing attorneys, are collaboration agreements. Carefully crafted collaboration agreements are essential to avoid preventable misunderstandings and various potential disasters. Because there are so many types of collaborations, the collaborators should carefully discuss the terms of their contract. The resulting collaboration agreement should be drafted to fit those terms, preferably by an experienced attorney. Fill-in-the-blanks or form agreements should not be used without thoughtful adaptation to the specific situation.

Ask Author Law

Q: What things should a collaboration agreement cover?
A: Collaborators should be sure that it's crystal clear who will be doing what. Their agreement should spell out the terms of the collaboration in considerable detail, by answering such questions as:

- Who will own the copyright in the finished work?
- What will the byline be?
- How will each party be compensated for work on the project? A professional writer whose living comes from writing will reasonably expect the initial work to be subsidized by the expert.
- What will the payment schedule be and what benchmarks along the way will trigger payments?
- Who will be parties to the publishing contract, if one results from the collaboration?
- Who will be responsible for such things as publicity and promotion?
- What will the writing schedule be and who will have the responsibility for moving it along?
- What will be the availability of the expert to work on the book, review the manuscript, and provide appropriate feedback?
- Who will be legally responsible for the content of the book?
- Who has final approval over editorial decisions and control of content?

- What will happen if one collaborator is unable or unwilling to complete the project?
- What standards should the work of the writer meet and who will decide if those standards have been met?

The answers should be spelled out as objectively and clearly as possible.

Sample Expert-Writer Collaboration Agreement

This agreement is made on the 00th day of Month, 1999, between Surgeon Author (hereinafter "Author") of Complete Address and Professional Writer (hereinafter "Writer") of Complete Address. These parties agree as follows:

1. Subject to the terms and conditions herein, Author and Writer agree to collaborate exclusively with each other in the preparation of a book-length manuscript about _____ tentatively entitled "Title of Book" (hereinafter "the Work") for which Author has entered into a publishing contract with Name of Publisher (hereinafter Publisher) and for which Author wishes to engage Writer for the writing of the manuscript.

2. It is understood and agreed that the actual writing of the manuscript shall be the responsibility of Writer. Author will cooperate with and assist Writer by providing all necessary information and Author's expertise regarding the content of the Work. Author agrees to make herself/himself available to Writer by telephone for sufficient time periods to permit Writer to meet the manuscript delivery date as stipulated in the agreement with the Publisher. Writer agrees to deliver the text of the Work to Author at set intervals for Author's input and approval, and Author shall promptly approve said text or detail reasonable revisions, if any. Writer agrees to revise the text, if necessary, according to Author's reasonable recommendations.

3. Author and Writer further agree to revise the text according the Publisher's reasonable requests, if any.

4. The names of both Author and Writer shall appear on the Work in all forms and languages throughout the world, separated by the word "and." The name of Author may precede the name of Writer, but both names shall be identical in size and style.

5. Copyright in the Work shall be registered in the name of Author.

6. Author agrees to indemnify Writer and hold her/him harmless against any claim, demand, suit, action, proceeding or expense of any kind arising from or based upon language, information, advice, citations, anecdotal matter, resource materials, or other content of the Work provided by Author.

7. Costs of typing, photocopying, postage and shipping, telephone, and other expenses associated with preparation of the Work shall be borne by Author. Any expenses in excess of one hundred dollars ($100) shall be approved by Author before being incurred.

8. All proceeds and revenues received from the sale, lease, license, or other disposition of any rights in the Work throughout the world shall be divided between Author and Writer as follows: (a) of the first installment of the advance stipulated in the publishing agreement, Author shall receive 20% (twenty percent), less only agency commission, and Writer shall receive 80% (eighty percent), less only agency commission; (b) of the remainder of the advance stipulated in the publishing agreement, Author shall receive 40% (forty percent), less only agency commission, and Writer shall receive 60% (sixty percent), less only agency commission.; (c) thereafter, Author and Writer shall each receive 50% (fifty percent), less only agency commission, of all revenues, from any source, received in connection with the Work. Author agrees to request Publisher to pay writer's share of all payments directly to writer, and, in the event Publisher refuses, to pay Writer's share of all payments to Writer within ten (10) days of Author's receipt of each payment. Author further agrees to request Publisher to send copies of all royalty statements and other payment records directly to Writer and, in the event Publisher refuses, to provide copies of

such statements and records promptly to Writer, along with any and all payments due to Writer.

9. Both parties agree that each shall have the right of first refusal to participate in any spinoff or ancillary projects based on the Work, including, but not limited to, merchandise, CD-ROMs, video, on-line, direct sequels, workbooks, and supplementary materials.

10. Should either Author or Writer become incapacitated or otherwise unable to complete the Work before it is finalized, the other party reserves the right to seek out a suitable successor. If Writer becomes incapacitated and the book is ultimately completed, she/he shall be paid a percentage of the total proceeds commensurate with the amount of Work she/he completed before his/her incapacitation. If Author becomes incapacitated and the book is ultimately completed he/she shall be paid a percentage of the total proceeds commensurate with the amount of Work he completed before his incapacitation. However, in the event Author is incapacitated and the book is ultimately completed, Author will receive a minimum payment of 50% (fifty percent) of what he/she would have received had he/she not become incapacitated.

11. The terms of this agreement shall be co-extensive with the life of the copyright in the Work and any extensions thereof.

12. This agreement sets forth the entire understanding of the parties and may not be changed except by written consent of both parties.

13. It is expressly understood and agreed that this agreement shall automatically be considered a part of any and all contracts and agreements made by the Author and Writer with respect to rights in the Work.

14. The terms and conditions of this agreement shall be binding upon, and the benefits thereof shall inure to the respective heirs, executors, administrators, successors, and assigns of the parties hereto.

15. Author and Writer each warrant that they have no other contractual commitment which will or might conflict with this

agreement or interfere with the performance of any obligations hereunder.

16. This agreement shall be construed in accordance with the laws of the State of New York.

17. Should any controversy, claim, or dispute arise out of or in connection with this agreement, such controversy, claim or dispute shall be submitted to arbitration before the American Arbitration Association in accordance with its rules, and judgment confirming the arbitrator's award may be entered in any court of competent jurisdiction, except that the parties shall have the right to litigate claims of $10,000 or less.

18. This agreement contains the entire agreement of the parties and there are no other promises or conditions in any other agreement whether oral or written. Any changes to this agreement must be made in writing and signed by both parties.

19. If any provision of this agreement is held invalid or unenforceable for any reason, the remaining provisions shall continue to be valid and enforceable.

IN WITNESS WHEREOF to this agreement consisting of _____ (number) pages, the parties have signed below.

Signature: _____ Date: _____
SURGEON AUTHOR

Signature: _____ Date: _____
PROFESSIONAL WRITER

Collective Works—As defined in Section 101 of the Copyright Act, a "collective work is a work, such as a periodical issue, anthology, or encyclopedia, in which a number of contributions, constituting separate and independent works in themselves, are assembled into a collective whole." Under section 201(c) of the Copyright Act, "copyright in each separate contribution to a collective work is distinct from copyright in the collective work as a whole, and vests initially in the author of the contribution." In practical terms, this means that freelance writers of articles for magazines and newspapers (periodical issues) and contributors to scholarly anthologies or journals are the owners of the copyrights in their works. Contrary to what many believe, a magazine or newspaper does *not* own a copyright in the independent freelance contribution and does not acquire any rights other than the right to publish the contribution as part of the issue or a later revision *unless the freelancer expressly grants additional rights. See* **digital rights, electronic rights, group registration.**

Commercial Speech—Speech is generally considered to be commercial in nature if it advertises a product or service or is used for another business purpose. Since 1975 commercial speech has enjoyed **First Amendment** protection from government regulation. The constitutional protection is not as great for commercial speech as for other types of protected speech. The courts have recognized that commercial speech is guided by the economic self-interest of businesses and that some government regulation may be justified to protect consumers from false or deceptive advertising. Therefore, in order to receive First Amendment protection, commercial speech must concern a legal activity and not be misleading. A court will determine whether a particular government regulation restricting the speech at issue serves a substantial government interest and, if so, if the regulation directly advances that interest and whether it is narrowly tailored to meet that interest.

**The Courts Say: Broadcast Advertising
of Lotteries Permitted**

Greater New Orleans Broadcasting Association, Inc., v. United States, 527 U.S. 173 (U.S. 1999)

The United States Supreme Court held that the Federal Communication Commission's prohibition on the broadcast of lottery information could not be applied to advertisements of private casino gambling that were broadcast by radio stations located in a state where such gambling was legal. The court found that the speech at issue was not misleading and involved a legal activity but that the government did not meet its burden of identifying a substantial interest and justifying the restriction.

Common Law—Common law is unwritten, nonstatutory law that derives its authority from usage and custom, often dating from the unwritten laws of antiquity or from the judgments of courts affirming such ancient laws. In the United States, common law refers to the laws, statutory or not, that were in effect in the colonies prior to the Revolutionary War. It is not surprising that modern American common law has deep roots in English common law. Courts may recognize common law in the absence of statutory law on a subject. Many modern statutes are codifications of basic common law principles.

Common Law Copyright—Prior to January 1, 1978, copyright was available under the common law of states for certain unpublished works until the work was published or registered with the Copyright Office, at which point federal copyright protection would begin. This common law copyright was not subject to the "limited time" restriction of the Constitution and theoretically could last forever if the work remained unpublished and unregistered. Other works that benefited from common law copyright included sound recordings, maps, reproductions of works of art, and commercial prints or labels. Common law copyright in the United States was generally abolished by the Copyright Act of 1976, which became effective on January 1, 1978. A common law copyright, in most instances, is no longer available due to federal **preemption** by the 1976 law. Federal copyright law now provides automatic protection of a work from the moment creation regardless of publication status. Common law copyright may still, under very rare circumstances, protect certain public performances, such as an extemporaneous speech, not eligible for federal copyright protection because they are not fixed in a tangible medium.

Commonwealth Rights—Some publishing contracts limit the grant of rights to specific territories. Commonwealth rights usually refer to rights in the British Commonwealth of Nations. This is a somewhat archaic designation.

Competing Works—A contract clause that restricts the author's right to write works that might compete with the work that is the subject of the contract is sometimes called a **noncompete clause** or a competing works clause.

Complaint—A lawsuit begins with the filing of a court pleading called a complaint. Under the Federal Rules of Civil Procedure, which govern the proceedings in the federal district courts in the United States, a complaint must contain a short and plain statement of the jurisdiction of the court over the case that the pleader, usually the **plaintiff**, is entitled to relief and a demand for judgment for the relief entitled to. The complaint must be signed by an attorney for the plaintiff or by the plaintiff who is representing herself on a **pro se** basis. A complaint must be filed with the court and properly served upon the **defendant**, along with a summons.

Sample Complaint for Copyright Infringement

Every lawsuit begins the same way, with the filing of a pleading document called a complaint. This particular complaint is for a writer whose work has been infringed on the Web site of a commercial business. In this case the infringer was a travel agency that posted the writer's magazine article on its Web site without permission. It is brought in a federal court because the Copyright Act is a federal law. This is called subject matter jurisdiction.

UNITED STATES DISTRICT COURT
SOUTHERN DISTRICT OF NEW YORK

WALTER WRITER,)

) **COMPLAINT FOR**

     Plaintiff,) **DAMAGES FOR**

) **COPYRIGHT INFRINGEMENT**

    v.   ) **AND RELATED CLAIMS**

) **JURY DEMANDED**

TRIPSEY TRAVEL, INC.,)

)

)

     Defendant.)

The first part of a complaint is called the caption. All papers filed in a case should carry a caption that identifies the court, parties, case, and the nature of the filing (a complaint, answer, motion, notice, etc.) Once this suit is filed, it will be given a case number to be included in every caption. Once filed with the court, the complaint must be served upon the defendant along with a summons provided by the court clerk. Complicated rules govern the filing of complaints and service of process. There is almost always a filing fee paid to the court. (In this federal case the fee is $150 and there may be additional charges.) Many state court filing fees are higher.

Plaintiff Walter Writer, by his attorney, Larry J. Lawyer, as and for his complaint, herein avers as follows:

JURISDICTION AND VENUE

1. This is an action for copyright infringement arising under the Copyright Act of 1976, 17 U.S.C. §§ 101, et. seq. This court has jurisdiction of this action under 28 U.S.C. §§ 1331, 1338(a) and 1338(b).

2. Venue is proper under 28 U.S.C. §§ 1391 and 1400(a). Upon information and belief defendant resides and can be found in the State

of New York. Further, Defendant committed acts of copyright infringement in the State of New York.

Complaints are composed according to standard procedure form. A complaint must indicate the jurisdiction and venue of the court, the parties, the claims made by the plaintiff (who is the filer of the complaint), and the relief the plaintiff is requesting.

PARTIES

3. Plaintiff Walter Writer is and was at all times relevant to the matter alleged in this complaint engaged in the business of freelance magazine writing. Walter Writer is a resident of the State of Florida.
4. Defendant TRIPSEY TRAVEL, INC. is a New York corporation with a place of business at 123 Sesame Street, New York, New York.

BACKGROUND FACTS

The background section tells enough of the plaintiff's story to justify the causes of action and relief requested. The goal of the complaint is to tell a compelling story within the constraints of the procedural rules. Such complaint drafting is an art.

5. Prior to August 2, 1999, Plaintiff created an original nonfiction article on the topic of hiking in the Adirondack Mountains entitled "Adirondack Adventures" (hereinafter referred to as the "Subject Work").
6. The Subject Work contains material wholly original with Plaintiff that is copyrightable subject matter under the laws of the United States. Plaintiff is currently, and at all relevant times, has been the sole proprietor of the right, title and interest, relevant hereto, in and to the copyright in the Subject Work. Plaintiff has produced and distributed the Subject Work in conformity with the provisions of the Copyright Act and other laws governing copyright.
7. On or about July 8, 2003, Plaintiff applied to the Register of Copyrights for a Certificate of Registration for the Subject Work. The Certificate was issued by the Register of Copyrights on August 2,

2003, and bears the registration TX 0-000-000. A true and correct copy of this Certificate is attached hereto as Exhibit A.

An exhibit is a copy of documentation attached to a court filing. In this case, the registration certificate must be filed with the complaint because copyright registration is a prerequisite to the filing of an infringement suit. If the certificate were not included here, the complaint would be fatally defective and the lawsuit would be subject to dismissal.

8. The Subject Work was published on July 4, 2003, in *National Hiker Magazine* a true and correct copy of which is attached hereto as Exhibit B.

Exhibits also can be used to document the facts. The supporting exhibits help in telling the "story" of the case.

9. On or about September 20, 2003, Plaintiff discovered the full text of the Subject Work on Tripsey Travel's Web site www.tripseytravel .bizz, a true and correct copy of which is attached hereto as Exhibit C.

10. Plaintiff has not authorized neither Tripsey Travel Inc. to copy, use, distribute or display the Subject Work.

COUNT I
COPYRIGHT INFRINGEMENT
AGAINST TRIPSEY TRAVEL, INC.

Each count must state a cause of action upon which, if proved, the court has authority to grant relief. Cases that fail to state a cause of action upon which relief can be granted can be dismissed, either by the court on its own initiative or upon motion of the defendant.

11. Plaintiff realleges and incorporates by reference as if fully set forth herein the allegations in paragraphs 1 through 10, inclusive as if set forth in full as Part of Count I.

Every cause of action has to have a separate case laid out. This is why every new cause of action incorporates all of the preceding allegations.

12. Upon information and belief, Defendant knowingly and willfully placed Plaintiff's Subject Work onto Tripsey Travel's Web site.

> *Facts don't have to be proved in the complaint, but they should be alleged in good faith. Whenever the plaintiff is not completely sure of the facts, they are pled "upon information and belief."*

13. Upon information and belief, Defendant has knowingly and willfully distributed, displayed, and reproduced the Subject Work via the Tripsey Travel website.

14. The natural and probable and foreseeable result of Defendant's wrongful conduct has been to deprive Plaintiff of the benefit of selling Plaintiff's Subject Work and to injure Plaintiff's relations with present and prospective customers.

15. Plaintiff is entitled to recover from the Defendant damages including attorney fees, it has sustained and will sustain and any gains, profits and advantages obtained by Defendant as a result of Defendant's acts of infringement. At present profits and advantages cannot be fully ascertained by Plaintiff.

COUNT II
CONTRIBUTORY COPYRIGHT INFRINGEMENT
AGAINST TRIPSEY TRAVEL, INC.

16. Plaintiff realleges and incorporates by reference as if fully set forth herein the allegations in paragraphs 1 through 15, inclusive as if set forth in full as Part of Count II.

17. Upon information and belief Defendant Tripsey Travel Inc. encouraged, facilitated and/or induced Internet users to display and reproduce unauthorized electronic reproductions of the Subject Work. Defendant knew that neither it nor the online users were authorized to distribute, display, and reproduce the Subject Work. Defendant derived substantial benefit from the infringing conduct of the online users.

PRAYER FOR RELIEF

> *Here the plaintiff lists the relief requested. All forms of relief justified by the facts should be included, even if they are contradictory or conflicting.*

WHEREFORE, PLAINTIFF prays for judgment against the Defendant as follows:

1. That the Court find that the Defendant has infringed the Plaintiff's copyright in the Subject Work.
2. That the Defendant, its directors and officers, agents servants, employees, and all other persons in active concert or in privity or in participation with them, be enjoined from directly or indirectly infringing Plaintiff's copyrights in the Subject Work or to participate or assist in any such activity.
3. That judgment be entered for Plaintiff and against Defendant for Plaintiff's actual damages according to proof and for any profits attributable to infringements of Plaintiff's copyrights in accordance with proof.
4. That judgment be entered for Plaintiff and against Defendant for statutory damages based upon Defendant's acts of infringement, pursuant to the Copyright Act of 1976, 17 U.S.C. §§ 101 et. seq.
5. That Defendant be required to account for all profits, gains, and advantages derived from its acts of infringement and for its other violations of law.
6. That all gains, profits, and advantages derived by Defendant from its acts of infringement and other violations of law be deemed to be held in constructive trust for the benefit of the Plaintiff.
7. That Plaintiff have judgment against Defendant for Plaintiff's costs and attorney's fees.
8. That the Court grant such other, further and different relief as the Court deems proper under the circumstances.

Dated:

LEGAL AND BEAGLE, LLP.

Larry J. Lawyer, Esq.
Attorney for the Plaintiff
Suite 1300
105 West 2nd Street
New York, NY 10000
(212) 555-2222

C

The federal rules require a complaint to be "verified." This means it must be signed by an attorney (or by the pro se plaintiff acting as his own attorney) who by signing verifies that the complaint is being filed in a good faith belief that a reasonable cause of action exists. Attorneys who file frivolous lawsuits are subject to sanctions.

JURY DEMAND

Many courts require that a jury demand be made at the time of the filing of the complaint, so it's usually included on the assumption that it can more easily be dropped than added later. The jury demand must also be verified by the attorney or pro se litigant.

Plaintiff hereby demands trial by jury on all issues triable to a jury.

Dated:

LEGAL AND BEAGLE, LLP.

_____

Larry J. Lawyer, Esq.
Attorney for the Plaintiff
Suite 1300
105 West 2nd Street
New York, NY 10000
(212) 555-2222

This complaint used exhibits to help tell its story. Another common device, not used here, is to have the plaintiff tell the story in a sworn and notarized affidavit, also attached to the complaint.

Compulsory License—The Copyright Act permits certain parties, musical artists, for example, to make use of certain copyrighted material, such as musical compositions, without the direct consent of the copyright owner upon payment of royalties set by a

copyright royalty panel, or after May 30, 2005, a **copyright royalty judge**. Literary works are not subject to compulsory licensing, although the digital revolution and the corresponding rash of electronic piracy of writers' work has led some author advocates and scholars to argue that compulsory licensing of literary works would protect digital rights. Others argue that authors should have control over the use of their work and that there are better ways, such as through organizations like the **Authors Registry** to handle digital licensing on behalf of writers.

Computer Programs—Computer programs are generally entitled to copyright protection as literary works, although there may be situations in which the program should instead be registered as an audiovisual work. A computer program, or software, is defined as a set of statements or instructions to be used directly or indirectly in a computer to bring about a certain result. The copyrightable expression in a computer is entitled to copyright protection, but protection does not extend to the underlying ideas, algorithms, or systems. Patent law protects the underlying processes, and if the patentable process is embedded in the program in such as way that the process and the expression are merged, then copyright protection is precluded by the patent. In addition, copyright protection may not be available for common elements such as menu command hierarchies, icons, and the use of multiple screen windows or menus to display and organize data.

Computer programs may be infringed in a nonliteral manner; that is, the look and feel of a program can be copied without copying the actual underlying code. Several courts have approached this issue from an analytical perspective, thoroughly reviewing all of the elements and levels of a program to filter out copyrightable expression from unprotected ideas and processes. A few courts, however, have taken a broader or narrower view of the extent of copyrightable expression in a computer program and have hesitated to rely on a formula that assumes that a basic amount of copyrightable expression will exist in every program.

Reverse engineering the object code of a computer program constitutes infringement, but a defense of fair use may be available if the reverse engineering is performed to discern the unprotected elements of the program, if the activities are limited in scope, and if the results are not used to commercially exploit the protected elements of the program. However, any fair use defense will fail if the person performing the reverse engineering does not possess an authorized copy of the program.

Due in part to the digital nature of a computer program and the way in which it is used and stored on the central processing unit (CPU) of a computer, the owner of a copy of a computer program is permitted to make a backup copy of the program for the purpose of running or storing the program on the computer, or if necessary, for the maintenance or repair of the computer itself. Any copies made in this manner should be destroyed and may not be transferred, leased, rented, or sold without the permission of the copyright owner.

In order to register a copyright in a computer program, a sample of the program must be deposited with the Copyright Office. This requirement may be met by printing out, or delivering in another readable format, the first twenty-five pages and last twenty-five pages of the program's source code or other scripted language used to create the program. If a user's manual or other documentation has been created, a copy must be deposited with the program's identifying material. If a computer program is contained on a CD-ROM, the entire CD-ROM package must be deposited in addition to the source code and any user's manual. If the program contains **trade secrets**, the registration application should include a letter to the Copyright Office stating that trade secrets are involved. The application should also include the page containing the copyright notice, and the requisite 50 pages of source code with the trade secret information blocked out. It is important, however, that the amount of source code blocked out is less than the amount of source code revealed and that the amount of visible code is an appreciable portion of the original computer code. If this is not possible, the Copyright Office will alternatively accept the first ten and last ten pages of source code with nothing blocked out; the first twenty-five and last twenty-five pages of object code, plus at least ten pages of source code with nothing blocked out; or for programs fifty pages or less in length, the entire source code with the trade secret material blocked out.

Separately published versions of a computer program containing new or revised material eligible for copyright protection should be registered separately with the Copyright Office. If the revised material is not contained in the first twenty-five or last twenty-five pages of source code, the deposit requirement may be fulfilled by submitting any fifty pages of source code containing the changes.

Condensation—A shortened version of a book or other literary work is called an **abridgement, abstract**, or condensation. A condensation is considered to be a **derivative work** and is independently copyrightable, but only with the permission of the owner of the copyright in the underlying work.

Confidentiality Agreement—When one party wants to protect an idea being shown to another party, a confidentiality agreement may help. Ideas are not protectable by **copyright**, so a confidentiality agreement may be useful to a limited extent.

Sample Confidentiality Agreement

When parties need to exchange information during the course of a negotiation and the information has value or needs to be kept secret, it can sometimes be pro-

---

C

tected through the use of a confidentiality agreement. The following agreement was drafted on behalf of a business executive to use before interviewing writers to collaborate on an autobiography.

CONFIDENTIALITY AGREEMENT

I _____ hereby acknowledge that Harry Squatter is seeking a professional writer to collaborate exclusively with him in the preparation of a nonfiction book proposal and, in the event of finding a publisher, a book manuscript based on Squatter's life story (hereinafter "the Work"). I am interested in being considered by Squatter as a potential collaborator.

This first section explains who is committing to a confidentiality agreement and, very important, why the information must be confidential.

For the purposes of evaluating the strength of Squatter's ideas for the Work and discussion of a possible collaboration agreement, Squatter is providing some detailed knowledge and information about his life to me. I agree that (a) all knowledge and information I may receive from Squatter, and (b) all information provided by Squatter, together with any other information acquired as direct result of any collaboration between me and Squatter, shall for all time and for all purposes be regarded as strictly confidential and held by me in confidence, and shall not be used by or directly or indirectly disclosed by me to any person whatsoever except with Squatter's prior written permission.

This paragraph spells out the requirements of confidentiality in specific detail.

I further agree that upon request, I will promptly return all confidential materials provided by Squatter and destroy or delete any copies. I also understand and agree that damages alone shall be an inadequate remedy to compensate Squatter in the event that I breach this confidentiality agreement. Accordingly, I agree that Squatter shall be entitled, without waiving any additional rights or remedies otherwise available to him at law or in equity or by statute, to injunctive relief in the event of my breach or threatened breach of confidentiality.

The final paragraph spells out the potential consequences of breaching this agreement and says that money damages may not be enough so Mr. Squatter will be entitled to seek a court injunction to stop the writer from breaching the confidentiality. What is the practical effect of this language? It might mean, for example, that if the writer doesn't get the collaborative job and decides to write an unauthorized biography, Mr. Squatter could ask the court to enjoin (stop) publication of the book. Injunctive relief is a powerful remedy and a court might be reluctant to impose it absent such an agreement.

Signature: _____ Date: _____

Printed name: _____

Note that this is a unilateral agreement and only needs to be signed by the party agreeing to its terms.

Contract—A contract is, very simply, an agreement between two parties that the courts will enforce. A contract has been compared to an exchange of promises that give each party rights and duties. If one or more of the promises are broken, the contract has been breached. When a contract is breached, the parties to a contract have a right to seek a remedy for the breach in court. In order to be legal and enforceable in court a contract must include certain essential basics, including competent parties of appropriate age and mental capacity, a clear indication of the subject matter of the contract (what the contract is actually for—publication of a book, for example, or an exchange of goods), consideration (something of value that changes hands when the contractual promise is kept), mutuality of agreement (offer and acceptance), and mutuality of obligation (performance—the keeping of the promises and the doing of duty). A contract must be legal (courts won't enforce a contract for a hired killer, for example) and possible for the parties to perform.

Ask Author Law

Q: My publisher has violated our contract in several ways. The most serious problem is that royalty payments are always late. On two different occasions, the payments were not enough and I had to raise a fuss in order to get what was owed me. The publisher is not marketing the book as aggressively as it could. Is there any way I can get out of this contract?

A: The first step is to consider diplomatic action. Talk to your agent if you have one. She should be able to apply pressure to the publisher.

If you seek a legal solution, you should be aware that the publisher must usually fall far short of its contractual obligations before the author can terminate or rescind the contract. A court will generally permit termination only in the event that the licensee has committed a material breach of the publishing agreement. Courts define a material breach as a breach of so substantial a nature that it "affects the very essence of the contract and serves to defeat the object of the parties." The breach must, in fact, constitute "a total failure in the performance of the contract." This is a high standard.

In various cases, courts have applied the above test and concluded that delays in royalty payments and certain monetary shortfalls do not amount to a material breach. Even though you may not be entitled to terminate the contract, however, you could be entitled to damages for the publisher's breach. Consult a knowledgeable attorney who can review your contract and advise you about your options.

Q: I've just been offered my first book contract from a small regional publisher. I didn't use an agent and I really want this deal, so I plan to go ahead and sign the contract, even though it's not perfect. I don't want to spook the editor by asking questions or making waves. A friend of mine said that if I don't have an agent I should have a lawyer look over the contract, but I don't want to pay a lawyer, who might just raise unnecessary questions. No offense, but my experience is that lawyers just make things complicated. And they charge an arm and a leg to muck things up.

A: First of all, any legitimate publisher is not going to be offended by reasonable questions about a contract and no good attorney is going to be offended by your concerns about the way she should approach a contract review or by a request to keep fees reasonable. That said, I can well understand that you might be uncomfortable raising contract questions, especially if there's nothing seriously wrong with the contract. But there's no reason you can't ask an attorney to do a quick review, look for any serious problems, flag any important questions arise, and suggest ways to address raise them with the publisher.

You may be more comfortable asking an attorney to handle all the negotiations on your behalf. If you tell the attorney you don't want to stir up any unnecessary trouble, he should be able to step in and spare you the agony of negotiation. The fee might be somewhat higher for the additional effort, but it can free you and the editor to concentrate on producing a good book while someone else handles the legal details. Many publishers actually prefer to deal with lawyers or agents, and having an attorney handle the negotiation for you is a way to communicate your status as a serious professional writer.

If you really don't have the resources to pay an attorney, or if you can't find an experienced publishing attorney to help you, you the **Authors Guild** provides a free legal evaluation of any book contract for its members. Your contract will be reviewed by a legal intern working under the supervision of a staff attorney, but it will be competent and very thorough.

Constitution, U.S.—The U.S. Constitution, adopted on September 17, 1787, is the foundation of federal law and government. The Constitution provides the structure for the three branches of the U.S. government and outlines the powers and responsibilities of the government and the basic rights of the people it represents.

The Constitution has been amended twenty-six times. The first ten amendments, added in 1791, make up the Bill of Rights.

Article I, Section 8, Clause 8 of the Constitution, commonly referred to as the copyright and patent clause, vests Congress with the power to grant authors and inventors, for a limited time, exclusive rights in their "Writings and Discoveries." The purpose of this provision is to promote progress in the arts and sciences. The drafters of the Constitution valued the hard work and creativity of individuals, and understood that a grant of rights as an incentive to authors and inventors would encourage progress and thus advance public welfare. The importance of the copyright clause to the drafters of the Constitution is clear when viewed in relation to the other powers they granted to Congress in the same section, including the power to declare war, the power to coin money, and the power to regulate commerce with foreign nations.

The **First Amendment** to the Constitution ensures freedom of religion, freedom of speech, **freedom of the press**, the right of assembly, and the right to petition the government for a redress of grievances.

Contributory Infringement—A person who knowingly encourages, causes, or materially contributes to someone else's infringing activities is liable for contributory infringement. Intention is a key factor in proving contributory infringement because unlike a direct infringer who is strictly liable under federal copyright law whether or not he or she has knowledge of **infringement**, the contributory infringer must actually know that a particular activity constitutes copyright infringement. The concept of contributory infringement has become especially important in the realm of **cyberspace** and new Internet-based technology. **Internet service providers** (ISPs) and bulletin-board-service operators have been found liable for contributory infringement for facilitating the infringing activities of their users and subscribers. However, courts have also held that when a bulletin-board-service operator cannot reasonably verify a claim of copyright infringement with regard to the distribution of a particular file on its system, either due to the lack of a copyright notice on the material at issue, the copyright owner's failure to provide documentation proving infringement, or because a fair use defense might be available, a lack of knowledge on the part of the operator will be found to be reasonable and no liability will be imposed.

The Courts Say: Contributory Infringement Requires Actual Notice and a Demonstrated Failure to Remove the Offending Material

A&M Records, Inc. v. Napster, Inc., 239 F.3d 1004 (9th Cir. 2001)

Napster, an Internet-based service that facilitated the transmission and retention of digital sound recordings in an easily downloadable, compressed digital format, by its users, was sued for copyright infringement by several record companies and music publishers. In addition to the plaintiff's claims of direct and vicarious infringement, the Ninth Circuit Court of Appeals concluded that they demonstrated a likelihood of success against Napster on the merits of a contributory copyright infringement claim, but determined that the injunction order by the district court was overbroad with regard to contributory infringement.

The court noted that contributory infringement exists if a defendant, with knowledge of the infringing conduct of another, induces, causes, or materially contributes to the infringement. The court cautioned that Napster did not have the requisite knowledge merely because the peer-to-peer file-sharing technology could be used to exchange copyrighted material, and concluded that actual notice of specific acts of infringement is required to hold a computer system operator liable for infringement. The court also determined that a computer system operator is liable for contributory infringement if the operator learns that specific copyrighted material is available on the system and fails to purge it. The Ninth Circuit held that liability for contributory infringement could be imposed only to the extent that Napster (1) received reasonable knowledge of specific infringing files with copyrighted musical compositions and sound recordings, (2) knew or should have known that these files were available on the Napster system, and (3) failed to act to prevent distribution of the works. The court determined that evidence supported the allegations that Napster had actual knowledge that specific copyrighted material was available by using its system, that it could block access to the system by suppliers of infringing material, that it failed to remove the copyrighted material, and that Napster materially contributed to the infringing activity of its users by providing the site and facilities for direct infringement to take place.

The Ninth Circuit ordered that the district court's injunction be narrowed to require A&M Records to provide notice to Napster of all of the copyrighted works available on the Napster system before Napster must disable access to the offending content. The court noted, however, that Napster has the burden to police its system within the system's limits.

CONTU—In 1974 the National Commission on New Technological Uses of Copyrighted Works (CONTU) was established within the Library of Congress. CONTU was established to research and report to Congress on how to best protect computer programs and photocopy machines.

The commission issued its report to Congress in 1979, concluding that computer programs, databases, and works created by computers are generally entitled to copyright protection. Congress implemented many of CONTU's recommendations in the Computer Software Copyright Act of 1980.

With respect to photocopying, the commission recommended amendments to federal copyright law to provide specific guidance for circumstances in which photocopies are made by commercial organizations on demand and for profit. CONTU also recommended that publishers, libraries, and government agencies increase public awareness regarding the copyright status of all published works.

Copyright—The first copyright was granted by a king to an early printer. It conveyed the right to own and use a printing press to reproduce and distribute various written works and established the legal rights related to the publication of written works. Copying technology has evolved exponentially since the printing press was invented; and copyright law has marched along with the advancing technology to create, preserve, and protect the property rights of authors in their creations. In the United States, copyright law is authorized in the Constitution and spelled out in a federal statute, the Copyright Act (Title 17 of the United States Code). Copyright is internationally recognized as a basic human right, essential to a civilized society. International copyright law—as embodied in treaties, organizations, associations, tribunals, laws, and agreements—plays an increasingly important role in a changing world by protecting the rights of individual human beings to property, prosperity, access to information, and freedom of expression.

The word copyright means, literally, the right to copy. It is the legal expression of a fundamental property right that has existed since the earliest civilizations, but only emerged as a distinct legal right after invention of the printing press. Before printing, the rights in words and symbols were perceived as a single property right that arose as soon as they were carved in stone, painted on skins, written on paper, or fixed in another tangible medium of expression. Printing technology didn't change the concept of written works as property, but it triggered awareness of an important distinction: the difference between the tangible object upon which written words were fixed and the intangible expression of a unique work created through the writer's selection and arrangement of those words. This distinction between physical property and **intellectual property** formed the basis of copyright law. Copyright was the first intellectual property right recognized in law as the technology revolution unraveled new strands in the ancient bundle of property rights.

Today, copyright law is so important to authors that it crops up throughout this book. Dozens of other alphabetical entries dis-

cuss copyright, including the first and last—**Abridgement** and
Zapruder. Copyright is found under **Berne Convention, Collaboration**, **Derivative Work**, **Electronic Rights**, **Fair Use**, **Graphic
Works**, **Infringement, Jurisdiction,** and so on through the alpha-
bet. Most of the sidebars and boxes are also related to copyright
issues in one way or another, providing information on how
courts, copyright owners, and society are responding to the challenges of the information age.

Ask Author Law: Copyright, A Relic of the Past?

*Q: Isn't copyright a relic of the past? Doesn't information want to be free?
Especially when it is used for the education and improvement of society?*
A: Since the advent of the Internet, there have been wild and misguided
claims that copyright law is outdated and that information wants to be
free. Such claims are simply not true. You are really asking if it's all right
to steal words, music and images, now that technology has made it
cheap and easy to digitize, download, duplicate, and distribute endless
copies. The answer is no. "Thou shalt not steal" is still engraved in
stone, although the Ten Commandments entered the public domain
long ago. Copyright infringement is stealing, pure and simple. Copyright
owners are just as entitled to protection from theft as are the owners
of jewelry, bicycles and soccer balls. Copyright law is clear and basic—
words, pictures, and sounds expressed in a distinctive way and written
down or otherwise fixed in a tangible medium of expression are the
property of the creator. "Thou shalt not steal," has been a universal
tenant of civilized society since the beginning of time and no one has
the right to steal the property of authors, regardless of the elaborate
rationalizations and excuses they concoct. No civilized society recognizes a right to steal physical property, even when it's easy to do so
and tempting to rationalize. No civilized society recognizes the theft of
intangible property, either. Copyright law has consistently adapted
along with technology. Just as laws, both civil and criminal, provide penalties and sanctions for the theft of jewelry, bicycles and soccer balls,
copyright laws provide penalties for the theft of authors' rights. Stealing
is stealing. And it's always been wrong.

Copyright Clearance Center—Billing itself as "the largest licenser of text reproduction rights in the world," the Copyright Clearance Center was formed in 1978 to facilitate compliance with U.S. copyright law. The CCC provides licensing systems for the reproduction and distribution of copyrighted materials in print and electronic formats throughout the world. Although viewed by some writers' organizations as a publisher-oriented organization, the CCC can be a very useful vehicle for rights management of literary works. 222 Rosewood Drive, Danvers, MA 01923. Phone: 978-750-8400, Fax: 978-646-8600, Web site: www.copyright.com.

Copyright Office—Copyright claims are registered with the United States Copyright Office, which has been a separate department of the Library of Congress since 1897. The Copyright Office also administers the copyright laws; provides advice and assistance to Congress on intellectual property issues, and provides technical expertise to other government agencies in negotiating and complying with international intellectual property agreements. Six separate divisions are headed by the **Register of Copyrights**. The Copyright Office is located in the Library of Congress at 101 Independence Avenue, S.E., in Washington, D.C. The telephone number is 202–707-3000. More information can be found on the Copyright Office's Web site at www.copyright.gov.

The Courts Say: Class Action Settlement Approved for Infringement of Electronic Rights

In re Literary Works in Electronic Databases Copyright Litigation, MDL No. 1379 (S.D.N.Y. March 31, 2005) (preliminary settlement)

Freelance writers won the right to share in a settlement of more that $18 million as payment for articles placed in online databases without permission. The settlement ended four years of class action litigation

---

and negotiations. Three different class actions suits were brought on behalf of all freelancers by twenty-one individual writers and three writers' organizations—the **American Society of Journalists and Authors**, the **Authors Guild**, and the **National Writers Union**. The suits were filed in 2001, shortly after the U.S. Supreme Court decided that publication of freelance writers' articles in digital databases without explicit consent constitutes infringement of their copyrights. See *New York Times Co. v. Tasini*, 533 U.S. 483 (2001) on page 183. Those cases were consolidated into a single class action that extended the battle over electronic rights for another four years.

Jim Morrison, the former ASJA president who represented his organization in the settlement negotiations, described the settlement as "an $18 million validation of how valuable electronic rights are to publishers. Freelance writers should remember that when negotiating their contracts."

The settlement was funded by the defendant databases, and publishers were brought into the suit for indemnification because they had licensed articles without authority of the freelancers. The hard-won settlement meant major money for freelancers who registered their copyrights within certain time limits and substantial money for those who had registered, but not within the time limits. Even writers who failed to register their copyrights at all qualified for up to $60 per article.

Course Packs—Course packs are selected excerpts of books and other copyrighted materials that have been compiled for use by students in college courses. The materials are selected by professors and then photocopied and distributed to students by a photocopy store. They provide professors with a way to create an **anthology** of course materials perfectly tailored to the content of the class, and they are a more economical solution for budget-oriented students who may otherwise be required to purchase many books for each course. Course packs are subject to copyright law, and it is therefore essential that permission is obtained from the copyright owner of each excerpt. While the photocopying of a selected excerpt may, in certain limited circumstances, be entitled to a **fair use** defense, most copying of this nature has been held to constitute copyright infringement.

The Courts Say: Academic Course Packs Are Not Fair Use

Basic Books, Inc. v. Kinko's Graphics Corp., 758 F. Supp. 1522 (S.D.N.Y. 1991)

The District Court for the Southern District of New York found that the activities of Kinko's with regard to the preparation and sale of course packs to college students in New York City constituted copyright infringement. Undertaking a comprehensive fair use analysis, the court determined that the multiple copying of excerpts from the plaintiff publishers' books without permission was not fair use because Kinko's merely repackaged the original material; no literary effort was made to expand upon or contextualize the copied selections; the books infringed were factual in nature, not fictitious; entire chapters of the books were copied; and the copying unfavorably affected the publishers' sales of these books and their collection of permission fees. The district court found that while students used the course packs for educational purposes, Kinko's did not; Kinko's was instead a commercial enterprise that intended to profit from the course pack business. The court also considered the Agreement on Guidelines for Classroom Copying in Not-for-Profit Educational Institutions that are part of the legislative history of the Copyright Act of 1976, but found that Kinko's had deviated from the spirit of guidelines designed to provide protection for some educational uses of copyrighted materials. Although the classroom guidelines expressly prohibit the creation of anthologies of unauthorized copyrighted material, the court stopped short of holding that *all* unauthorized anthologies are prohibited without a fair use analysis. The district court enjoined Kinko's from infringing future copyrighted works and awarded the plaintiff publishers statutory damages, attorney's fees, and costs.

Princeton University Press v. Michigan Document Services, Inc., 99 F.3d 1381 (6ᵗʰ Cir. 1996)

In a similar case brought in Michigan, the Sixth Circuit Court of Appeals also held that a copy shop's preparation and sale of course packs were not fair use of the copyrighted works. The owner of the copy shop, who felt that the *Kinko's* case in New York had been wrongly decided, chose not to request permission to use the copyrighted materials and did not pay permission fees. In its fair use analysis, the court determined that the market effect of the copying is the most important consideration of the fair use doctrine. Noting that the unauthorized course packs diminished the potential market value of the copyrighted works because the publishers were collecting permission fees at a rate of nearly $500,000 per year from the complying copy shops, the court enjoined the defendant from future infringement but did not award statutory damages given the unsettled nature of the fair use doctrine and the defendant's sincere belief that the copying was fair.

Court System in the United States—Article III of the U.S. Constitution establishes the judiciary as one of the three separate branches of government, along with the legislative branch and the executive branch. The judicial branch has evolved into a three-tiered system of federal courts: the Supreme Court, the circuit courts of appeal, and the district courts. Each state also has its own courts to decide matters arising from state law.

The dual federal-state structure of the United States court system ensures that nearly all cases have a fair opportunity to be heard and resolved. The two court systems are sufficiently interconnected that certain cases originating in a state court may be transferred or appealed to a federal court if federal issues are involved. Likewise, federal cases can be transferred to a state court if necessary.

Federal Courts. The U.S. Supreme Court is located in Washington, DC. The Court is composed of a chief justice and eight associate justices. The justices are appointed by the president and confirmed by the Senate for a life term. Each year, the Court hears a limited number of cases that have originated in the lower courts and involve important issues of constitutional or federal law. When a party appeals a case from a circuit court to the Supreme Court, the Court will grant or deny a writ of certiorari since the decision as to whether to hear a case on appeal is a matter of discretion. The Supreme Court has original **jurisdiction** over matters involving ambassadors or consuls, and cases where a state is a party. The Court has appellate jurisdiction over all other cases involving federal law and the **treaties** of the United States.

There are twelve circuit courts of appeal, or circuit courts, each authorized to hear appeals from the district courts or from federal administrative agencies within the circuit. Court of Appeals judges, like Supreme Court justices, are appointed by the president and confirmed by the Senate for life. The Court of Appeals for the Federal Circuit is the thirteenth appellate court. This special circuit court exercises national jurisdiction over appeals in specialized cases, including patent cases and those decided by the Court of International Trade, a trial court that decides cases involving international trade and customs issues, and the Court of Federal Claims, which hears cases involving claims for money damages against the United States, disputes over federal contracts, and other claims against the United States.

There are ninety-four regional district courts. Eighty-nine situated within the fifty states, and the others are located in Puerto Rico, the Virgin Islands, the District of Columbia, Guam, and the Northern Mariana Islands. Each state has a least one district court and many have more than one. The district courts serve as trial courts and have jurisdiction to hear nearly all federal cases, including both civil and criminal matters. Like other federal judges, district court judges are appointed by the president and confirmed by the Senate for a life term. Magistrate judges are appointed by a majority vote of the active district judges of the court to hear cases assigned by statute as well as those delegated by the district judges. Full-time magistrate judges serve for eight years.

In addition to a district court, each judicial district within the United States has its own bankruptcy court. Bankruptcy judges are appointed for fourteen-year terms by the majority of judges of the circuit courts to specifically hear bankruptcy matters.

When a case has been decided by the district court, the losing party generally may appeal that decision to the regional Circuit Court of Appeals. If the circuit court's decision conflicts with the decisions of its sister circuit courts, the Supreme Court may agree to hear a case (grant certiorari) to determine the matter once and for all. The Supreme Court may also decide to grant certiorari to a case on appeal from a circuit court if constitutional issues are involved.

State Courts. Each of the fifty states has its own state court system to hear matters arising from state law. A state's court system is often modeled on that of the federal government and consists of three levels, although some states have only two levels. In general, the state's trial court will be a county court or the county circuit court. States have different names for intermediate appelate courts and their highest courts.

Cover Price—The cover price of a book usually refers to the retail price, or **list price**. A royalty rate based on a percentage of the cover price is considered to be more valuable than one based on a discounted or **net price**.

Credit—The author of a book or article usually expects appropriate recognition in the form of a credit of some sort, sometimes called a **byline**, credit line, or **authorship credit.** Authors often protect their name and reputation by seeking control over such credit. Sometimes it will be important to get appropriate credit and at other times an author might not want his name to appear on a particular work.

Cross-Collateralization—The practice of accounting for all sums owed to a publisher by a single author under more than one contract rather than keeping each contract separate is called **bucket accounting**, **joint accounting**, or cross-collateralization. This is fundamentally unfair to authors because it can have the effect of holding back royalty payments on one book until the **earn out** of another.

Cyberspace—Surf's up, so plug in and log on! The **Internet** has not only created new modes of communication and opportunities for home shopping, but it has created an entire digital culture, complete with its own language. The term cyberspace was coined by science fiction author William Gibson in his 1984 novel, *Neuromancer*. The word quickly came to describe the network of links that constitute the essence of the Internet, lending the text and graphics appearing on the user's two-dimensional, small computer screen an air of mystery and excitement. The average computer user became a "pioneer" exploring the "frontier" of a new digital world. Cyberspace has come to represent the online global community, which stretches across the world unconstrained by traditional political and geographic borders.

Tips and Tools: Copyright in Cyberspace

There has been a great deal of controversy over the role of copyright in cyberspace. Many people hailed the Internet as a new medium that would revolutionize the dissemination of information and "free" information from the constraints of copyright ownership. Copyrighted material can be linked, copied, cut and pasted, transmitted and downloaded from the privacy of one's own home or business. Critics of copyright in cyberspace argue that nobody can prevent unauthorized copying in cyberspace, and efforts to enforce copyright laws in cyberspace are bound to be futile.

In reality, however, copyright laws function the same way online as

---

they do in the world of paper and photocopy machines. Text, photographs, images, sound recordings, and other material found in cyberspace are protected by copyright because they have been fixed in a tangible medium of expression. Internet-based technology has indeed made copying easier, cheaper, and better in quality than ever before, but it has not changed the fact that copyright does exist and is enforceable in cyberspace. The Internet's success as a commercial venue has greatly influenced the public's perception of cyberspace and the early ideals of getting information for free are fading into history. Still, as illustrated by the advent of downloading music files, people do not usually stop to think about copyright ownership as a property right, similar to the ownership of real estate; instead, they feel entitled to use and benefit from the work of others while paying little or nothing for the privilege. Authors who upload copyrighted material to the Internet find themselves having to protect the products of their creativity from theft.

Cyberspace has created an opportunity for authors to receive an unprecedented level of public exposure that can result in increased sales and income for the copyright owner. On the other hand, online publication can result in rampant infringement unless authors get serious about seeking out and prosecuting infringers. Many methods are currently available to protect online works from unauthorized uses. For example, digital watermarking deters downloading because it prevents the printing of a clean copy. Another option is to display work in PDF format rather than in traditional HTML code because users can read and even print PDF documents, but are prevented from cutting and pasting text or graphics to other documents. Copyright owners can register with the **Authors Registry**, **Copyright Clearance Center,** or another rights clearance center to facilitate grants of permission and the collection of fees associated with the legal use of copyrighted material. Digital rights management has become big business as attempts are made to find new methods of protection as quickly as others find ways to circumvent existing technology. Although the **Digital Millenium Copyright Act** prohibits the circumvention of copyright management systems, circumvention is still a concern.

Cybersquatting—The deliberate, bad-faith, and abusive registration of **Internet** domain names in violation of the rights of trademark owners is known as cybersquatting. The **Anticybersquatting Consumer Protection Act** (ACPA) was enacted in 1999 to protect trademark owners from a new form of blackmail involving the bad-faith registration of a well-known brand name as a domain name in order to force the trademark owner to buy it in order to do business on the Internet under its own brand name.

The ACPA imposes liability on cybersquatters with a bad-faith intent who register, traffic in, or use a domain name identical or confusingly similar to a distinctive mark, or identical, confusingly similar to, or dilutive of a famous mark. The law establishes nine factors that may be considered in determining whether a person has acted with bad faith: (1) the trademark or other intellectual property rights of the person, if any, in the domain name; (2) the extent to which the domain name consists of the legal name of the person or a name that is otherwise commonly used to identify that person; (3) the person's prior use, if any, of the domain name in connection with the bona fide offering of any goods or services; (4) the person's bona fide noncommercial or fair use of the mark in a site accessible under the domain name; (5) the person's intent to divert consumers from the mark owner's online location to a site that could harm the goodwill represented by the mark, either for commercial gain or with the intent to tarnish or disparage the mark; (6) the person's offer to transfer, sell, or otherwise assign the domain name to the mark owner or any third party for financial gain without having used the domain name in the bona fide offering of any goods or services; (7) the person's provision of material and misleading false contact information when applying for the registration of the domain name; (8) the person's registration or acquisition of multiple domain names that the person knows are identical or confusingly similar to marks of others; and (9) the extent to which the mark incorporated in the person's domain name registration is or is not distinctive and famous.

The ACPA also contains a safe harbor that protects an innocent user from a finding of bad-faith intent where the person reasonably believed that the use of the domain name was fair use or otherwise legal.

The Courts Say: Bad Faith Is a Key Factor in Determining Liability for Cybersquatting

Virtual Works, Inc., v. Volkswagen of America, Inc., 238 F.3d 264 (4th Cir. 2001)

The Fourth Circuit Court of Appeals affirmed the decision of the district court finding that Virtual Works, an Internet service provider, violated the ACPA by registering the vw.net domain name and later trying to force Volkswagen to buy it back. The court found that it was not limited to considering the nine factors enumerated in the ACPA in determining whether or not a party acted in bad-faith. The court determined that at the time Virtual Works proposed to sell its domain name to Volkswagen, it was motivated by a bad-faith intent to profit from the fame of the VW mark, despite the fact that Virtual Works had used it for two years in its own business, because Virtual Works registered the name with the knowledge that it was similar to a famous mark and the intent of selling it someday for a profit. The court also determined that there were other domain names available to Virtual Works that it could have registered just as easily instead, including vwi.net, and that Virtual Works threatened Volkswagen that the domain name would be sold to the highest bidder within twenty-four hours if it did not make an offer. The court found that the fact that the domain name resembles a famous mark and the fact that Virtual Works offered to sell the name to Volkswagen did not constitute violations of the ACPA by themselves, but the totality of the circumstances revealed that Virtual Works had acted in bad faith.

D

Damages—Damages is a legal term for money—financial compensation paid by one party to another for an injury or injustice. Damages are awarded by courts after liability has been proved. There are numerous kinds of damages.

Actual Damages must be proved by a successful **plaintiff** and generally must bear a close relationship to specific harm caused by the **defendant.** Actual damages in copyright infringement cases, for example, must reflect the reasonable value to the plaintiff of the work infringed or the amount by which the defendant was unjustly enriched.

Punitive Damages are designed to deter tortious behavior by punishing defendants for wrong acts. In order to have a deterrent effect, punitive damages should be large enough to hurt the defendant. They are often determined as a percentage of a defendant's profits or corporate value. Many corporations are supporters of tort reform designed to cap or eliminate punitive damages, which they see as a way for trial lawyers to earn huge contingency fees by unfairly attacking businesses. Trial lawyers, on the other hand, see punitive damages and contingency fees as a necessary check on corporate excess and a way to ensure justice for individuals who might not be otherwise able to assert their legal rights.

Special Damages are sometimes awarded on top of actual damages to compensate victims for such intangibles as pain and suffering or loss of consortium.

Statutory Damages are specifically provided for by statute. For example, statutory damages are may be elected in lieu of actual damages in certain copyright infringement actions when the copyright was registered within three months of publication or prior to the infringement. Statutory damages for copyright infringement can range from $250 for "innocent" infringement all the way up to $150,000 for willful infringement. A plaintiff can prove actual damages or elect statutory damages but cannot receive both for the same infringement. Punative damages are not available as a remedy for copyright infringement.

Liquidated Damages is the amount that a party to a contract has agreed to pay in the event of a breach. The purpose of liquidated damages is to secure performance of the contract and to designate a specific amount in the event of nonperformance.

Database—A database is a collection of data that is arranged in a specific manner to facilitate research and retrieval of the information. Databases are often stored on computers. They are traditionally considered to be compilations and are thus entitled to copyright protection. Copyright protection, however, only extends to the copyrightable elements of expression in a database and not to the underlying ideas, concepts, or formats, so the resulting protection may be thin. A compilation of facts will be entitled to copyright protection to the extent that it constitutes original authorship, and some or all of the contents of the database may be protected as well. A similar level of international protection is also provided for databases by the **Berne Convention** and the **Agreement on Trade-Related Aspects of Intellectual Property (TRIPs)**.

Since copyright protection for a particular database is dependent on **originality** and thus may not extend to all elements of the work, there are some alternative methods of protection that have been at least recognized by the courts. For instance, common law protection may be available under individual state trespass to chattels laws for a database that has been accessed in an unauthorized manner. Protection may also exist under the Computer Fraud and Abuse Act if the owner of the database can prove that the intentional unauthorized access to its computers by another party permitted that party to obtain or alter information it could not legally access, or that the unauthorized use caused damage to the computer system. Protection of a database under contract law is becoming an increasingly popular method of controlling access to and subsequent use of data. Database owners may establish the terms of use for a database and deny access to anyone who does not agree to the terms, but the extent of protection is dependent on the contract law of each state and the database owner will most likely have to prove damages as part of a breach of contract claim. A very few databases may also be entitled to protection as trade secrets, provided that the information contained in the database is sufficiently confidential.

Should Databases Receive Copyright Protection?

The copyright protection of databases has proved to be a challenging issue for several reasons. First, much of the data stored in a database, such as names, phone numbers, and other bare facts, lack the originality that is a prerequisite for copyright protection. For instance, a white pages telephone directory is not entitled to copyright protection. Second, automated databases, which usually exist on a computer, may be subject to nearly constant revision. The Copyright Office has developed a special group registration process for automated databases that allows for three months of revisions to be registered at one time. Third, the fact that information contained in computerized databases can be easily retrieved and copied poses problems of unauthorized access and copying.

Just what sort of protection should be given to databases under U.S. copyright law has been a subject of vigorous discussion. It may be argued that databases do not deserve copyright protection because they lack originality and therefore fall outside the scope of the constitutional mandate for the federal protection of creative works. However, because they have traditionally received at least some protection under copyright law as compilations, it is doubtful that this protection will be further reduced. It is more likely that protection for databases will be expanded, either within the framework of copyright law or through the application of other available laws. Gaps in protection exist in many databases because portions of the structure or content of the database are not sufficiently creative to meet the originality requirement for copyright protection. This uneven protection claims of economic losses by some businesses. It has also encouraged developers to find ways of creating original copyrightable content, selection methods, and formats for their databases.

The European Union provides copyright protection to the structure of a database and has also established sui generis protection for the content of the database, which is not dependent on the originality of the data. This protection, however, is only available to EU nationals and to others if their country of origin provides reciprocity or if they establish a commercial presence in the EU. This stronger European protection places database owners in the United States at a disadvantage in the global market.

Lawmakers are still grappling with and information users are still debating the degree of protection that can or should be afforded to databases.

Deal Points—Specific contract terms related to a particular agreement between an author and publisher are often called deal points, as opposed to **boilerplate** terms, which are likely to be standard in all a particular publisher's contracts. Deal points are almost always the subject of negotiation, but authors should also evaluate the whole contract and make sure the boilerplate is acceptable. Many boilerplate clauses can also be negotiated and should not be overlooked by authors and their agents or attorneys. Typical deal points include the **royalty rate**, **advance**, and rights acquired.

Declaratory Judgment—Damages are not the only thing disputed by litigants in copyright infringement cases. Federal courts can also be asked to determine ownership of a copyright. Asking a court to make such a determination is done by filing a **complaint** for a declaratory judgment.

Deep Discount—Publishers sometimes pay lower royalty rates on books they provide to distributors at a discount exceeding a certain percent off the **cover price** that is considered to be greater than the publisher's normal discount to the bookselling trade. Such deep discount sales can be the norm rather than the exception in these days of megabookstores and wholesale club sales.

Tips and Tools: Negotiating a Reasonable Deep Discount Clause

Authors should pay close attention to the deep discount clauses in their publishing contracts. Here are some ways to blunt the unfortunate impact of deep discounting:

- Do some projected calculations to see what will happen to the income from your book at various discount rates and point out the negative effect when you negotiate with your publisher. This may help you to negotiate some concessions and will at least give you a more realistic view of the value of your contract.
- Try to establish a minimum royalty or a floor below which the rate may not drop.

- Try to raise the royalty rate for deep discount sales. For example if the proposed contract calls for royalties on a certain discount to be reduced to, say, 5 percent from 10 percent, ask for a reduced rate of 7 or 8 percent instead of accepting the 5 percent.
- Try to raise the deep discount threshold or the range of discounts that will trigger royalty reductions. For example, if the publisher proposes to lower the royalty rate on all discounts over 45 percent, try to get that threshold increased to 50 percent or more. Or try to get the rate changed in more gradual increments than in the offered contract.
- Try to make up for the projected impact of deep discount sales by asking for other concessions from the publisher, such as a better escalator clause.

Deep Linking—The practice of linking from one Web site to an internal Web page of another Web site is called deep linking. In contrast, the creation of a link to the home page of another Web site is not considered a deep link. Deep linking does not generally violate copyright law or unfair competition laws where the link transfers the user to a Web page on a different Web site but does not copy any of the material from that Web page or attempt to confuse the user as to the source of that material. *See also* **framing**.

The Courts Say: Deep Linking Does Not Violate Copyright Owner's Right to Reproduce or Publicly Display a Work

Ticketmaster Corp. v. Tickets.Com, Inc., 2003 WL 21406289 (C.D.Cal. March 7, 2003)

Ticketmaster brought a lawsuit against Tickets.com, a company that sells tickets to events and provides information on all events regardless of whether they sell the tickets through its Web site. Tickets.com provided deep links to specific Web pages within Ticketmaster's Web site where users could purchase tickets to particular events. The court held that the unauthorized deep links created by Tickets.com were not copyright infringement because they did not violate Ticketmaster's exclusive rights of reproduction and display since the user was transferred directly to one of Ticketmaster's Web pages, which clearly identified itself as part of the Ticketmaster Web site. The court also found significant the fact that the Tickets.com Web page clearly displayed a notice stating that the tickets were not available through Tickets.com but rather through another online ticketing company. Although the issue was raised as to whether "framing" the material in a separate, smaller window affected the decision, the court noted that the frames in question were created by some browsers based on the settings of the individual user and were not created by Tickets.com to confuse the user by disguising the sale of tickets through Tickemaster.

Defamation—Libel, or injuring someone's reputation with the written word, is the major form of defamation and the most serious potential liability faced by writers, reporters, and broadcasters. **Slander** is another form of defamation related largely to spoken words. The law of defamation varies from jurisdiction to jurisdiction.

Default—Failure of a **defendant** to respond to a lawsuit filed against him is called a default and can result in a default judgment being entered by the court. As painful as it is to face a lawsuit, it can be far more painful to ignore a summons and risk a default judgment. If you are sued, consult an attorney.

Defendant—In a civil lawsuit, the defendant is the party who is sued by the **plaintiff.** In a criminal case the defendant is the person charged with a crime and prosecuted by the people through the state. Individuals cannot bring criminal charges against other individuals.

Demand Letter—A formal letter that makes a demand for payment or for the meeting of a legal obligation in a straightforward and timely manner, with the demand supported by appropriate facts and arguments, is a potentially effective first step in the process of enforcing a legal right. A good demand letter should be carefully phrased, brief, and clear, with the potential consequences of failing to respond appropriately identified. While demand letters are usually written by lawyers on behalf of clients, there is no reason why an individual who has suffered a legal wrong can't make an effective written demand.

Tips and Tools: Creating an Effective Demand Letter

- Address it by name to someone with the authority and motivation to respond. This might be the president, publisher, editor in chief, CEO, legal counsel, vice president of public relations, or an executive with a similar title. Research appropriate recipients by visiting the firm's Web site or simply calling and asking for a name.
- Verify the correct spelling of the recipient's name.
- Keep the tone civil but firm.
- Keep it brief and clear.
- Specify exactly how you have been wronged with just enough carefully selected supporting detail to make your point without saying too much.
- Specify exactly how you expect the wrong to be remedied.
- Set a reasonable time limit for a response.
- Explain what your next step will be in the event of a failure to respond. You can hint at dire consequences, but don't make a threat that you don't intend to keep.
- Indicate your willingness to discuss potential solutions to the problem and invite the recipient to contact you with any questions or concerns.
- When you've finished your letter, set it aside for a day or two and then revise it. You want to polish it until it is transformed into a lean, mean fighting machine.

- Don't use up all your ammunition in a first letter. Keep something in reserve.
- Keep track of the time limit you set and follow up appropriately.
- Consider adding your attorney to the carbon copy line, but only if your attorney gives you permission.
- If you have a lot at stake, consider consulting your attorney *before* sending a demand.

An early step in resolving a potential dispute is to put the other party on notice that the problem exists. Under our system of justice, there is a core principle that adversaries are entitled to know the nature of the claims against them and have a chance to respond. Sometimes notice is a requirement before a complaint can be filed. Other times it is an optional step used to precipitate a settlement discussion and avoid litigation. A demand letter is one method of putting a potential adversary on notice. A cease and desist letter is another variation. The following demand letter was sent directly by the writer to his publisher. The writer could also engage an attorney to send a demand letter on his behalf.

Demands can also be made in a series, escalating from polite requests and subtle hints of consequences to firm demands and a pointed discussion of the consequences of ignoring them. Regardless of the stage, the tone should always be businesslike and civil. Stridency is almost never effective and any threats should be ones that the writer intends to follow through on. Phrasing should be very careful.

A Sample Demand Letter

This particular demand letter is written to a vanity print-on-demand publisher masquerading as a traditional publisher. While the publisher does not charge for printing and editorial services, it does offer promotion packages and publicity "packages," which are overpriced and undereffective. Print-on-demand technology has blurred the lines between traditional and vanity (or subsidy) publishing and potential authors should be very careful of publishers claiming to offer opportunity to undiscovered writers. Such tricks as token advances, requesting lists of friends to whom to offer "discounts," and charging for promotion should raise red flags on the part of authors.

Walter R. Writer
123 Sesame Street, New York, NY 10000

A demand letter should be professionally formatted on a business letterhead and in business style.

July 18, 2004

Peter R. Printshop, CEO
POD Publishing Co.
447 Twilight Lane
Roseville, OH 44567

RE: *The Great All-American Novel*
VIA: Facsimile (418-555-1234)
and First Class Mail

Dear Mr. Printshop:

I am an author who is not satisfied with the promotional services provided by your firm in relation to publication of my book, *The Great All-American Novel*. In spite of my repeated attempts to communicate my problems to various members of your staff, I have not been able to get any satisfaction or the delivery of services for which I have paid.

The first paragraph spells out the problem clearly and simply. The author believes that the promotional package for which he paid was not what he expected and didn't get the implied results.

Accordingly, because POD Publishing has failed to provide me with the services for which I contracted, I must demand a refund of all monies paid to POD and a reversion of all rights in my work.

> *Next comes the formal demand, again spelled out in clear, simple terms. He is asking for a refund of the money he has paid and, more important, a reversion of his rights that are now tied up by this vanity publisher.*

I will follow up with you soon. In the meantime, if you have any questions or anything you'd like to discuss, please do not hesitate to contact me. I sincerely hope we are able to resolve this matter without the necessity of legal action.

> *This ending invites a negotiation and indicates a willingness to discuss potential solutions. Legal action, the consequence of failure to respond, is merely hinted at rather than directly threatened. This leaves an opportunity for another letter with more explicit threats and the legal action could be another interim step, perhaps the involvement of an attorney, before filing of a lawsuit. This letter has been cleverly designed to be flexible and useful. Note that it doesn't leave a response up to the publisher, but indicates that the demand will be followed up.*

Yours very truly,
Walter R. Writer

cc: Angela Editor
     Pamela Publicity
     Larry Lawyer
     Association of American Publishers

> *Note that these people are openly sent copies in an attempt to put pressure on the recipient. If you send a copy to your lawyer, make sure that you have his consent to do so. If the dispute escalates later, you may want to send copies to writers organizations or publish-*

> *ing associations (organizations that represent the inter-*
> *ests of either party). Careful thought should be given as*
> *to when and whom to CC. This tactic can sometimes*
> *backfire and should be prudently used.*

Derivative Work—A derivative work modifies or adapts a pre-existing work, and the original authorship contained in the derivative work is protected by copyright. However, the author of a preexisting work has the right to prepare or authorize derivative works based on that material. This means that a derivative work can only receive copyright protection if it was prepared with the authorization of the owner of the copyright for the preexisting work. If the author of the derivative work does not obtain consent from the original copyright owner, derivative work created will be considered infringing.

Translations, sound recordings, dramatizations, motion picture versions, abridgments, and condensations are examples of derivative works. A work may also be considered derivative if it incorporates editorial revisions or other changes that amount to an original work of authorship.

The Courts Say: A Work Is Considered Derivative if It Is Substantially Similar to a Preexisting Work

Tufenkian Import/Export Ventures, Inc. v. Einstein Moomjy, Inc., 338 F.3d 127 (2d Cir. 2003)

A district court held that a floral rug design was not an infringing derivative work because both the preexisting work and the derivative work were adaptations of the same public domain sources and were only substantially similar with respect to the public domain elements. The Second Circuit, vacating and remanding the decision, concluded that although the district court considered the total concept and feel of the two works, it failed to determine whether material portions of the derivative work infringed the preexisting work. After performing a close visual inspection of the works, the court found that the particular combination of public domain elements in the preexisting work amounted to expression entitled to thin copyright protection, and that the derivative work infringed this copyright by copying the original and particular selections of public domain elements embodied in the preexisting work. The court considered the overwhelming number of motifs in the two works that were selected or eliminated in the same way from the public domain works, as well as the essential similarity in the structural layout of both designs.

Digital Millenium Copyright Act—The DMCA was signed into law on October 28, 1998, to implement the **World Intellectual Property Organization** (WIPO) Copyright Treaty and the WIPO Performances and Phonograms Treaty. The act also limits the liability of **Internet service providers** (ISPs) for copyright infringement, creates an exemption for making a copy of a computer program by activating a computer for purposes of maintenance or repair, and adds several provisions relating to the functions of the Copyright Office, distance education, the exceptions in the Copyright Act for libraries and for making ephemeral recordings, **Webcasting** of **sound recordings** on the **Internet**, and the applicability of collective bargaining agreement obligations in the case of transfers of rights in motion pictures. The act also establishes a ten-year term of protection for the design of vessel hulls.

The DMCA prohibits the circumvention of technological measures that control access to protected works and the manufacturing or trafficking in technology designed to circumvent those measures. It permits nonprofit libraries, archives, and educational access to a copyrighted work solely for evaluation or for acquisition permits; certain enforcement or intelligence activities of state or federal governments; and permits certain reverse engineering purposes. The DCMA bars the provision or distribution of false copyright management information with the intent to induce or conceal infringement. It provides exemptions for law enforcement and intelligence activities of state or federal governments, and for certain analog and digital transmissions by broadcast stations or cable systems. The act establishes civil and criminal penalties for violations of these provisions.

The DMCA exempts an ISP from liability for copyright infringement for transmitting material through its network, or for the temporary system caching of the material if that transmission was initiated by a person other than the service provider, and if the transmission is carried out by an automated process. An ISP will also not be held liable for data stored on its network at the direction of a user if the ISP does not have actual knowledge that the material or the use of the material is infringing a copyright. In order to benefit from the liability limitations, an ISP must provide contact information of a designated agent to the public and to the Copyright Office to facilitate notification of infringement, comply with the notice and take-down requirements of the act (see Tips and Tools, below), implement and inform subscribers of a policy for terminating repeat infringers, and accommodate standard technical measures used by copyright owners to identify or protect copyrighted material.

Tips and Tools: Protect Your Rights with Notice and Take Down

The notice and take-down provisions of the DMCA offer authors a way to protect their works online while limiting the liability of ISPs for copyright infringement. Notice and take down requires you to police the Internet and search for infringing materials.

If infringing material is found, you must submit a notification, under penalty of perjury, to the ISP's designated agent. The notification must:

- bear your physical or electronic signature, or that of your agent; see **digital signature**

- identify the work that you claim has been infringed, or if more than one work is infringed on a single Web site, a representative list of the works at that site;
- identify the infringing material that is to be removed, and include any information necessary so the ISP can locate the material;
- provide your address, telephone number, and e-mail address, so that the ISP can contact you;
- state that you have a good faith belief that use of the material on the Web site has not been authorized by you, your agent, or the law;
- state that the information in the notification is accurate, and under penalty of perjury, that you are the owner of the copyright that has been infringed or that your agent who is filing the notification is authorized to act on your behalf.

If you fail to comply substantially with the statutory requirements, the notification will not be considered by a court in determining whether the ISP has the requisite level of knowledge to support a liability claim.

Upon receiving your notification, the ISP must promptly make a good faith effort to remove the infringing material from its network or disable access to the material. This is called take down. The ISP will not be liable for any action based on the fact that the material was removed. The timely removal or blocking of the infringing material also means that the ISP will not be liable for monetary damages if you file an infringement action in court.

After removing the infringing material, the ISP must take reasonable steps to promptly notify the subscriber that the material has been removed or blocked. If the subscriber responds with a counternotification, the ISP must provide you with a copy of that response and notify you that it will replace the removed material or cease disabling access to it in ten business days. Unless you notify the ISP's designated agent that you have filed an action seeking a court order to restrain the subscriber from infringing your work on the ISP's system or network, the ISP must replace the material within ten to fourteen business days.

The DCMA permits the subscriber to respond to the notice and take down by issuing a counternotification. The counternotification must:

- bear the physical or electronic signature of the subscriber;
- identify the material that has been removed or blocked and the location at which the material appeared before it was taken down;
- state under penalty of perjury that the subscriber has a good faith belief that the material was removed or disabled as a result of mistake or misidentification;
- provide the subscriber's name, address, and telephone number, and a statement that the subscriber consents to the jurisdiction of federal district court for the judicial district in which the address is located, or, if the subscriber's address is in another country, for any judicial district in which the ISP may be found, and that the subscriber will accept service of process from you or your designated agent.

The DCMA imposes damages, including costs and attorneys' fees, incurred by the alleged infringer, the copyright owner, or the ISP against any party who knowingly misrepresents material facts in either the notification or the counternotification.

Digital Performance Right in Sound Recordings Act of 1995— The DPRS act, which took effect on February 1, 1996, created a public performance right in a sound recording under federal copyright law. While this right previously received recognition in other countries as part of the limited bundle of rights known as **neighboring rights**, the right to publicly perform a sound recording was never given protection in the United States. The DPRS act specifically recognized the right to publicly perform a sound recording by means of a digital audio transmission, subject to certain limitations including a new compulsory license for nonexempt, noninteractive, digital subscription transmissions. The **Digital Millennium Copyright Act** of 1998 expanded the scope of the license. *See* **The Courts Say,** page 144.

Digital Rights—Digital rights encompass a wide range of uses of a work based in digital media as opposed to traditional print media. Digital rights for literary works protect the use or display of a work on a **Web site**, on CD-ROM, in an electronic database, or in some other electronic form. Works appearing in a digital format can be downloaded or copied at relatively low cost and with virtually no reduction in the quality of the work compared with the original. The unprecedented availability of digital works and the ease of copying them make digital rights a very valuable piece of the bundle of exclusive rights included in a copyright. *See also* **electronic rights**.

Tips and Tools: Negotiating for Digital Rights

With growing frequency, publishers are insisting on grants of all rights or at least both print and digital rights in their contracts with authors. Digital rights permit the publisher to reproduce or license the author's work to appear online or as part of an electronic database or CD-ROM. Because authors rely on the sales of their work to earn a living, publishing contracts that demand grants of all rights are often a result of unequal bargaining power. For instance, a freelance magazine author is often forced to accept a slightly larger payment from one publisher in return for his or her digital rights in lieu of the ability to resell the same article to several other publishers. With a more limited, print-based grant of rights, authors were able to earn substantially more per article by selling it to multiple publishers. In some cases, authors receive no compensation for their digital rights except the opportunity to continue to do business with that publisher again.

So how can freelance writers interested in earning a living protect their digital rights? The first rule in negotiating a sound contract is to read it and understand what rights you are licensing and how you are going to be compensated for them. Have the contract reviewed by an attorney before you sign it. If you are dissatisfied with the terms, offer a creative compromise. Find out exactly how the publisher intends to use your work and see if there is a solution that could be beneficial to

---

both parties. If your negotiations are stalling or if you feel the publisher is not willing to negotiate in good faith, you can enlist the assistance of your attorney to provide some leverage.

The **Authors Guild, ASJA, National Writers Union**, and other organizations have taken strong positions on the issues of digital and **electronic rights**.

Digital Signature—A digital signature is a specific type of electronic recognition that uses encrypted public and private "keys," or mathematically unique sequences, to verify the identity of the sender and also to confirm that the content of the related document has not been altered during transmission. A digital signature can be time-stamped, and because the sender of a digital signature can confirm that the message arrived, the transaction cannot easily be repudiated later.

An electronic signature can be any symbol, sound, or process used in conjunction with a contract or other document that is executed by the person intending to sign the document. A digital signature can include anything from a typed name at the bottom of an e-mail message or a click on an "I Agree" or "I Disagree" box on a Web site, to an encrypted file.

The Electronic Signatures in Global and National Commerce (E-SIGN) Act became effective in October 2000. E-SIGN validates the use of electronic signatures for many purposes and does not distinguish between digital signatures and other types of electronic signatures. Under the law, an electronic assignment of copyright verified by the digital signature of the author will satisfy the writing requirement of the Copyright Act since the assignment is in writing and signed by the owner of the rights conveyed.

Many states have also enacted laws that relate to the use of digital and electronic signatures in business transactions.

The public-private key technology involved with creating digital signatures can be costly and management of the process can be time consuming. Furthermore, there are many different processes available that offer different levels of security for the transaction.

Before entering into an agreement by means of a digital or electronic signature, it is essential to understand what method will be used and what the binding legal consequences of using the signature will be. Courts have not yet had the opportunity to rule on issues involving the use of electronic signatures. While it is always a good idea to consult an attorney before signing any contract, it is especially important to do so before entering into a contract by means of any type of electronic signature.

Tips and Tools: How to Set Up a Digital Signature

Creating a digital signature can be a daunting task because there are many different standards and procedures currently in use. Before proceeding with any method, it is essential to discuss the issue with the other party involved and agree on what level of security will be required for the transaction. If a digital signature will be required, will the digital signature attach to the document itself or will the contents of the document be cut and pasted into an e-mail message that will then be digitally signed? In addition to the digital signature, must the e-mail message be encrypted for added security? Encrypting the message will allow the receiver to verify that the contents of the message were not altered or intercepted during transmission.

To create a digital signature for a publishing contract, you must first obtain a private-public key pair from a reputable authority to establish the encryption method. This is known as a digital ID. Independent certification authorities such as Verisign and Thawte can issue digital IDs. A list of certifying authorities can be found at: http://office.microsoft.com/en-us/assistance/HA010547821033.aspx. The private key will remain confidential, known only to you. The public key, however, is not confidential and you should provide this key to your publisher.

You will next need to cut and paste the contract or other document to be signed into an e-mail message. Alternatively, you may choose to digitally sign the document before attaching it to your e-mail message.

The next step is to generate the digital signature. This requires special software that will perform a hash function to create a mathematical summary of the message. Many e-mail programs provide this function. Microsoft Outlook, for example, has the ability to create a digital signature for you once you input your digital ID and follow the instructions.

If you want the added protection of encrypting the resulting signature and the entire original message, your private key will allow you to do that as well. Send the message to your publisher.

When your publisher receives the message, he or she will run a program that contains the same hash function that you used to create the digital signature. Again, many e-mail programs such as Outlook provide the capability to perform this function. The publisher will then use the public key to read the message if it is encrypted. If not, the publisher can simply verify the digital signature of the message or document. This process will generate a message digest. If the publisher can read the message, then he or she will be able to verify that the message came from you, and the digital signature was a success. If you chose to encrypt the message as well, the publisher's software will then create a second digest of your message with the public key and compare it with the decrypted message. They will match if the message has not been altered or intercepted during the transmission.

Document Delivery Service—A document delivery service acquires articles, often those appearing in scholarly journals, and delivers the articles to a third party. The document delivery service maintains a database of available titles that the user can search and then select the articles to be delivered. A legal document delivery service seeks reprint permission and pays a royalty to the copyright holder, or to a copyright clearinghouse if appropriate. The fee charged to the individual requesting the article may be based on the royalty payment and how quickly the article is needed.

The Courts Say: Document Delivery Services Must Obtain Reprint Permission from the Author of an Article

Ryan v. CARL Corporation, 23 F.Supp.2d 1146 (N.D. Cal. 1998)

The U.S. District Court for the Northern District of California held that four authors had standing to proceed as a class action against a document retrieval and delivery service, UnCover, with their claim that the defendant failed to pay them royalties for the use of their articles and thereby violated their copyrights in the individual articles. UnCover requested permission from and paid royalties to the publishers of the periodicals, but did not deal directly with the authors. The court found that the authors had standing to sue even though they requested their own articles from UnCover because they did not authorize the reproductions of their articles and suffered injury by the service's failure to pay them royalties. The court determined that publishers of a collective work such as a periodical do not have the right to reproduce individual contributions; the right of reproduction lies solely with the author.

Due Dilligence—Due diligence refers to the comprehensive investigation conducted before filing a lawsuit, buying property or investments, or entering into a contract. It is a subjective legal standard of performance that is measured by what can be expected from an ordinary reasonable person in a similar situation. Due diligence requires a thorough review of all the facts of a situation and may involve extensive research to uncover all the necessary information. An attorney must engage in due diligence prior to filing a lawsuit to avoid wasting the court's time with a frivolous claim, and also during the discovery process. Patent law requires an inventor to perform due diligence with respect to the existence of prior inventions and courts will consider the exercise of due diligence where there are competing claims.

E

Earn Out—When a book has generated **royalties** in excess of the **advance** paid to the author, it is said to have earned out.

Editing—Editing includes a variety of tasks that are undertaken by a publisher to prepare a manuscript for publication. In large publishing houses, editing responsibilities may be divided between several people. An acquisitions editor usually builds a relationship with the author and is responsible for negotiating the publishing contract and ensuring the timely delivery of the manuscript. A manuscript editor then reviews the manuscript, performs fact checking, and makes any necessary changes to the manuscript. At this point, the manuscript may be reviewed by an attorney or other expert to ensure that it contains no material that would trigger liability for copyright or trademark infringement, defamation, obscenity, or any other violation of law. A production editor may physically prepare the manuscript for the printing process. The author usually has an opportunity to review the manuscript before it goes to press to approve any changes and to check for errors.

Tips and Tools: Working with Your Editor

It is wise to build a strong relationship with your editor because he is often your only contact with the publisher of your manuscript. Your editor will represent the publisher when negotiating your contract, and you should be able to freely discuss the terms of the contract and request clarification or modifications of the terms as necessary. It is always a good idea to have your own attorney review a publishing contract before you sign it, and this is especially important if your editor is unavailable or unwilling to discuss the terms of the contract with you. If you feel that the relationship is starting out badly, try to discuss this with your editor at this point to avoid more serious problems in the future.

Your job is to submit the manuscript to the editor by the deadline stated in the contract. An editor may be able to provide an extension in certain circumstances, or work with you to find a way to overcome whatever hurdle is jeopardizing your meeting the deadline.

Your editor can help you with any issues you may have during or following the publication process. Your editor should be able to follow up on marketing efforts, sales statistics, and that royalty check that was lost in the mail.

Of course not all relationships go smoothly, and if you develop problems with your editor, it is important to know your rights as an author and to keep a written record of your communications with your editor. An editor's personality may simply differ from yours, or there may be a deeper problem with the publisher that is preventing your editor from addressing your concerns.

Edition—Books are published in one or more editions. Many textbooks and nonfiction reference books are regularly revised and updated and may go through multiple editions during the period of publication. *See* **revision, derivative works.**

Editor Clause—Authors who have a long-standing relationship with a particular editor and a record of producing good sales may have enough clout to get a guarantee from a publisher that a particular editor will handle the book and that if the editor leaves the publishing house, the author will be permitted to break the contract and go with the editor.

E

Electronic Books—Electronic books, or e-books, are created by converting digitized text into a format that can be read on a computer, personal digital assistant, or dedicated e-book reading device. Although e-books may contain many elements found in a traditionally formatted book, such as a cover page, a title page, and a copyright page, e-books provide the user with many additional features as a result of their digital nature. For example, an e-book user may be able to change the font type and size, search for key words, electronically highlight or bookmark certain text, or type his or her own notes, which are then stored with the related text. E-books use hyperlinks to interconnect portions of the text, to allow the reader to jump between the table of contents and the main text, or to access external material such as **Web sites**. The electronic book format will soon offer such features full audio and video capabilities.

The format of an electronic book differs significantly from that of a printed book and the enhanced features provide the user with a truly unique reading experience. The rights relating to the creation and distribution of an e-book are likewise separate and distinct from the rights an author grants a publisher to publish a work in book form. While these electronic and digital rights may be included in a broad "all rights" assignment, authors have the power to retain these rights or to negotiate them separately.

The Courts Say: The Right to Publish a Work "in Book Form" Does Not Include Publication of an E-book

Random House, Inc. v. Rosetta Books LLC, 150 F.Supp.2d 613 (S.D.N.Y. 2001), *aff'd*, 283 F.3d 490 (2nd Cir. 2002)

A district court held that the rights held by Random House to publish various books "in book form" did not prevent the authors of those books from negotiating with another company for the publication of their works in e-book format. Applying New York State contract law and considering publishing industry custom, the court determined that the grant of the right to publish a book in book form is a limited grant. The court found that the rights granted by the authors to Random House did not encompass new uses of the work resulting from technological advances unforeseen at the time the contract was signed.

Electronic Reserves—Some academic libraries have converted to a system of digitizing reserve material and putting it on a Web site for patrons to visit. Even if access to the Web site is tightly restricted, such electronic reserves are of highly questionable legality unless the library has obtained permission from the copyright holder or restricts access to the material to a single computer on the actual library premises. It is also required that libraries make copies only of materials they have in their own collections and that the number of copies be limited. Many writers are finding their work on the Web sites of academic institutions. "I don't care if it's for education, it's still infringement," says one such writer. "We need to preserve our fair use rights," claims a librarian. "Copyright law shouldn't interfere with the rights of students and scholars." Who's right? The consensus among copyright experts gives the edge to the copyright owners in this debate. This issue hasn't yet been tested in the courts.

Electronic Rights—Electronic rights are a valuable part of the bundle of exclusive rights that make up a copyright. Authors may retain or separately negotiate the rights to have their works published in an electronic database, on a CD-ROM, as electronic books, or in another electronic format. The terms electronic rights and **digital rights** are sometimes used interchangeably since works that exist in electronic media are usually stored or transmitted in a digital format.

As a result of the Supreme Court's 2001 holding in *New York*

Times Co. v. Tasini, many publishers now grab all electronic rights from authors. While some publishers may remain stubborn on this point, a grant of all electronic rights is so broad that your publisher could certainly negotiate a narrower, more tailored grant of rights. As with any grant of rights, it is essential that you understand exactly what rights you are assigning and how you will be compensated for those rights.

The Courts Say: Publication in an Electronic Database Is Not a Permissible Revision of an Existing Work

New York Times Co. v. Tasini, 533 U.S. 483 (2001)

In a case closely followed by freelance writers, the U.S. Supreme Court ruled that under federal copyright law, the inclusion of individual articles previously published in periodicals in a variety of electronic and CD-ROM databases constituted copyright infringement. The Court concluded that the databases were not reproduced and distributed as part of "revisions" of individual periodical issues from which the articles were taken. Therefore, when the authors had not expressly transferred the electronic rights, the publishers of the periodicals could not relicense the individual articles to the databases.

The Court rejected the publishers' argument that they were acting within the scope of their privilege to reproduce and distribute the articles as part of a revision of their collective works and found that the owner of a collective work is only presumed to have acquired the right to reproduce and distribute the author's contribution as part of that collective work. The Court noted that unlike microfilm or microfiche, electronic databases provide the user with a single requested article and thus do not provide the same context that exists when the article is viewed as part of the periodical in which it was published. See *In re Literary Works in Electronic Databases Copyright Litigation,* p. 148.

Employee—The status of an individual as an employee or independent contractor is essential when determining whether a work qualifies as a **work made for hire**. In determining the employment status of the author of a work, courts will apply the law of agency and consider the following factors: (1) the skill required, (2) the source of instrumentalities and tools used, (3) the location of the work, (4) the duration of the relationship between the parties, (5) the hiring party's right to assign additional projects to the hired party, (6) the extent of the hired party's discretion over when and how long to work, (7) the method of payment, (8) the hired party's role in hiring and paying assistants, (9) the regular business of the hiring party, (10) whether employee benefits have been provided to the hiring party, and (11) the tax treatment of the hired party. Greater weight is normally given to certain factors, including the hiring party's right to control the manner and means of creation, the skill required, the provision of employee benefits, the tax treatment of the hired party, and whether the hiring party has the right to assign additional projects to the hired party.

Entire Agreement—A **contract** will often have a clause saying that the contract constitutes the entire agreement between the parties, that the contract supercedes any prior agreements, verbal or written, between the parties, and that any changes to the contract must be in writing and signed by both parties. Even when a contract does not have such restrictive language, it is never wise to rely on spoken promises, especially any that may conflict with what's in the contract, and it's always a good idea to confirm any later changes, such as a deadline extension, in writing.

Errors and Omissions—A common type of business insurance is a policy that covers any loss resulting from a mistake or oversight. Publishers usually have such a policy and it may be possible for an author to ask the publisher to include him as a "named insured" on its errors and omissions policy. Although this is often possible, many such policies have such high **deductibles** that such insurance is of limited value to authors. *See also* **libel, warranty**.

Escalator Clause—Many **publishing contracts** call for **royalties** to escalate as sales increase. An escalator clause in the contract will typically identify certain **break points** that will trigger an increase in the royalty rate when sales pass those points.

Excerpt—An excerpt is a selected passage taken from a larger work. Excerpts of copyrighted materials generally must not be used without the permission of the copyright owner, although the **fair use** doctrine may provide a valid defense in some situations.

Exclusive License—A property owner, such as the holder of a copyright or a patent, may grant an exclusive license to another party to do a particular thing, and may not then grant that same right to anyone else. *See* **nonexclusive license**.

Execution—In the world of contract law, execution is actually a good thing. The signing, dating, witnessing, and taking of all necessary steps to put a contract into effect is called execution. Most contracts are created in multiple originals so that each party can retain a signed original. Most contracts can be executed by simply signing and dating them, but some contracts should be witnessed or even notarized. Both parties to a contract should be sure that the other has the **authority to sign**. Some employees of a company may not, for example, have the legal authority to sign a binding contract on behalf of the company.

Exhibit—Supporting papers attached to contracts and court documents are often called exhibits. The main contract or document will usually refer to the exhibit and incorporate the exhibit by reference. Attachments to court documents are almost always called exhibits and labeled by number or letter. Attachments to contracts are sometimes called appendices, **riders**, or schedules.

F

Failure of Consideration—Consideration is something of value (usually money) that is legally necessary to support a **contract.** When the consideration isn't forthcoming the contract sometimes fails for failure of consideration. A writer who signs a work made for hire agreement, for example, and then isn't paid may be able to claim that ownership of the copyright did not transfer to the commissioning party without the consideration being paid.

Failure to Deliver—When an author misses her contractual deadline and fails to deliver an acceptable manuscript, the publisher may have the option of rescinding the **contract** and demanding return of the **advance.**

Failure to Publish—When a publisher fails to meet the contractual deadline for publishing, the author may have the option of rescinding the contract and getting the rights back. Very often, the author will be able to keep any advance already paid.

Fair Use—The U.S. Supreme Court has called the fair use doctrine "the most troublesome in the whole law of copyright." Fair use is subtle and complex because its meaning must be determined by context. In fact, one federal court justice called it "so flexible as virtually to defy definition." To make things more complicated, courts have not hesitated to expand or restrict the scope of fair use protection to serve the "interests of justice." Is all this complexity really necessary? The answer is yes. The fair use doctrine is a judicial and legislative attempt to balance the interests of copyright holders, society at large, and individual information users. Fair use cannot do that if it is overly simplistic.

So exactly what is fair use and how does it apply to the work of freelancers? Fair use is an **affirmative defense** to copyright infringement. In legal terms, an affirmative defense acknowledges wrongful behavior but provides an excuse. Self-defense is an affirmative defense for murder because the accused admits to killing the victim but offers an excuse. This means that the fair use does not apply to material that cannot be protected by copyright in the first place. Copyright cannot protect ideas, facts, or events, but only creative description and expression. Ideas and facts, therefore, may be freely copied. Fair use comes into play only when an existing copyright has been infringed. Fair use is codified in statute form as section 107 of the U.S. Copyright Act, but it is actually a case-based doctrine that existed in common law long before Congress revised the present copyright law in 1976. The copyright statute does not define the term fair use or provide definitive rules for its application. Section 107 was intended, according to a congressional report at the time, merely to "restate the preexisting judicial doctrine of fair use, not to change, narrow or enlarge it in any way."

Section 107 starts with a statement of purpose and then lists four factors to be considered by the courts. The statute, however, does not explain how to weigh the purpose and the four factors to decide whether any given use of copyrighted material is fair or infringing.

Purpose of Fair Use. The purposes for which it may be fair to use a copyrighted work include "criticism, comment, news reporting, teaching, scholarship, or research." This list of purposes, however, is not exhaustive but merely illustrates some examples of fair use. In order for a use to be fair, the general rule is that it must result in a public benefit or an increase in knowledge beyond the contribution of the original work. When viewed in light of the statute's stated purpose, a use is not fair, for example, simply because it is a single or small infringement, or a private noncommercial use.

The Four Factors

1. Purpose and Character of the Use

The first factor requires you to consider "the purpose and character of the use, including whether such use is of a commercial nature or is for nonprofit educational purposes." In keeping with the goal of social benefit resulting from the unauthorized use of copyrighted material, the courts have been less likely to rule that commercial uses are fair. Despite this, the courts have recognized that virtually all publications are run for profit, and that most uses will exist on a continuum of commercial and nonprofit uses. At the commercial end of the spectrum, the court in the case of *Amana Refrigeration, Inc. v Consumers Union of United States, Inc.* 431 F. Supp. 324 (N.D.Iowa 1977) said that quoting a portion of an article published in *Consumer Reports* is not a fair use when used to promote sales of products—it is mainly a commercial use. At the opposite extreme is a purely nonprofit use such as education. If you intend to use copyrighted material, therefore, you must assess the commercial motive and purpose of the work.

2. Nature of the Work

The second factor is "the nature of the copyrighted work." It is more likely fair use to quote factual works, news reports, and biographical facts than a work of fiction. In part, this distinction embodies First Amendment considerations and more broadly the public interest in dissemination of important facts. A dramatic illustration of the weight of the public interest in information is found in the case of *Time Inc. v. Bernard Geis Associates* (293 F.Supp.130 (S.D.N.Y. 1968), which dealt with the unauthorized publication of still-frames from the **Zapruder film** that showed the Kennedy assassination. The exclusive rights to the Zapruder films belonged to Life Magazine, Inc., which had purchased them from Abraham Zapruder for $150,000. Several years later, the defendant Thompson approached *Life* for permission to use frames from the film for a book he was writing about the assassination. When *Life* declined his offer, Thompson used his access to *Life*'s archives to secure photographs of the desired frames that he reproduced in his own book. *Life* sued for copyright infringement and Thompson asserted the fair use defense. Even where Thompson's behavior in obtaining the images was egregious and the infringement was clear, the court held that the public's interest in the dissemination of information about Kennedy's assassination outweighed *Life*'s proprietary interest in the images.

3. Amount Infringed

The third factor, is "the amount and substantiality of the portion used in relation to the copyrighted work as a whole." Although courts will sometimes point out that an infringing use constituted a certain percent of the entire work, there is no magic number. Both the quality and quantity of the portions used are at issue. One illustrative case involves a videotape of the Reginald Denny beating shot by the Los Angeles News Service from one of its helicopters. The news service licensed several television stations to use the footage but denied permission to KCAL. KCAL, however, aired a purloined version of the video during its coverage of the riot and later argued that its airing constituted fair use because the portion it showed was a relatively small part of the entire video. The court rejected this argument because the news station had aired the most valuable segment of the video and held KCAL's limited use to be infringing.

4. Market Value

The fourth factor is "the effect of the use upon the potential market for or value of the copyrighted work." A use is unfair when it diminishes the marketability of the original by serving as a substitute. A good illustration of fourth factor analysis is with abstracts of longer works. You have to consider how and why the abstracting is done. In a bibliographic abstract, for example, little of the original work is used and the use is likely to be fair. A synopsis, on the other hand, is likely to contain more material from the original, and you need to take care. There is a higher likelihood that the synopsis will destroy the market for the original work, which means that the use is less likely to be fair.

Fair use is a flexible doctrine. Whether or not a particular infringement can be excused as fair use depends heavily on the facts of each case. In each case, you must consider the underlying purpose of the fair use provisions of the Copyright Act and a balancing of the four factors cited in the statute, as well as the case law interpreting each factor.

See **archives, course packs, electronic reserves, parody**.

The Courts Say: Use of Unpublished, Copyrighted Material Is Generally Not Fair Use

Harper & Row Publishers, Inc., v. Nation Enterprises, 471 U.S. 539 (1985)

The publisher of President Gerald Ford's memoirs sued *The Nation* for copyright infringement based on its unauthorized publication of verbatim quotes from the book in an attempt to scoop the exclusive first serial right to license prepublication excerpts granted to another magazine by the publisher. The Supreme Court found that the magazine's use of the material was not a fair use. The Court concluded that the unpublished nature of the work was a key, though not necessarily determinative, factor tending to negate the magazine's defense of fair use, and emphasized that under ordinary circumstances, an author's right

---

to control the first public appearance of his unpublished expression will outweigh a claim of fair use. The Court observed that the right not to publish is a very important one and that the right of first publication permits the author to choose when, where, and in what form to first publish a work. Rejecting the First Amendment arguments of the magazine based on the theory that the book was of great political importance to the public, the Court declined to expand the concept of fair use to create what would amount to a public figure exception to copyright. The Court applied a traditional fair use analysis and determined that each of the four factors favored the publisher. In considering the first factor, the purpose of the use, the Court noted that the magazine actively sought to exploit the headline value of its infringement. The Court also noted that although the magazine's quotations only amounted to three hundred or four hundred words, the quotations represented essentially the "heart" of the unpublished book.

Home Videotaping of Television Programs for Time-Shifting Purposes Is Fair Use

Sony Corp. v. Universal Studios, Inc., 464 U.S. 417 (1984)

Universal Studios and Walt Disney Productions, the owners of many copyrights on television programs, sued Sony, a manufacturer of Betamax home videotape recorders (VTRs), and others for copyright infringement, claiming that consumers had been recording their programs when they aired on television and that the petitioners were liable for copyright infringement because of their marketing of the VTRs. The Supreme Court ruled that Sony demonstrated a significant likelihood that substantial numbers of copyright holders who licensed their works for broadcast on free television would not object to having their broadcasts time-shifted by private viewers. The Court also held that Universal and Disney failed to demonstrate that time-shifting would cause any likelihood of nonminimal harm to the potential market for, or the value of, their copyrighted works and therefore the Betamax VTR was capable of substantial noninfringing uses. The Court further concluded that Sony was not liable for vicarious or contributory infringement based on its sale of VTRs. In its fair use analysis, the Court characterized time-shifting for private home use as a noncommercial, nonprofit activity. The Court reasoned that a plaintiff must demonstrate, by a preponderance of evidence, that some meaningful likelihood of future harm exists and if the intended use is for commercial gain, that likelihood may be presumed; however, if it is for a noncommercial purpose, the likelihood must be demonstrated. Concluding that Universal and Disney failed to meet their burden, the Court determined that time-shifting for private home use is a fair use.

Reverse Engineering Can Be Fair Use

Atari Games, Corp., v. Nintendo of America, Inc., 975 F.2d 832 (Fed. Cir. 1992).

Nintendo sued its competitor, Atari, for copyright infringement and other intellectual property violations when Atari reverse-engineered the security system contained in the Nintendo Entertainment System. The Court of Appeals for the Federal Circuit held, among other things, that Nintendo's computer program contained protected expression and that the reverse engineering of object code constitutes fair use insofar as it does not exceed what is necessary to understand the unprotected elements of a computer program. The court observed that fair use to discern the underlying ideas of a work, however, does not justify extensive efforts to profit from replicating protected expressions. The court ultimately ruled against Atari on the fair use issue because it did not use an authorized copy of Nintendo's program in the reverse engineering process, in violation of copyright regulations. The court noted that reverse engineering cannot be used as an excuse to commercially exploit a program.

Quoting and Paraphrasing Unpublished Letters Is Not Fair Use

Salinger v. Random House, Inc., 811 F.2d 90 (2d Cir.), *reh'g denied*, 818 F.2d 252 (2d Cir.), *cert. denied*, 484 U.S. 890 (1987)

J. D. Salinger sought a preliminary injunction barring the publication of a biography that included quotations and paraphrases from his copyrighted, unpublished letters. The court granted the preliminary injunction and concluded that the biographer could not establish a valid fair use defense. In its fair use analysis, the court found that although the first factor, the purpose of the use, favored the biographer's claim that the material he copied enriched the scholarly biography, it did not entitle him to the generous application of the fair use doctrine. In determining that the second factor, the nature of the copyrighted work, favored Salinger, the court emphasized the unpublished nature of the letters. The third factor, the court found, also favored Salinger because the biographer extensively quoted and paraphrased the letters; material from the letters made up approximately 40 percent of the biography. The court observed that the fourth factor slightly favored Salinger since the potential market for his letters would be relatively unaffected by the material published in the biography. In finding no fair use on the part of the biographer, the court emphasized that the biographer could report the facts contained in the letters, but not quote or paraphrase the author's expression of those facts.

Third-Party Distribution of Shareware for a Fee Is Not Fair Use

Storm Impact v. Software of Month Club, 13 F. Supp. 2d 782 (N.D.Ill. 1998)

Storm Impact, the owner of a copyright in computer software marketed as "shareware," sued the Software of the Month Club (SOMC) for copyright infringement, unfair competition, and false designation of origin under the federal trademark law, and deceptive trade practices under Illinois law. SOMC provided to customers, for a fee, collections of newly introduced shareware on a monthly basis. The court awarded statutory damages to Storm Impact and concluded that SOMC's use of software was not fair use, and Storm Impact did not impliedly consent to such use by posting its shareware on the Internet. Conducting a fair use analysis, the court found that the first factor, the purpose and character of the use, favored Storm Impact since SOMC's use was not transformative and even if SOMC's use increased distribution of the shareware programs, their inclusion in SOMC's collection adversely affected the market for Storm Impact's copyrighted software. The court determined that the other three factors favored Storm Impact as well. Furthermore, as a matter of first impression, the court considered whether material placed on the Internet for free distribution is entitled to protection and held that the shareware at issue is entitled to copyright protection in light of Storm Impact's valid and enforceable express reservation of distribution rights on its Web site.

First Amendment—The First Amendment to the Constitution ensures freedom of religion, freedom of speech, **freedom of the press**, the right of assembly, and the right to petition the government for a redress of grievances. These rights are also applicable to the states under the due process clause of the Fourteenth Amendment. At first glance, there appears to be a tension between the First Amendment guarantee of free expression and copyright law's protection of expression. It is the delicate balance of these two bodies of law, however, that allows for the free flow of information in the United States. Both work together to prevent censorship: the First Amendment protects most types of speech, even **commercial speech,** from government interference, while copyright law protects it from private infringement. Copyright law also preserves individual First Amendment rights by protecting only the expression of an idea rather than the idea itself. This protects the free exchange of ideas and ensures that individuals are always free to express what is on their minds, just not in the same way. The concept of **fair use** is also founded on First Amendment principles of freedom of expression. Without fair use, copyright law would restrict research and debate by preventing criticism, commentary, and scholarly debate. This would lead to censorship and ultimately deter future expression from authors and artists. Because these First Amendment checks and balances exist within the framework of copyright law, First Amendment claims raised as a defense will usually be dismissed by the court in copyright infringement cases.

Government regulation of speech may be content-based or content-neutral. Content-based regulation of speech is permitted under the First Amendment, but a strict level of scrutiny will be applied. A court will uphold a content-based law only if it is justified by a compelling government interest and then only if it is narrowly tailored to serve that interest. On the other hand, content-neutral regulations, which restrict the time, place, and manner of speech, are subject to an intermediate level of scrutiny and will be upheld if they burden no more speech than necessary and serve a significant government interest. A government regulation of this type may be upheld in certain instances if the law leaves open ample alternative channels of communication.

The First Amendment's protection of free speech is not absolute, and there are some types of speech that are not entitled to constitutional protection. **Obscenity**, for example, is not protected by the First Amendment. Neither is libel or so-called fighting words, which are considered to inflict harm when uttered and are inherently likely to invoke a violent response from the listener.

The Courts Say: The Communications Decency Act (CDA) of 1996 Violates the First Amendment

Reno v. American Civil Liberties Union, 521 U.S. 844 (1997)

The CDA was enacted in 1996 to, among other things, criminalize the act of transmitting obscene or indecent material through a telecommunications device, such as a modem, to a person under eighteen years of age and the act of sending or displaying "patently offensive" material over the **Internet** to persons under eighteen years of age. Several plaintiffs challenged the constitutionality of these two provisions. The Supreme Court ruled that the challenged provisions violated the First Amendment because they were overbroad. The first provision, prohibiting the transmission of obscene or indecent material, could be saved by delting the "or indecent" language. The Court noted that although the government demonstrated a compelling interest in shielding minors from access to indecent materials, the statute was not narrowly enough tailored to serve that interest. The Court noted that the statute was not limited to commercial transactions, and did not allow parents to consent to their children's use of restricted materials. Furthermore, the CDA failed to define "indecent" and incompletely defined "patently offensive."

Speech May Not Be Entitled to First Amendment Protection in Every Context

FCC v. Pacifica Foundation, 438 U.S. 726 (1978)

The broadcaster of a prerecorded twelve-minute monologue by George Carlin, entitled "Filthy Words," sued the Federal Communication Commission in response to its determination that the language of the broadcast was indecent and prohibited by statute. The Supreme Court upheld the government's restriction and ruled that the FCC's action did not constitute censorship. The Court also affirmed the FCC's conclusion that indecent language was used, even though the monologue did not rise to the level of obscenity. Although the monologue was entitled to First Amendment protection, the Court determined that its offensive content was not entitled to absolute constitutional protection in the context of an afternoon radio broadcast. The Court found that of all forms of communication, broadcasting has the most limited First Amendment protection, in part because it has a uniquely pervasive presence in the lives of individuals, is particularly accessible to children, and it is impossible to completely avoid patently offensive transmissions.

Use of the Copyrighted Works of Others Is Not Protected by the First Amendment

Eldred v. Reno, 537 U.S. 186 (2003)

Several businesses and individuals that used formerly copyrighted works that had subsequently fallen into the public domain sued the attorney general, challenging the constitutionality of the **Sonny Bono Copyright Term Extension Act** of 1998, which extended the term of copyright protection by twenty years. The Supreme Court ruled that the CTEA was a valid exercise of power under the copyright clause of the Constitution. The Court also concluded that the statute did not violate the Constitution's limitation on the duration of copyright protection because it did not create a perpetual copyright, and that it did not violate the plaintiffs' First Amendment rights to freedom of speech because it did not alter the traditional contours of copyright protection. The Court found that rather than violating the First Amendment, the CTEA actually supplements copyright's traditional safeguards by allowing libraries and archives, in certain circumstances, to reproduce, distribute, display, or perform a published work during the extended copyright term for purposes of research, preservation, or scholarship. The court reasoned that the statute protects an author's original work from unrestricted exploitation.

Cable Programmers and Operators Are Entitled to First Amendment Protection

Turner Broadcasting System, Inc., v. FCC, 520 U.S. 180 (1997)

Cable television system operators and programmers sued the Federal Communications Commission, challenging the constitutionality of the must-carry provisions of the Cable Television Consumer Protection and Competition Act that required carriage of local broadcast television stations on cable television systems. The Supreme Court applied intermediate scrutiny and held that Congress's interests in preserving the benefits of free, over-the-air local broadcast television, promoting the widespread dissemination of information from a multiplicity of sources, and promoting fair competition in the market for television programming were important governmental interests for First Amendment purposes. The Court also concluded that substantial evidence supported the statement that the must-carry provisions were designed to address a real threat under a First Amendment analysis. The Court determined that the content-neutral must-carry requirement thus served the government's interests in preserving cable carriage of local broadcast stations, and that the provisions did not burden substantially more speech than necessary to achieve those interests.

The Press Has No Special Immunity Under the First Amendment to Laws of General Applicability

Cohen v. Cowles Media Co., 501 U.S. 663 (1991)

A candidate for a gubernatorial race in Minnesota provided information regarding an opponent to reporters from two newspapers on the condition that his identity remain confidential. The confidentiality agreements were independently breached by both newspapers, and the candidate sued for fraudulent misrepresentation and breach of contract. The Supreme Court held that the First Amendment did not prohibit the candidate from recovering damages under Minnesota law for the breach of a promise of confidentiality given in exchange for information. The Court found that enforcement of general laws against the press is not subject to stricter scrutiny than would be applied to enforcement against others. The Court determined that the promissory estoppel law was generally applicable to the daily transactions of all Minnesota citizens and that the First Amendment did not bar its application to the press.

First Negotiation Right—Many publishing contracts have an **option clause**, right of first refusal, or a first negotiation right designed to give the publisher of an author's book a first look at the next book. Such clauses are not considered favorable for authors and many publishers will delete them on request.

First North American Serial Rights—In the era before electronic publication, databases, and Web sites, the standard rights offered by freelance magazine writers were first North American serial rights, which meant, literally the right to publish the article first in a North American periodical. But although the copyright law itself limits the transfer of more than one-time rights without a written agreement to the contrary, many publishers have indulged in a rights grab that has writers fighting hard to preserve their electronic rights. Although the Tasini decision (*see* **electronic rights**) was a hard-fought victory for freelancers, many publishers have attempted to evade the spirit of the law with onerous **work made for hire** or **all rights** contracts.

First Printing—The initial print run of a book is called the first printing. Many books never sell out their first printing or earn out their advances, and publishers end up **remaindering** them as "bargain books." First printings of surprise bestsellers or early books by authors who later break into bestsellerdom often become highly valued collectibles.

First Proceeds—When a book is canceled by the publisher for cause, the writer is often expected to pay back the advance. Sometime a publisher will permit the author to pay it back from the first proceeds, if any, from the sale of a book to another publisher.

Fixation—Fixation occurs when a work is displayed or communicated by the author in a sufficiently permanent manner so that it can be perceived by the naked eye or with the aid of any machine. In order to be eligible for copyright protection in the United States, a work must be fixed in a tangible medium of expression. A live public broadcast, such as news coverage, is considered to be fixed if the work is recorded or otherwise fixed simultaneously with the transmission.

Flow-through—The author's share of income from sales of subsidiary rights can be passed directly on to the author within a short time of receipt by the publisher, but sometimes these funds are held until the end of the royalty period before being sent to the author. It's always better when sub rights payments flow through to the writer right away. *See* **secondary rights**.

Force Majeure—This is a legal **term of art** for something that's not the fault of the parties to a contract that excuses them from their obligations to perform or from failing to meet a contractual deadline.

Foreign Rights—In most publishing contracts, the grant of foreign rights or foreign language rights is a subsidiary right. Foreign rights can be quite lucrative, and authors should ask their editors and/or agents to try very hard to sell the foreign rights.

Forum—The court of law or tribunal where a matter is litigated.

Forum Shopping—The practice of comparing the laws of various counties, states, or federal circuit courts in order to find the court that will provide the plaintiff with the most favorable verdict. It is essential to file your case in the proper court, but sometimes more than one court may properly exercise **jurisdiction** over the case. An attorry can help you choose the court most likely to favor your claim.

Framing—Framing occurs when the creator of a **Web site** presents material from the external Web site of another in a frame as part of the creator's Web site. Framing can be compared to **linking**, where a user of one Web site is transported to another Web site by clicking on a hyperlink. The frame does not transport the user to the external site; rather, it brings the material on that site into the first site. When frames are used, the user clicks on a link and the selected material from the external site pops up in a new window, or frame.

Frames raise many intellectual property issues. A frame may infringe the reproduction and adaptation rights of a copyright

200

owner if it creates an unauthorized derivative work of the material used in the frame. The author of the framed material no longer has control over how the work is displayed when it is used in a frame. The frame isolates a portion of the work, and the user views the framed material out of its original context. Since the user is not transported to the external site, the framed material is surrounded by the items on the Web page that contains the link. Framing may also infringe the public performance and public display rights of a copyright owner. In addition to copyright issues, framing may also infringe the trademark rights of the creator of the external Web site. Because the creator of the frame can choose to display selected portions of the external Web site, the creator may cause confusion or dilution of the mark. The creator of the frame may choose to delete or rearrange the advertising included on the external site, or use the framed material in conjunction with the advertising contained on his or her own Web site. The creator of the external Web site may also be able to establish a claim of trade dress infringement if the Web site is entitled to trademark protection for its look and feel. *See also* **linking, deep linking.**

The Courts Say: Framing May Constitute Trademark Infringement

Hard Rock Cafe Intern. (USA) Inc. v. Morton, 97 Civ. 9483 (RPP), 1999 WL 717995 (S.D.N.Y. 1999)

The Hard Rock Café sued Morton, the owner of the Hard Rock Hotel and Casino and the recipient of a license to use various service marks and trademarks, over his operation of the hardrock.com Web site. Among other things, Morton offered a link to enable users to purchase compact discs from the Web page of a third party, Tunes Network, Inc. The Tunes link appeared in a frame on Morton's Web site, surrounded by a border containing the Hard Rock Hotel Logo. The United States District Court for the Southern District of New York noted that the two Web sites were combined through framing to present a single visual presentation, and that the Hard Rock Hotel mark was used to promote the sale of the Tunes merchandise. The court determined that a user would be confused as to who was actually offering the merchandise for sale and noted that the Hard Rock Hotel's domain name remained on the screen, while its logo appeared not only around the frame but also in the Tunes toolbar on the Tunes page itself. The court concluded that the Hard Rock Hotel mark was used to sell merchandise in violation of the license agreement with the Hard Rock Café, and ordered Morton to permanently stop framing the Tunes Web page or to do it in a manner consistent with the license agreement.

Pop-up advertisements use framing technology to display targeted ads on a computer user's computer screen, triggered by that user's visit to a particular Web site, which obscure a portion of the underlying Web site. Several district courts have held that pop-up ads generally do not violate copyright law for two reasons. First, they do not infringe the Web site owner's exclusive right to display the Web site because pop-up ads appear in a separate window and do not alter the content of the Web site in any way. Second, a pop-up ad screen display cannot constitute an infringing derivative work because it is too transitory in nature to receive copyright protection.

Freedom of Information Act (FOIA)—Sometimes called sunshine laws, FOIA and state FOIL laws (Freedom of Information Law) are designed to free up the flow of public information by creating a process whereby news organizations and citizens can request government documents and files. These laws are sometimes difficult to enforce. The **Reporters Committee for Freedom of the Press** has extensive information about sunshine and open meetings laws on its Web site at www.rcfp.org.

Freedom of the Press—The First Amendment of the U.S. Constitution provides for freedom of the press in order to benefit citizens by ensuring a free flow of communication, especially concerning the functioning of government. Freedom of the press is a fundamental right that protects every sort of publication that may be used to convey information or express an opinion from abridgement by the federal government. Back in the 1800s freedom of the press gave individuals the right to publish their views anonymously. The First Amendment right to freedom of the press, however, has been broadened over the years. It protects open debate and has even been used to strike down a use tax on the cost of paper and ink products consumed in the production of publications. The right is not unlimited, however, and at trial, the government may, in exceptional cases, be able to demonstrate that there is a legitimate public policy reason for the limitation it imposed.

The First Amendment freedoms of speech and the press have additionally been recognized as falling within the liberty safeguarded by the due process clause of the Fourteenth Amendment from invasion by state action.

The Courts Say: Freedom of the Press Extends to Motion Pictures

Joseph Burstyn, Inc., v. Wilson, 343 U.S. 495 (1952)

The U.S. Supreme Court held that a New York statute authorizing appointment of an education department censor to issue licenses for motion pictures was an invalid abridgment of free speech and of free press. The Court recognized the value of motion pictures as a medium for the communication of ideas and political opinions and found that the fact that they are created for private profit by large companies had no effect on their eligibility for First Amendment protection.

Front Matter—Material at the beginning of a book, such as a copyright page, title page, table of contents, foreword, introduction, dedication, acknowledgments, and so forth is called front matter. *See* **back matter**.

Future Technologies—The issue of whether a publisher or other party can make new uses of a work as a result of technologies developed after the publishing contract or license agreement was signed is often referred to as a new use problem. Interpreting the language of the contract, a court will look to the applicable state contract law, the surrounding circumstances, and publishing industry custom. A court will also consider whether the future technology was reasonably anticipated at the time the contract was signed. If the language of the contract is broad or if the new use reasonably appears to fall within the same medium of the previously granted rights, a court will likely find that the new use is valid. *See also* **all rights.**

The Courts Say: Future Technologies Not Included in License

Rey v. Lafferty, 990 F.2d 1379 (1st Cir. 1993)

The First Circuit Court of Appeals held that videocassette sales were not covered by an agreement licensing production of 104 film episodes of the Curious George character. The court determined that the license did not grant the defendants any specific rights in future technologies or methods of exhibition. The court also considered the differences between viewing television and viewing a videocassette, and found that while videocassettes are often viewed on home television screens, they embody different types of technology. In rendering its decision, the first circuit also noted the unequal bargaining power of the author in relation to the licensee, a professional investment firm accustomed to licensing agreements.

G

Galley Proofs—*See* **page proofs.**

GATT Treaty—The General Agreement on Tariffs and Trade is an international treaty, adhered to by most trading nations, that deals with all aspects of global trade. GATT was established in 1947, and since then the treaty has been updated through a series of multilateral trade negotiations known as GATT Rounds. The latest cycle, the **Uruguay Round**, concluded in December 1993. The purpose of GATT is to reduce trade barriers and to promote free global trade. The general principles of the original GATT treaty relating to intellectual property have been incorporated into the **Agreement on Trade-Related Aspects of Intellectual Property Rights (TRIPS)**, which is administered by the **World Trade Organization**.

Ghostwriter—*See* **collaborator.**

Governing Law—Governing law is the law that is applied to a case in a particular **jurisdiction**. If a case is filed in state court, that state's laws will be applied by the court in deciding the matter. If a case is brought in federal court, federal laws will govern, and any state claims will usually be decided under the governing law

205

of the state in which the claim arose. A contract often contains a **choice of law** clause that specifies which state's law will govern in the event of a dispute.

Government Bodies—In the United States, both state and federal governments comprise government bodies, or agencies, that carry out the regular functions of the government and implement the laws. On the federal level, government bodies include agencies such as the Department of Justice, the **Copyright Office**, the Patent and Trademark Office, and the State Department.

Graphic Artists Guild (GAG)—The GAG is a national union that is committed to improving conditions for all creators of graphic art and raising standards for the entire industry. Open to all graphic artists, the organization's membership includes illustrators, designers, Web creators, production artists, surface designers, and other working artists. The organization advocates for artists' rights and provides education and networking opportunities at conferences and seminars and through its active local chapters. GAG publishes the *Graphic Artists Guild's Handbook of Pricing and Ethical Guidelines,* which offers invaluable guidance on subjects ranging from copyright law and contract negotiation tips to industry pricing. The Graphic Artists Guild Legal Defense Fund provides support for members involved in legal disputes and participates in collective bargaining negotiations to ensure the rights of artists are protected. The organization is headquartered in New York City and has chapters across the country. GAG can be contacted at 90 John Street, Suite 403, New York, NY 10038-3202, 212-791-3400. You can learn more about GAG on its Web site at www.gag.org.

Graphic Works—Copyright protection extends to two- and three-dimensional graphic works such as maps, globes, charts, diagrams, models, and technical drawings, including architectural plans. The artistic craftsmanship of a graphic work is entitled to protection, but the mechanical or utilitarian elements of the work are not. The copyrightable features of the graphic work must be able to be distinguished from, and be capable of existing independently of, the utilitarian aspects of the work.

A graphic design may be protected under both copyright and trademark law if the requirements for each type of protection are met. The copyright protects the artist's creation and the trademark protects the use of the design to identify its creator.

Graphs—Graphs are entitled to copyright protection as **graphic works** if they contain copyrightable features that are separate from their utilitarian or mechanical elements.

Grant of Rights—When an author licenses rights in a work to a publisher, the contract/license agreement often refers to this as the "grant of rights." The rights to an author's work and the underlying copyight in it are actually a **bundle of rights** that can be licensed or retained in a variety of ways. The rights granted by the author can be exclusive or nonexclusive, primary or secondary, and unlimited or limited by factors such as time, territory, and type of publication.

Tips and Tools: Negotiating a Reasonable Grant of Rights

Many publishers initially seek the broadest possible grant of rights but will compromise if they can get the rights they really think they need to have. If the contract offered to you asks for more rights that you're willing to grant, try these tactics:

- Explain that you're happy to license any rights the publisher legitimately needs and intends to exploit but that you would prefer to retain the rights they don't need.
- Instead of identifying the rights you'd like to retain, hit the ball

---

back to the publisher by asking it to identify the specific rights it needs.

- In a pleasant manner, ask the publisher why it needs a particular right and how it intends to exploit it.
- Suggest that you might make additional rights available if a separate fee can be established or if the publisher is limited in time or has other restrictions.
- Repeat that you want the publisher to have what it really needs, will use, and will pay for, but that you aren't willing to give a blanket grant, especially when it's not necessary.
- Suggest that you will negotiate in good faith if the publisher needs a right in the future that isn't contemplated now.

Group Registration—Freelance writers can register all of their articles published during one twelve-month period in a single Copyright Office registration for one $30 fee by using Form GR/CP as an adjunct to Form TX (see sidebar).

Tools and Tips: Why and How to Register Your Articles

Prepared by the ASJA Contracts Committee

First Things First: The One-Paragraph Copyright Primer

As a freelance writer, unless you've signed a work-made-for-hire agreement or otherwise transferred copyright, what you write belongs to you. You need not put a little C in a circle on it. You need not register it with the Copyright Office. The work need not even be published for your copyright to take effect. The copyright is yours immediately. If your work appears in a periodical, the publisher owns the copyright in the entire issue *as a collective work*, but not in your individual work. The publisher may use the copyright symbol © with its company name and file the issue with the Copyright Office, but its protection covers the issue *as an issue*, not the articles within. The copyright in your writing is *yours* unless and until, induced by cash or cowed by threats, you sign it away.

Why Register?

Under the law, if your copyright is infringed, you can't sue unless the work has been registered with the Copyright Office. You can, of course, wait until there's a problem before you bother filing a registration application. But there's a good reason to file as a matter of routine.

In copyright infringement cases, courts may assess two distinct kinds of damages.

STATUTORY DAMAGES

Up to $150,000 if the infringement is judged to be willful—available only if the work was registered no later than three months after first publication or, if the work was registered later than that, if the infringement begins after registration. ("Publication" means public availability, which may be earlier than the cover date.) In cases where statutory damages apply, the court may also award attorneys' fees.

ACTUAL DAMAGES

Monetary losses suffered by the infringed party—losses that are likely to be small as well as time consuming and difficult to prove. What's more, courts are not free to award attorneys' fees in conjunction with actual damages.

So for infringement of articles not registered in time, it is rarely cost-effective to hire a lawyer and sue in federal court. (A suit in small claims court, based on contract rather than copyright, may make sense in such cases.) If you've registered your copyright in time, you're in a better position to inflict pain in a real lawsuit; thus, you have far greater clout.

In short: As a defensive move against infringement—such as unauthorized electronic use of an article—it can be wise to register each magazine and newspaper article you write.

Isn't Registration an Expensive Pain?

Actually, it's neither as costly nor as onerous as you may think. Registration costs $30, but you can group articles on a single application to save on fees and drudgery. If you're a prolific article writer, the cost per story is quite low. To meet the within-three-months requirement, you need to file four times a year, each time listing your previous three months' published work; thus, four filings and $120 give you maximum protection on a year's output.

HOW TO DO IT

To group register, you need two official U.S. Copyright Office forms:

Form TX for nondramatic literary works (use the long form; the streamlined **Short Form TX** may only be used for a single work); **Form GR/CP** for grouping published works on a single application.

You can obtain the forms directly from the Copyright Office by phoning 202-707-9100 (available twenty-four hours a day). Leave a message; wait two to three weeks for the forms to arrive. You can also download forms from the Copyright Office's Web site: www.loc.gov/copyright or www.copyright.gov. Photocopy them at will, but use a good grade of $8\frac{1}{2} \times 11$ inch white paper, use both sides of the sheet, and match the layout of the originals. Type or print in black ink.

On Form TX, question 1, if you are registering two or more articles at the same time, enter "See GR/CP, attached." In question 2, under Nature of Authorship, you should typically enter "Entire Text" or "co-author of Entire Text," whichever applies. If you're group registering: in 3a, use the latest applicable date; in 3b, enter "See GR/CP, attached." In question 4, Copyright Claimant, is ordinarily the same as the author: you. In question 5, under Previous Registration, check "No" (remember that registration of the entire issue by the publisher does *not* constitute specific registration of your work). For most magazine or newspaper articles, ignore question 6.

On Form GR/CP, list articles chronologically, from earliest to latest, numbering the lines consecutively; no more than twelve months may separate the first from the last.

The Copyright Office's separate instruction sheets say that you must include the entire magazine or newspaper section in which each submitted article appeared—but that needn't actually be done. The office advises that you may instead submit simple tearsheets or even photocopies. Just be sure to include with your application a letter asking that the office "please accept the enclosed tearsheets [or photocopies] as part of ongoing special relief from the deposit requirement"; the request is routinely granted.

Enclose a check for $30, payable to Register of Copyrights. Mail your application to the address on Form TX.

FOUR FREQUENTLY ASKED QUESTIONS

How long will it take?
Perhaps as long as several months.

When does registration take effect?
As soon as the application and supporting materials are received by the Copyright Office. That's why you want to use certified mail, so you know the date of receipt.

What do you do if an article appears in more than one periodical?
Submit any published version, the earlier the better; if different published versions reflect only minor changes, you need *not* register each version.

What about unpublished works?
You may also submit the manuscript version(s), but you may *not* use form GR/CP, *nor* may you mix published and unpublished works. Unpublished works may be grouped using Form TX alone; simply use a descriptive title for the group, such as "unpublished writings, Jan–Mar 1996."

(Adapted from an information sheet prepared by the Contracts Committee of the American Society of Journalists and Authors and used with permission.) *See* **The Courts Say**, p. 148

H

Hardcover—The version of a book published by a traditional publisher has hard covers and a jacket. Today many publishers bring a book directly out as **paperback** and may forego hardcover publication altogether.

Harry Fox Agency—Harry Fox Agency, Inc., was established in 1927 as a musical copyright information source and licensing agency for the music industry. The agency represents more than twenty-seven thousand music publishers and is the premier licensing resource for the mechanical use of music reproduced in all formats and media. www.harryfox.com.

Heading—*See* **caption.**

Home Recording Act of 1992—*See* **Audio Home Recording Act of 1992**.

Hyperlink—A hyperlink, or link, directs the user of a **Web site** to a specific **Web page** within the Web site or to material located on another Web site anywhere in the world. Using a mouse, the user clicks on a word, image, or icon, which is usually displayed in a different color or underlined to distinguish it from the surrounding material. When the user has accessed a link, that link will often appear in a different color to provide a record of which links have already been visited. Links are commonly used in directories, indices, and tables of contents to direct the user to specific information. Links also are commonly used to provide support for an idea or to call attention to additional material on a particular matter. Linking uniquely connects information on the **World Wide Web** in ways that they could not be connected otherwise.

I

Imprint—An imprint is a separate publisher within a larger publishing organization.

Indemnity—*See* **warranty.**

Infringement—Infringement is the violation of copyright. *See* **plagiarism, copyright, Digital Millennium Copyright Act.**

Injunction—An injunction is a court document that stops a party from continuing to engage in a specific unlawful activity. An injunction may be temporary or permanent. A preliminary injunction is a temporary type of injunction that is issued at the discretion of the court prior to trial to halt the alleged illegal activity and thus prevent further harm, until the case is decided. In order to obtain a preliminary injunction, the plaintiff must demonstrate (1) irreparable harm if the injunction is not granted, (2) a likelihood of success at trial, and (3) that a balance of the hardships favors the plaintiff. The court will also consider **public policy** issues in determining whether to issue a preliminary injunction.

A permanent injunction is issued as equitable relief if the court finds that the defendant is liable for copyright infringement. The injunction prevents the defendant from ever engaging in the un-lawful activity again. In rare cases, the court may decide not to grant a permanent injunction if it would violate public policy. *See* **prior restraint**.

The Courts Say: A Preliminary Injunction Will Not Be Granted if There Is No Proof of Irreparable Harm

Bourne Co. v. Tower Records, Inc., 976 F.2d 99 (2d Cir. 1992)

The Second Circuit reversed the district court's order of a preliminary injunction barring the Walt Disney Company and Buena Vista Home Video from using the song "When You Wish upon a Star" to advertise EuroDisney on videocassette trailers. The court concluded that the use of the song was not a "new use," to which an objection was promptly brought because for decades, Bourne failed to complain about Disney's use of the song in a wide variety of media in ways that were inconsistent with Bourne's view of its agreement with Disney. Although Bourne had complained a couple of times to Disney in the previous ten years, it never filed suit. In denying the injunction, the court found that Bourne failed to prove that it would suffer irreparable harm if the injunction was not granted. The court found that the lengthy delay in filing suit against Disney to enforce its copyrights rebutted any presumption of irreparable harm, even though Bourne had established a prima facie case of copyright infringement. The Second Circuit determined that the perceived harm from a new use of copyrighted material must be so qualitatively different from the harm following from a prior uncontested use that the injured party could not reasonably foresee the new harm.

In Print—*See* **out of print; cessation of publication, remaindering.**

Insurance—*See* **errors and omissions, libel, warranty.**

Integration Clause—The integration clause of a contract, also known as a **merger clause**, has the effect of merging all previous agreements and even future oral agreements into the contract, effectively nullifying them and ensuring the superiority of the merged contract unless and until it is superceded by another written agreement.

Intellectual Property—Intellectual property is intangible property created by a through application of intellect and protected in the United States under the Constitution and federal law. Intellectual property includes **copyrights, trademarks, trade secrets,** and **patents**, all similar in that they represent the product of human intellect but different in the way they are protected.

Interactive Rights—Some types of literature in which the reader can pick an ending or make plot choices along the way are called interactive. These types of literature might also be published in hypertext or electronic form. *See* electronic rights or **digital rights.**

Interlibrary Loans—An interlibrary loan takes place when one library borrows material from another library on behalf of a patron. When libraries photocopy or fax articles and book excerpts, copyright owners worry that such interlibrary loans may cross the line of infringement. Under the copyright act, libraries are limited in the number of times they may copy a work in their collection for interlibrary loan purposes. Basically, libraries should not use copying and pooling of resources to avoid paying for content. This restriction is more important than ever in today's digital climate. *See* **electronic reserves.**

International Law—International law governs relations between foreign countries and multinational organizations such as the United Nations. International law comprises treaties and international customs. For instance, there is no formally codified international copyright law, but international copyright protection exists through treaties such as the **Berne Convention**, which has established an international standard of protection that many countries have agreed to uphold.

Internet—The Internet is a global computer network that allows individuals and organizations around the world to communicate with one another. Originally known as ARPANET, the Internet was created in 1969 by the Advanced Research Projects Agency (ARPA) of the U.S. government to facilitate communication between users of research computers at various universities. The network could remain functional in the event of a military attack or other disaster. Today, the Internet is made up of the World Wide Web, e-mail, chat rooms, bulletin board services, instant messaging services, Internet telephone technology, and other forms of computer-based digital communication. *See* **electronic rights, defamation,** and **digital rights.**

Internet Service Providers (ISP)—An ISP provides individuals and organizations with access to the Internet and other related services including high-speed lines, Web server management, and **Web site** construction and monitoring. ISPs may be liable for copyright infringement carried out with the use of their services. An ISP may be liable for **contributory infringement** for facilitating the infringing activities of its users and subscribers. *See* **Digital Millennium Copyright Act.**

Invasion of Privacy—You may have a First Amendment right to write truthfully about people, but individuals also have a right to privacy. You should be careful not to reveal private facts about people in your reporting, such as medical information. The right to privacy is strongest in a person's own home and more limited in public places, but you should be careful about revealing any highly personal details without permission. Of course, the right to privacy varies from one jurisdiction to another.

A note related to privacy and defamation: some states have enacted "false light" laws that allow plaintiffs who might have difficulty winning a defamation suit, including public figures, to seek damages for statements that they claim are unfairly embarrassing, even if true. If you write stories about people who might be eager to sue you, check on any "false light" laws in your state.

The Courts Say: Invasion of Privacy Recognized

Time, Inc., v. Hill, 385 U.S. 374 (1967)

In an action involving a New York privacy statute, the U.S. Supreme Court recognized invasion of privacy as a wrongful tort and considered its interaction with the press's First Amendment privilege to provide the public with news. The Court concluded that the New York statute was valid because it could be construed to avoid the constitutional protections of speech and press. The Court distinguished invasion of the right to privacy from libel, noting that while a libel action seeks a remedy for injury to a reputation, in an action for invasion of privacy, the primary damage is mental distress from having been exposed to public view, although injury to reputation may be an element. The Court further emphasized that for an invasion of privacy claim, the published material does not need to be defamatory in nature, and might even be laudatory and still warrant recovery of damages.

Inventions—New devices, methods, or processes that have been created through human endeavor. An invention may be patentable if it meets the requirements for a patent established under federal law.

Investigative Reporters and Editors (IRE)—A grassroots non-profit organization dedicated to improving the quality of investigative reporting, IRE was formed in 1975 to create a forum in which journalists throughout the world could help each other by sharing story ideas, news gathering techniques, and news sources. The IRE offices are based at the University of Missouri School of Journalism. Staff members include professional journalists, database experts, office professionals, and graduate and undergraduate students. IRE also counts on members with varied expertise to assist in its many training programs. The Web site is www.ire.org.

Invoice Price—The invoice price of a book is the discounted price publishers charge booksellers. This is generally equivalent to net price, as opposed to list, retail, cover, or catalog price.

ISBN—The International Standard Book Number is a unique machine-readable identification number, which marks any book unmistakably. For thirty years the ISBN has revolutionized international book trade. One hundred fifty-nine countries and territories are officially ISBN members. Publishers usually obtain ISBNs on behalf of their authors and each edition of a book has its own bar-code ISBN. Its Web site is www.isbn.org.

J

Joint Accounting—Sometimes known as **bucket accounting** or **cross-collateralization,** joint accounting is a method that is unfair to authors in which publishers withhold funds due to an author under one contract if the author owes money to the publisher under another contract.

Joint Authorship—*See* **collaborator, copyright.**

Judgment—A judgment is any final decision of a court. It is also a term used to describe an award of **damages** by a court.

Jurisdiction—Jurisdiction refers to the power of a court to decide a case. A court must be able to exercise control over the subject matter of the case and the parties involved. *See also* **choice of venue.**

Tips and Tools: Who Can You Sue and Where Can You Sue Them?

You can sue anyone you believe has infringed your copyright, or has contributed to the infringement. You can also sue someone who has violated a transfer of copyright rights, a license agreement, or other

---

contract. The defendant can be a person, multiple people, or a corporation or organization. It does not matter if the person resides in the United States or not, but if he does not, then you will need to sue him in federal district court and establish the requisite level of contacts so that the court can properly exercise jurisdiction.

Subject matter jurisdiction

Copyright protection is a federal question, created by federal law, so federal courts have jurisdiction over copyright cases. This means that you must file your action in a federal district court and not in a state court. This is true even if your claim also contains state law issues such as breach of contract. However, if your case is really a breach of contract claim with "incidental" copyright issues, then you might file in a state court. Federal district court is also the appropriate venue for a case that does not involve a federal question if all the plaintiffs are from different states than all the defendants, and the amount of the controversy exceeds $75,000.

If you decide that federal court is the correct choice for your case, there are many district courts in the United States and it is up to you and your attorney to determine the appropriate district court.

If you sue for breach of contract or any other state law action, then you must file your case in a state court.

Personal jurisdiction

A court can hear a case only if it can exercise authority over the defendant. This requires that the defendant has established minimum contacts within the forum state, even if a federal court will be hearing the case. The long-arm statute of the forum state will provide guidance as to which contact requirements must be met. The defendant's minimum contacts with the state usually must be meaningful in some manner and may arise from the circumstances that resulted in the lawsuit, such as the state where the contract was signed, or they may be more general. For instance, minimum contacts may be found to exist if the defendant owns property in the state.

> If your contract specifies that a particular court will be used to settle any and all disputes, then your choice is limited to that court.

Jury—A jury is a panel of individuals who have been sworn to impartially render a verdict in a particular case. Criminal defendants have the constitutional right to a trial by jury, and they must be found guilty by all twelve jurors. A few states, however, permit a conviction or acquittal to be decided ten to two. In civil cases, juries traditionally comprise twelve jurors; however, in many jurisdictions, only six or eight jurors may be selected for civil trials. A jury in a civil trial usually must return a unanimous verdict, but this may not always be the case. A jury trial is not available in cases where an **injunction** is the sole relief requested or in many family-related matters; however, in most civil cases either party may demand a jury trial. If a jury is not called the judge will decide the case. This is called a bench trial. A jury trial is often preferred when the issues at hand are emotional in nature or when a party believes that an ordinary person would favor her arguments. A trial before a judge, on the other hand, is often preferred when a case involves complex or technical legal matters.

The individual members of a jury are chosen through a process called voir dire during which the attorneys for both sides, or in many cases the judge alone, will have the opportunity to ask the members of the pool of potential jurors questions in order to select jurors who will be fair and impartial in deciding the matter at hand. Jurors may be questioned about matters such as their background, occupation, or previous jury service. In most jurisdictions, each party may make a certain number of preemptory challenges to rule out a potential juror for no given reason, as well as challenges for cause.

Juvenile Books—Books for young readers are sometimes called juvenile books.

K

Kill fee—A kill fee is a contractually specified amount paid to a freelancer whose work is accepted but not used by a publication. Kill fees for work delivered as agreed are considered unfair by many writers' organizations.

L

Laws—Laws are the rules and principles that govern conduct. They may be established by custom as **common law**, by the courts **as case law**, or by the action of a government entity such as Congress or an administrative agency. Federal laws, including the Copyright Act, ensure the consistent regulation of certain types of conduct on a national level, while individual states regulate other types of conduct, such as the execution of a contract. *See also* **choice of law**.

Tips and Tools: Where Do Laws Come From?

Laws can be established by case law, statute, or traditional values and customs. Case law precedents and standard industry practices are recognized and interpreted by courts, even though they have not been codified. Laws can be enacted by federal, state, or local legislatures. In addition, administrative bodies may enact regulations that pertain solely to that entity.

When a court applies common law or industry custom in a case, that case becomes part of the permanent record of judicial decisions forming the basis for future decisions in that court. Some cases may be designated as "unpublished" if they do not contain a new or significant interpretation of the law. Unpublished cases normally cannot be cited as precedent in a future case but may provide insight into how the court might rule on a related matter.

A federal law begins as a bill proposed by a member of either the Senate or the House of Representatives. The bill is sent to a committee that handles issues pertaining to the topic of the bill, and it is discussed, debated, and often revised or amended. Public hearings may be held. If the committee agrees on the bill, it is reported to the full Senate or House for further debate or amendment and a vote. If the bill is passed, it is then sent to the other house and the process is repeated. If the other house votes to pass the bill, it is returned to the original house for concurrence. When a bill is passed in the same form in both houses, it is considered enrolled in the house in which it originated, and it is sent to the president for signature. When the president signs the bill into law, it is then added to the session laws and the statutory code.

Administrative regulations are established by the agencies themselves. Some administrative bodies have their own administrative law courts to interpret their regulations.

Tips and Tools: How Can I Find a Law?

Federal and state judicial decisions are published in volumes of case reporters and summarized in case digests. Access to these cases is available in electronic legal databases such as LEXIS, WESTLAW or LoisLaw, on the Internet and in volumes shelved in law libraries.

Federal statutes are published chronologically as session laws in *Statutes at Large*, and also organized according to subject matter in the *United States Code*. Two other versions, both from private legal publishers, *United States Code Annotated*, and *United States Code Service*, are also supplemented with useful interpretative material. When a new law amends an existing statute, it is not printed in the *United States Code* in its entirety. Instead, the changes are incorporated directly into the existing statute. Each state has its own published series code. Like case law, federal and state statutes are available in electronic and printed form.

Federal agency regulations are organized into in the *Code of Federal*

Regulations and published in the *Federal Register* whenever they are created or revised. Federal regulations are also available in electronic versions or print. Federal administrative agency decisions are usually
available from the agencies themselves. State administrative bodies may
not always publish their regulations or administrative law decisions, and
you may need to contact the agency directly to get the information you
need. Look for state regulations in a law library within that state or
online.

Lawsuit—An action brought before a court to address a grievance is called a lawsuit. A lawsuit is commenced by the filing of a
complaint.

Lawyers—Lawyers, or attorneys, advise clients in legal matters
and represent them in court. A lawyer can review your publishing
contract and assist you in patenting your invention or registering
your copyrights or trademarks. You can also hire a lawyer to bring
a lawsuit against someone who you believe is infringing your intellectual property rights, or to defend your work and to protect
your rights in court. *See* **attorney**.

Lecture—*See* **speech**.

Legalese—Highly technical language that has a specific legal
meaning is sometimes referred in a derogatory manner as legalese. While it is important that contracts and other legal documents be clear and straightforward, consistent use of language
even if repetitive or redundant is still a good idea. Legalese often
incorporates **terms of art**, words that have a specific legal meaning. "Time is of the essence," for example, is a term of art that
means that a contract can be canceled completely if a particular
deadline is not met. Writers sometimes fall into the trap of want-
ing variety in contract language to their legal detriment. This
doesn't mean that lawyers shouldn't strive to draft clear and

straightforward agreements; it just means that a certain level of legalese is not only acceptable, but often preferable.

Legislation—Legislation refers to a law, or a group of related **laws**, proposed or enacted by Congress or a state legislature. *See also* **common law**, **case law**, and **administrative law**.

Libel—Libel is written **defamation** of someone's character through publication of something untrue that might hold an individual up to ridicule. Defamation is libel (written) or slander (spoken). A statement is defamatory if it adversely affects the reputation of the person in question in the estimation of ordinary persons; deters ordinary people from associating or dealing with that person; or injures the person in his or her occupation, grade, office, or financial credit. Defamation affects the entire chain of publication: author, editor, publisher, distributor, vendor, even a radio announcer. As with most things legal, the law of defamation varies from jurisdiction to jurisdiction. That means that it is different in Massachusetts than it is in New York. Between countries, the differences are even greater.

In trying to decide whether a particular statement you are about to make might be defamatory, first look at the plain meaning of the words. Second, ask if the innuendo is defamatory? Third, given the overall context of the story, ask if it is defamatory? Defamation must be specific. Does your statement refer to the plaintiff? You need not refer to the plaintiff by name but can refer to her indirectly. Even fiction can be defamatory if readers can figure out on whom your character is based. You cannot defame a group, however, only individuals. Defamation must be published. Publication can be in writing or speech. Saying something defamatory is not actionable unless it is heard by someone else. Publication may be accidental, and repeating a defamatory statement is, in many countries, just as bad as making the original statement.

If you are accused of libel, you have a few defenses. First, if what you said it true, you're in the clear, although you should be careful about what constitutes truth. There are also several legal justifications for defamation such as consent of the subject of the statement and privilege. Certain statements are protected by law. For example, judges and members of Congress or state legislatures are all protected for what they say in the course of litigation and debate. However, a statement made on the floor of Congress could be the source of a lawsuit if repeated outside the Capitol.

Some statements are protected by the qualified privilege of fair comment. If you are reporting on important matters of public interest, you may also have a qualified privilege if your reporting is fair and accurate, substantially correct, and on an important matter of public interest. In the United States, a defamatory statement made about a public figure must also have been made maliciously. The law assumes that public figures have chosen to be in the public eye and so are not entitled to the same level of protection.

If you defame someone, there are some ways you can make it better—and hopefully avoid large a large damage award. First, apologize and retract the statement. Doing so *before* you are sued carries more weight than afterward. As long as the apology is "full and fair," you may be able to avoid an award of general damages. If you're clearly in the wrong, the publication that printed the defamation or the broadcaster that aired it will probably offer to settle the case.

The Courts Say: Libel Must Be Measured by Standards That Satisfy the First Amendment

New York Times v. Sullivan, 376 U.S. 254 (1964)

The U.S. Supreme Court considered the extent to which freedom of speech and freedom of the press limit a state's power to award dam-

---

ages in a libel action brought by a public official against critics of his official conduct, and held that an Alabama statute was unconstitutional where it provided that the standard for libel is met if published material harms a person's reputation by criticizing his official conduct, even though it provided that the truth of statement is a defense. The Court found that a defense that compels the writer to guarantee the truth of each fact presented would lead to self-censorship and would restrict both true and false speech. The Supreme Court concluded that a public official cannot recover damages for a defamatory falsehood relating to his official conduct unless he proves that the statement was made with actual malice.

The Court further concluded that the New York Times did not act with actual malice in printing a full-page advertisement on behalf of the African American right-to-vote movement and the African American student movement, even though some of the statements were false, because it relied upon the good reputations of the sponsors of the advertisement. The Court recognized that the newspaper may have been negligent in not fact checking the advertisement but that it did not act with the requisite recklessness to amount to actual malice.

Although the advertisement did not mention the defendant by name, he alleged that as the police commissioner for Montgomery County, many of the statements that referred to police activities were directed at him. The Court determined that since he was not mentioned in the advertisement, the defendant could not claim that the statements were about him.

Libel Defense Resource Center—The name of this organization has been changed to the **Media Law Resource Center**, 80 Eighth Avenue, Suite 200, New York, NY 10011. Phone: 212-337-0200, Fax: 212-337-9893, Web site: www.medialaw.org.

Library of Congress—The Library of Congress is the largest library in the world, with almost 130 million books and other holdings on approximately 530 miles of bookshelves. Most of its core holdings are obtained as copyright deposits. Recognized as the national library of the United States, the library also acts as the research arm of Congress. Its stated mission is to make its resources available and useful to Congress and the American people and to sustain and preserve a universal collection of knowledge and creativity for future generations. It is headed by the Librarian of Congress, who is appointed by the president of the United States and confirmed by the Senate. The **Copyright Office** has been part of the Library of Congress since 1870 and a separate department of the library since 1897. The Library of Congress is located at 101 Independence Avenue, SE, Washington, DC 20540. Phone: 202-707-5000, www.loc.gov.

Licensing Rights—A license is a contract that transfers to another party fewer rights than are held by the owner of a copyright or a patent. A license can be as narrow or broad as desired, but even a broad license stops short of transferring the entire copyright or patent to the licensee. For instance, a license may assign digital rights, reproduction rights, or performance rights. An author may enter into an **exclusive license** or a **nonexclusive license**, and in the case of certain music and broadcast transmissions, compulsory licensing requirements established by law and administered by the Copyright Office may need to be met. A court will interpret a license pursuant to state contract law.

Linking—Links unify the World Wide Web into a single body of knowledge by allowing a **Web site** user to access another document or **Web page** located anywhere on the **Internet** with the click of a mouse. While linking can promote new ideas and ways of thinking, it can also lead to confusion as to the authorship and accuracy of linked material.

Tips and Tools: The Law of Linking

Linking does not, in itself, infringe the copyright of the linked material. The linked material is not copied and it remains in its original location

---

at all times. The issue of infringement may arise, however, if the creator of the link has directly copied any of the linked material onto the original Web site. Linking can also raise questions of authorship. When following a link, it may not always be clear whether the author of the original material is also the author of the linked material.

Current case law suggests that a person may generally create a link to your home page or, indeed, even a **deep link** to a Web page within your Web site, if it is clear that the material on your page belongs to you and they are merely directing people to your site.

If someone has included a link to material on your Web page to which you object, you may be able to bring an action for unfair competition or a trademark violation if you believe that a user would likely be confused as to the source of the material or if the material is confidential in nature. For example, an action for trademark infringement may be brought if the linked material pops up in a new box and is thus framed by the original Web site. This practice is called **framing** and it makes it particularly difficult for users to discern authorship of the linked material. Further, if the linked material is something that a user on your site would normally pay to access, then that activity would be actionable under unfair competition and even criminal laws.

List Price—The list price of a book is the cover price, catalog price or retail price.

Litigation—Litigation, very simply, is the pursuit of a lawsuit in court. Litigation can be costly, frustrating, and frightening. Some lawyers are litigators, while other lawyers concentrate on transactional work or counseling. If you are sued or need to sue someone, you will need help from both a litigator and lawyer who is an expert in publishing law or the field in which you plan to litigate.

Lyrics—Lyrics are protectable by copyright. Because it's so easy to infringe and because lyrics, like poetry, are likely to be short, it's important to seek the permission of the author of a lyric or a poem before quoting even a small portion. *See* **fair use**.

M

Magazines—Magazines are periodicals, serials, and collective works. Magazines are subject to copyright protection for the publication as a whole, but copyrights in the individual articles are owned by the authors unless they have been otherwise assigned.

Manuscripts—A manuscript is the text of a work in the form as written by the original author. **Copyright** in a manuscript vests when the author has fixed it in a tangible medium of expression. It's not usually necessary to register the copyright in an unpublished manuscript, but it can be done for a $30 fee and by sending one copy of it to the **Copyright Office** along with a completed Form TX. Copyright Office Web site, www.copyright.gov, has more information about copyright protection and registration of copyright in manuscripts.

Markup—Once a publishing deal has been offered and negotiated, it's important to be sure that the contract includes all the elements of the deal and that all the terms have been agreed to by both parties. The process of incorporating such changes is called marking up. Many publishing contracts are marked up by hand, with changes written in the margins and initialed and dated by the parties. No law that says a contract must be neat as long as it is understandable and that changes are acknowledged, and heavily marked-up contracts are perfectly legal. Another way of marking up a contract is to redline or **blackline** it. Redlining generally means incorporating proposed changes by drawing a line through proposed deletions and underlining proposed additions, so all parties can see and understand all changes. Redlining is usually done using the change tracking feature of a word processing program that allows proposed changes to be highlighted, then accepted or rejected prior to final printing and **execution** of the contract.

Mask Work—A mask work is a series of related images representing the three-dimensional pattern of the material contained within the layers of a semiconductor chip when it is fixed in a semiconductor chip product. Each image within the mask work bears the pattern of the surface of one form of the semiconductor chip product. A mask work is considered to be fixed when its embodiment in a semiconductor chip product is sufficiently stable to permit the mask work to be perceived or reproduced from the product for a period of more than transitory duration. *See also* **Semiconductor Chip Protection Act**.

Media Law Resource Center—Formerly the Libel Defense Resource Center, this organization changed its name to the Media Law Resource Center in 2003. According to Executive Director Sandra Baron, "when this organization was founded in 1980, libel was our membership's primary concern. Since then, the practical concerns of media and media counsel have broadened substantially to include, among other things, privacy and news gathering issues, as well as a myriad of new Internet-related law issues. The center reports on issues such as privacy, news gathering, fair use, and international liability. With the goal of supporting members in day-to-day media law operations. The MLRC tries to deliver practical and useful information and services.

Contact the center at 80 Eighth Avenue, Suite 200 New York, NY 10011. Phone: 212-337-0200, Fax: 212-337-9893, Web site: www.medialaw.org.

Mediation—Like **arbitration**, mediation is form of **alternative dispute resolution** where the parties to a dispute agree to work with a neutral third party to resolve the differences between them. Mediation and other forms of ADR are thought to be less expensive, more confidential, and less disruptive than **litigation**.

Merger Clause—A contractual provision that says something to the effect that the contract terms may not be changed by oral agreement or prior terms because those terms are deemed to have been merged into the contract at issue. Another term for a merger clause is **integration clause**.

Merger Doctrine—A **copyright law** principle that says when an underlying idea and its expression have merged, or become so closely entwined that it is difficult to separate the idea that is *not* copyrightable from the expression that *is* copyrightable, then any copyright protection that might exist in the merged concept is thin to nonexistent as a matter of public policy. Courts have repeatedly recognized application of the merger doctrine as a way to avoid private ownership of ideas or let copyright law create a monopoly on a common subject. Otherwise it would be almost impossible to write about such things as how to bake a loaf of bread or how to study the Bible, even when such writing is uniquely expressed.

Metatags—Metatags are key words chosen by a Web site creator and embedded in the code of the Web site in order to identify the content of the site to Web search engines. Metatags are hidden from the plain view of the Web site's users. Search engines view metatags to determine if a specific Web site contains content that satisfies the search request of a user. The more words in the metatags that overlap with the search terms input by the user, the more likely that the Web site will appear as a match.

The Courts Say: Use of a Competitor's Trademark in the Metatags of a Web Site Is Likely to Cause Initial Interest Confusion

Brookfield Communications, Inc., v. West Coast Entertainment Corp., 174 F.3d 1036 (9th Cir. 1999)

The Ninth Circuit Court of Appeals held that the use of a competitor's "MovieBuff" trademark in the metatags on the defendant's Web site was likely to cause initial interest confusion among users and concluded that initial interest confusion is actionable under the Lanham Act. The court determined that initial interest confusion occurs when a sizable number of consumers who were originally looking for the trademark owner's product simply decide to use the defendant's offerings instead. The defendant thus improperly benefits from the goodwill that the trademark owner has developed in the mark. The ninth circuit noted that although the defendant could not use the MovieBuff mark as a metatag, the company could legally use an appropriate descriptive term such as Movie Buff.

Microfilm, Microform, and Microfiche—The photographs of actual pages of a publication that are made available by using a special viewer.

Moral Rights—Moral rights are derived from the French concept of *droit moral.* While moral rights have long been recognized in Europe, they are relatively new to U.S. intellectual property law. There are three basic types of moral rights: the right of attribution, the right of integrity, and the right of withdrawal. With the enactment of the Visual Artists Rights Act of 1990 (**VARA**), Congress recognized the moral rights of integrity and attribution for authors of visual works only. Moral rights are conferred on the artist, for her lifetime, rather than on the work of art itself, and cannot be transferred because they exist independently of the artist's copyright in the work. Moral rights may, however, be waived with the author's express written agreement.

Tips and Tools: Do You Have Any Moral Rights?

If you are the author of a work of visual art as defined by U.S. copyright law, you may exercise the moral rights of attribution and integrity, as provided by VARA. If you are an author of any other type of work, however, you are not entitled to moral rights under federal copyright law. Some states, however, recognize moral rights for their authors of fine art, and some moral rights have been indirectly recognized under federal law. For example, courts have recognized the right of integrity inherent in the false advertising provisions of the Lanham Trademark Act. As a practical matter, any moral rights that you may wish to claim should be specifically negotiated through a written contract.

Motion—A motion is a formal request to a court to issue an order.

Multiple Authors—*See* **joint authorship, collaboration, copyright.**

Multiple Submission—Work submitted to more than one publisher or agent at once is a multiple submission. Some publishers frown on this practice, but writers and writers' organizations consider it necessary in today's publishing climate.

Musical Work—The copyright of a musical work includes both the lyrics and the score and may be expressed in either sheet music or a phonorecord such as a CD or a cassette tape. It protects the generic sound that would necessarily result from any performance of the piece. Federal copyright law has established a compulsory licensing requirement for the use of musical works in broadcasting or in jukeboxes. The copyright for a musical work differs from that for a **sound recording** because the copyright for a musical work protects the actual music itself. A copyright for a sound recording extends only to the specific arrangement of sounds as they occur on a phonorecord. While one person can copyright a musical work, another person may copyright the sound recording of his performance of that musical work.

N

National Association of Science Writers (NASW)—NASW was established in 1934 and formally incorporated in 1955. The organization works to improve science reporting, encourages communication among science writers, and promotes the free flow of accurate science news and information to the public. NASW members include science reporters, freelance writers, and public information officers from government labs, universities, and other entities. NASW works closely with its sister organization, the Council for the Advancement of Science Writing, to provide its members with access to the latest developments in scientific research through seminars and fellowships. NASW also offers a job mailing list to assist member writers in finding work. The organization presents three annual Science in Society awards to recognize outstanding reporting about science and its impact on society. NASW can be contacted at 304-754-5077. More information can be found on the organization's Web site: www.nasw.org.

National Commission on New Technological Uses of Copyrighted Works—*See* **CONTU.**

National Libel Defense Resource Center—*See* **Media Law Resource Center.**

National Writers Union—The National Writers Union bills itself as "the only labor union that represents freelance writers in all genres, formats, and media." The NWU has a membership of about 5,000 members and is affiliated with the United Automobile Workers (UAW). The NWU works to advance the economic and working conditions of writers. Its Web site is www.nwu.org.

Negligence—The underlying cause of action for many legal wrongs, negligence is very simply the failure of a person who has a legal duty of some sort to use reasonable care in the carrying out of that duty and whose negligent conduct results in harm to another.

Negotiation—The process of making and seeking concessions in order to reach an agreement with another party, negotiation is a key skill for a savvy writer to have and use in dealing with contract issues. Sadly, many writers lack the skill or motivation to negotiate, but fortunately this is a skill that can and should be learned and improved by education, practice, and networking with other writers.

The Voice of Experience: Tips for Smart Negotiating

Timothy Perrin, writer
Westbank, British Columbia

Timothy Perrin is a working freelance writer and "recovering lawyer" from Canada whose expertise in negotiation has helped many of his fellow writers. He says, "Negotiation is a learned skill, and even for professionals, it's still a challenging task." The following tips are adapted from an article he wrote for *Writer's Digest* magazine, an article for which he retained reprint rights. These tips are reprinted here with his permission, permission he is free to give because of his own negotiating skill.

Oh, Is That All?

Whenever you're negotiating the money for an assignment, let the other side make the first offer, then, no matter what the offer, pause about five seconds and say, "Oh, is that all? I was thinking more like . . . ," and triple whatever he offered. Make sure your voice drips with disappointment. I can virtually guarantee he'll boost his offer substantially.

Time Is on Your Side.

The party not in a hurry generally has an advantage. Always say, "I'll think about it and get back to you." Ignore artificial deadlines, particularly ones imposed by the client's failure to get to the project in time.

Don't Take It or Leave It.

When someone tells you a contract isn't negotiable, ignore him and start negotiating. He's already invested time and money in your idea. Your being businesslike and reasonable in your requests for changes in contract positions won't drive away a client. Go for the ideal by taking out everything you don't want and put in what you do want. Then throw in a few things you can give away later!

It's Not about Price.

Editors aren't buying what you think you're selling. Like anyone else, they're buying a solution to a problem and the good feeling they get from solving the problem. So ask questions of your customer and of others who have dealt with your customer to find out what problem you can help solve.

Pressure Is Mutual.

You're not the only one feeling pressure. The editor has a magazine to fill with quality material on a budget that is undoubtedly too small. A book editor has to buy enough profitable books to hang on to the job. Don't let yourself be intimidated.

Neighboring Rights—Exclusive rights that are closely related to copyright are called neighboring rights. Neighboring rights include the rights of performers in their performances, recording companies in their sound recordings, and radio and television broadcasters in their broadcasts. The United States is not a signatory of the Rome Convention, the primary international treaty addressing neighboring rights. Since most internationally recognized neighboring rights are protected under federal copyright law, there has been no need to expressly recognize neighboring rights for literary works in the United States. The lack of neighboring rights under U.S. law, however, means that a few U.S. recording artists don't get payments for foreign broadcasts of some musical performances.

Net Price, Net Proceeds, Net Receipts, Net Income—The net price of a book is typically the **retail, cover**, or **list price**, less the retail discount offered. A publisher's net price does not typically include standard overhead. Similarly, net proceeds, receipt, or income refers to the amount actually received by a publisher for the license of subsidiary rights or the sale of books as opposed to the catalog or retail amount. When used in a contract, net terms should be defined so that there is no ambiguity about the meaning and what factors are involved in the calculations.

Net Royalty—When royalties are calculated on the basis of net income or net price, rather than on the basis of list or cover price, the actual dollars paid in net royalties are generally much less (often about half). It used to be that most trade publishers calculated royalties on the basis of cover price, but many have now switched to paying net royalties. The method of calculation is not as important as is a clear understanding of how that rate, whatever it is, actually translates into earnings.

Newspaper—Like a magazine, a newspaper is a **collective work**, serial publication, or **periodical.** Newspapers sometimes acquire content from freelancers, although they are more likely than magazines to be staff written. Freelancers who license rights to newspapers should be aware of the rights issues involved. Copyright in a newspaper covers the overall issue and most staff-written content, but not individual freelance contributions, unless the paper has acquired the copyright by **work made for hire** or **assignment.**

Next Book—Some publishing contracts have a clause requiring that the book being contracted for is the author's next book, meaning that the author agrees not to work on other books until the contracted-for book is submitted. The purpose of such a clause is to protect the publisher from authors becoming overextended. A writer shouldn't agree to a next-book clause unless he is sure that he will not be working on another book in the interim. Even then, a next-book clause can be unfair and most publishers will permit the clause to be stricken. The next-book clause is sometimes intended as an **option clause**.

Noncompete Clause—Most publishing contracts have some sort of competing works or noncompete clause that restricts the right of an author to write another book or article and protects the publisher from having the writer produce another work on the same subject that would unfairly compete with the contracted-for work. A publisher is certainly entitled to have an exclusive right to such a book or article, but authors should be careful that such a clause is not overly restrictive.

Tips and Tools: Negotiating Tips for Next Book and Noncompete Clauses

Publishers can rightfully require an author not to license the same or very similar rights to another publisher, so a noncompete clause is, from the publisher's point of view, an essential protection. A reasonable noncompete clause is perfectly fine but should be fair and not overly restrictive for the writer. Here are some ways to ensure a fair noncomplete clause:

- Ask that the definition of a competing work be narrow in terms of subject. Rather than agree not to write a book on the same subject, for example, specify the exact topic, perhaps "personal financial management techniques for mutual fund investors."
- Narrow the definition in terms of audience or market by saying that you will not write a children's book or textbook on the same subject as an adult trade book, for example.
- Narrow the definition of "compete." Look for language that says "will" interfere with sales rather than "might" interfere.
- Shorten the time frame of a noncompete period. Be wary of such an unlimited period as "the term of the copyright" or "as long as the work remains in print."

Nonexclusive License—An owner of such intellectual property as a copyright patent or trademark may enter into a nonexclusive license with several different parties for use of the same property. The licensor may grant the same rights to multiple licensees. For example, you could permit a professor to copy an **excerpt** from your new book for use in a **coursepack**. If you make it a nonexclusive license you could also permit other professors to use the same excerpt. An **exclusive license**, however, can only be used to grant the permission to a single licensee.

Notice and Takedown—The process outlined in the Digital Millennium Copyright Act by which a copyright owner notifies an **Internet service provider** (ISP) of infringing material on its network and the ISP subsequently removes the infringing material. The ISP must promptly notify the subscriber who posted the infringing material that the material has been removed or can no longer be accessed. The subscriber may then respond by filing a counternotification. If the ISP in fact receives a counternotification indicating that the material was removed through mistake or misidentification, it must restore access within ten to fourteen business days. *See* **Digital Millenium Copyright Act** for a discussion of how to protect your rights with Notice and takedown.

Notice of Copyright—A notice of copyright, usually consisting of the copyright symbol © with the name of the author and the year of publication or completion of the work, is no longer legally necessary for the work to be protected by copyright, but it's usually a good idea for a published work to carry an appropriate copyright notice. Just because a work does not carry a copyright notice does *not* mean that it isn't protected. *See* **copyright**.

O

Obscenity—A work is obscene, legally speaking, if its content is so offensive and lacking in redeeming value that it would seriously offend, in a patently offensive way, contemporary community standards of decency. The standard for obscenity to be considered illegal is standard to meet. Not all **pornography** or **x-rated** material, for example, will rise to the level of obscenity. Truly obscene material, however, can be legally banned.

The Courts Say: Obscene Material Is Not Protected by the First Amendment

Miller v. California, 413 U.S. 15 (1973)

When the U.S. Supreme Court sent a defendant's conviction for mailing unsolicited sexually explicit material in violation of a California statute back to the trial court for review, it held that a work describing or depicting sexual conduct may be considered obscene, and thus subject to state regulation only when taken as a whole, it (1) appeals to the prurient interest in sex; (2) portrays, in a patently offensive way, sexual conduct specifically defined by the applicable state law; and (3) does not have serious literary, artistic, political, or scientific value. The Court found that if a state obscenity law is thus limited, First Amendment values are adequately protected by ultimate independent appellate re-

---

view of constitutional claims when necessary. The Court rejected the "utterly without redeeming social value" test for obscenity and the concept of a national standard saying instead that the determination whether a work is obscene must be considered from the perspective of an average person, applying contemporary community standards. The Court noted that, at a minimum, prurient, patently offensive depictions or descriptions of sexual conduct must have serious literary, artistic, political, or scientific value to merit First Amendment protection.

The Courts Say: A Ban on Virtual Child Pornography Violates Freedom of Speech

Ashcroft v. The Free Speech Coalition, 535 U.S. 234 (2002)

The U.S. Supreme Court struck down the Child Pornography Prevention Act of 1996 (CPPA), a federal law that expanded the federal prohibition on child pornography to include a broad range of sexually explicit images that appear to involve a minor, and any sexually explicit images that are advertised or distributed in such a way as to convey the impression that they involve a minor engaging in sexually explicit conduct. The Court ruled that the law abridged the freedom to engage in a substantial amount of lawful speech, and thus was overbroad and unconstitutional under the First Amendment. The intent of Congress in enacting the CPPA was to prohibit virtual child pornography as well as actual child pornography. The Court noted that pornography can only be banned if it is obscene, but pornography depicting minors can be prohibited whether or not the images are obscene. The Court determined that the CPPA was unconstitutionally overbroad because it regulated speech that was not obscene and prohibited speech without regard to its serious literary, artistic, political, or scientific value. The Court noted that under the CPPA, William Shakespeare's play *Romeo and Juliet* would be banned, as well as recent movies such as *Traffic* and *American Beauty*. Child pornography, the Court reasoned, may be regulated regardless of the value of the work because the images themselves are the products of child sexual abuse, but virtual child pornography is not intrinsically related to the sexual abuse of children.

O

The Courts Say: Public Libraries Must Use Internet Filters to Block Access to Obscene Material

United States v. American Library Association, 539 U.S. 104 (2003)

The U.S. Supreme Court upheld the constitutionality of the Children's Internet Protection Act (CIPA), requiring public libraries to use Internet filtering software as a condition of receiving federal funding. The Court determined that the law did not violate the First Amendment rights of library patrons because a Web site can be unblocked, or the filter disabled, by a librarian at the patron's request. Congress passed CIPA to protect minors from being exposed to pornography on the Internet through the use of library computers. The Court noted that the government has a legitimate interest in protecting young library users from exposure to inappropriate material. The Court recognized that while public libraries have broad discretion to decide what material to include in their collections, they do not normally include pornography or other materials of inappropriate quality. The Supreme Court also said the law was a valid exercise of congressional spending power.

Offer—Technically, a proffered contract is an "offer" that doesn't take effect until it is "accepted" by the other party. When the other party proposes changes rather than accepting the proffered contract, it becomes a "counteroffer."

Open Meeting Laws (Sunshine Laws)—Laws that require government bodies to deliberate in public are called open meeting or sunshine laws. Such laws are designed to protect the public interest by making sure public business is conducted in an open and above-board manner. See also FOIA.

Operas—Dramatic performances set to music are called operas. Operas are entitled to copyright protection as dramatico-musical works because they are acted as well as sung. The opera as a whole may be protected by copyright, and in addition, the li-

247

bretto and each musical composition contained in the opera may be protected individually through registration with the Copyright Office.

Option Clause—An option clause in a publishing contract requires the author to offer his next book to the publisher. Sometimes called a **right of first refusal**, an option clause can be quite unfair. It is almost never in an author's best interest to agree to an option clause because it restricts that author's future freedom to some extent. Option clauses are sometimes imprecisely referred to as **next book** clauses.

Tips and Tools: Negotiating an Option Clause

Some first-time authors are flattered by an option clause because they assume, erroneously, the publisher sees the author in terms of a publishing career rather than a single book. What an option clause really means, however, is that the author is restricted from approaching other publishers while the publisher has no corresponding obligation. When negotiating an option clause, try to

- Eliminate it altogether. Many publishers will agree, and asking to strike an option clause is unlikely to derail contract negotiations.
- Limit the time of an option clause both in terms of the option period (a year or two might be reasonable) and in terms of the publisher's time to respond to the option work offered (sixty to ninety days may be reasonable, but longer is not).
- Limit the terms and conditions of the option contract. Avoid agreement to offer the option book on the same terms as the present contract.
- Limit the subject and audience of the option book to, for example, your "next work on the subject of personal finance for a consumer audience."
- Limit the submission form of the option work to a description or proposal, rather than a complete manuscript.

Originality—In order to qualify for copyright protection, a work must be original to the author and have at least a modicum of creativity. The author must have independently created a work that doesn't need to be new or unusual, but must have creative spark, no matter how tiny.

A higher standard of originality applies to certain derivative works when the preexisting work is popular. In such cases, the courts have considered whether the derivative work is a substantial variation of the preexisting work.

The Courts Say: Copyright Rewards Originality, Not Sweat of the Brow

Feist Publications, Inc., v. Rural Telephone Service Co., 499 U.S. 340 (1991)

A telephone utility sued a competitor, Feist, for copying entries from its residential telephone directory for use in its own directory. The U.S. Supreme Court held that the utility's white pages were not entitled to copyright protection and thus Feist's use of the names, towns, and telephone numbers culled from the utility's directory did not constitute copyright infringement. The Court noted that while facts are not entitled to copyright protection, factual compilations may be eligible if they meet the originality requirement mandated by the U.S. Constitution. The Court rejected the established "sweat of the brow" theory, which rewarded the hard work that went into creating a factual compilation, because it extended copyright protection to the underlying facts themselves. The Court determined that the utility's alphabetical arrangement data and its selection of which information to include for each resident was dictated by the nature of the directory and lacked even a modicum of originality.

Orphan Book—When a book's acquiring editor leaves a publishing house before shepherding it through the publishing process, the book is said to be orphaned. The new editor may not share her predecessor's enthusiasm for the book. *See* **acceptable manuscript** clause and **editor clause**.

Out of Print—When a book goes out of print the rights should revert to its author, but many publishing contracts fail to adequately spell out what triggers a **reversion of rights** upon **cessation of publication, remaindering**, or an out of print declaration.

Tools and Tips: Negotiating an Out of Print Clause

You should be entitled to get the rights to your work back when the publisher is no longer interested in or able to exploit them. Avoid having your rights unfairly tied up by carefully negotiating a reversion or out of print clause.

- Make sure "out of print" is fairly defined. You don't want your rights tied up because there are a few copies in Swahili sitting in some warehouse. A fair definition would specify that an English-language version of the book be listed in the publisher's current catalog and available for sale through normal channels of distribution.
- Make sure that print-on-demand technology doesn't mean that your book stays perpetually in print. Get language saying a book is deemed out of print when annual sales drop below a certain level or that existence only in a digital or on-demand format does not mean it's in print.
- Make sure the process of rights reversion isn't unduly burdensome on the author. Few publishers will make reversion completely automatic, and most will require that the author make some sort of written demand that the book be reprinted. But a demand without a timely response should trigger an automatic reversion.

Over the Transom—This expression dates from the era when office entrances had ventilation transoms over doors and authors would submit books to publishers by sliding them under a door or tossing them over the transom. It is a term for an unsolicited manuscript. Over-the-transom submissions often end up in a slush pile.

P

Packager—A packager is a hybrid between an publisher, editor, book designer, and agent who arranges to have a book written, edited, illustrated, designed, and sometimes printed prior to turning it over to a publisher for distribution *See* **book packager**, and **Tools and Tips: Book Packaging**, page 108.

Page Proofs—Page proofs, also called galley proofs, or galleys, are printed out for proofreading after a book has been set into type and organized into a preliminary layout.

Paperback Books—Paperback books have paper covers and are often smaller and more cheaply produced than hardcovers. However, the distinctions between paperback and hardcover have blurred in recent years with a greater variety of paperback formats such as paperback original, **mass market paperback**, **trade paperback**, and rack paperback, sold from special display racks in a variety of nontraditional retail outlets.

Parody—A parody is work that imitates the characteristic style of another author or work for the purpose of humor or commentary. Therefore, a parody by nature must use some elements of the prior work in order to create the new one. In determining

251

whether parodies constitute fair use, a court will analyze each work on a case-by-case basis, applying the four fair use factors set forth in the copyright statute. *See* **fair use.**

The Courts Say: Parody May Be Entitled to an Affirmative Defense of Fair Use

Campbell v. Acuff-Rose Music, Inc., 510 U.S. 569 (1994)

The U.S. Supreme Court held that a rap song parody was fair use. Acuff-Rose Music, the copyright holder of Roy Orbison's song "Pretty Woman," sued the rap music group 2 Live Crew for copyright infringement. The threshold or basic inquiry for a determination of parody is whether the parodic character of the work can be perceived; the good taste or bad taste of the work does not matter. Applying the first of the fair use factors, the Court found that the purpose and character of the rap song, which commented on and criticized the original version, was transformative in that it gave a new level of meaning to the work. The Court reasoned that the more transformative a work is, other fair use factors such as commercialism become less important because transformative works lie at the heart of the fair use doctrine's guarantee of breathing space within the confines of copyright. Considering the commercial nature of the work, the Court concluded that it is merely one element of the fair use analysis and does not create a presumption against the fair use of a parody.

The Court determined that the second fair use factor, the nature of the copyrighted work, was not very useful when applied to parodies since they must copy a well-known work to be effective. The third factor, the amount and substantiality of the portion used, the Court recognized, encompasses not only the quantity of the material used in the parody, but also its quality and significance.

The Court found that 2 Live Crew's use of the words of the first line of the song was not excessive and sent it back to the district court to determine whether repeated use of the opening bass riff from the original was excessive. In considering the fourth fair use factor, the Court concluded that when a use is transformative as opposed to merely duplicative of the original, market substitution is less certain and market harm is not readily inferred. The Court noted that with regard to pure parody, it is likely that the new work will not affect the market for the original. As part of its inquiry, the Court considered the derivative market for rap music and found that there was no evidence that the parody harmed the potential rap market for the original song.

HOW MUCH APPROPRIATION IS TOO MUCH?

Suntrust Bank v. Houghton Mifflin Company, 268 F.3d 1257 (11th Cir. 2001) The Eleventh Circuit Court of Appeals vacated a preliminary injunction issued by the district court and held that *The Wind Done Gone*, a parody of Margaret Mitchell's *Gone with the Wind*, established a viable fair use defense. The Eleventh Circuit noted that the parody was not a general commentary on the Civil War-era American South, but rather a specific criticism of the depiction of slavery and the relationships between blacks and whites in *Gone with the Wind*. In finding that the parody was a transformative work, the court considered its use of first-person narrative and very different language from the original, and the fact that the last half of the book contained a completely new story. In its fair use analysis, the court determined that the third factor, the amount and substantiality of the portion of the original used in the new work, was the most critical.

Once enough has been taken to ensure identification, the court noted, how much more is reasonable will depend on the extent to which the overriding purpose and character of the work is to parody the original, or the likelihood that the parody will become a market substitute for the original. The court said that the new work was indeed a parody, but the appropriation numerous characters, settings, and plot twists from the original book, including seemingly nonrelevant details, made a ruling as to whether the quantity and value of the materials used were reasonable in relation to the purpose of the copying difficult to make on the basis of the record. The court decided the issue of market substitution in favor of the parody.

Pass Through—This is a term that applies when payments for subsidiary rights are passed through to the author by the primary publisher. From the author's point of view, it's advantageous to have such payments passed on promptly by the publisher, rather than being held until the next royalty period, or worse, applied against an advance.

Patent—A patent is issued to an inventor by the federal government and grants the inventor the right to exclude others from making, selling, or using the invention. A patent does not protect ideas but rather the structures or methods that express the idea. There are three types of patents: **utility**, design, and plant. While a utility patent protects the functional aspects of a product or process, a design patent protects industrial design, and a plant patent protects a new type of living plant.

Pay on Acceptance—Most professional magazine writers expect publishers to pay for their work upon acceptance rather than on publication. First-tier publications usually do pay when work has been accepted. It's a good idea for a contract to specify what constitutes acceptance.

Pay on Publication—It's considered unfair for a periodical to hold up payment for work until it's actually published. ASJA says "Pay on publication may mean never." The practice ties up the rights in a piece for an indefinite time, which is also very unfair.

PDF—The acronym PDF stands for portable document format, a universal file format that preserves the appearance of any original document, including graphics and layout, regardless of the program used to create it. PDF was created by Adobe in the early 1990s. A PDF file can be read by anyone who downloads the free Adobe Reader from www.adobe.com. Many vendors in addition to Adobe offer software to create, view, and modify PDF files. While a PDF file provides a way to essentially post anything, even photocopies, on the Internet, it can also allow such security options as a **digital signature** to authenticate the accuracy of the PDF file in relation to the original and to protect the PDF file from unauthorized alteration or copying.

PDF is quickly becoming a standard for archiving and electronic document management in corporations and government entities around the world. Many federal and state courts across the United States have implemented electronic case filing systems, which will replace traditional paper filings and case dispositions with the electronic transmission of PDF documents.

Pen American Center—A writers' organization that bills itself as "a fellowship of writers working for more than eighty years to advance literature, to promote a culture of reading, and to defend free expression." PEN American Center is a member center of International PEN, an association of prominent literary writers and editors. PEN's goals are to promote intellectual cooperation and understanding among writers, to create a world community of writers that would emphasize the central role of literature in the development of world culture, and to defend literature against the many threats to its survival from the modern world. The Web site is www.pen.org.

Pen Name—A pen name, or **pseudonym**, is literally a false name used by an author. Authors use pen names for a variety of legitimate reasons ranging from shielding identity to protecting privacy to using different names for different types of work.

Performance Rights—The owner of a copyright has the exclusive right to perform it publicly. Performance rights encompass reciting, rendering, playing, dancing, or acting a work, either directly or by means of a device. Authors of musical works routinely join **performing rights societies** that license these rights to others for a fee. Performance rights are generally available to all works under federal copyright law; however, the copyright for a pictorial, graphic, or sculptural work does not include the right to perform it publicly, but rather to display the work. The **Digital Performance Right in Sound Recordings Act** of 1995 recognizes a public performance right in sound recordings.

Performing Arts—Works of performing art are intended to be performed in public and are protectable by **copyright.** They include musical works, dramatic works, pantomimes and choreographic works, motion pictures, and other audiovisual works.

Performing Rights Societies—Performing rights societies represent songwriters and publishers. They protect the rights of their members by licensing and distributing royalties for the nondramatic public performances of their works. Licenses are regularly granted to radio networks, television stations, nightclubs, and Web site operators. Members of performing rights societies include composers, songwriters, and music publishers. *See* **ASCAP, BMI, SESAC.**

Periodical—A **magazine, newspaper**, or other **collective work** that is published regularly on a **serial** or periodical basis is called a periodical.

Periodical Writers Association of Canada (PWAC)—PWAC is a organization of about five hundred freelance writers and journalists across Canada. The organization's goals are to develop and maintain professional standards in editor-writer relationships; encourage higher standards and fees for all types of freelance writing; offset the isolation of freelance writers; provide professional development programs and information on issues, trends, and new technology; mediate grievances between writers and editors; work actively for the survival of periodical writing in a highly competitive communications market; and lobby for freedom of the press and freedom of expression in Canada. PWAC, 215 Spadina Ave.,

Suite 123, Toronto, ON, M5T 2C7, Canada. Phone: 416-504-1645, Fax: 416-913-2327, e-mail: info@pwac.ca, www.pwac.ca.

Permissions and Permissions Services—*See* **Author's Registry, Copyright Clearance Center (CCC), ASCAP, BMI, SESAC.**

Photocopies—The dawn of the Xerox era, the proliferation of the photocopier, and the easy duplication of endless copies ushered in an new world of copyright infringment unrivaled until the beginning of digital technology. One writer who has found herself repeatedly infringed in academic **coursepacks** contends that the technology that makes piracy easy has also resulted in the renewed efforts of authors, musicians, and other copyright owners to enforce their work. "We may be behind, but we're catching up," she says. "I can't understand people who think it's okay to steal just because it's easy."

Photographs—Like **literary works**, photographs are protected by **copyright law** from the moment they are fixed in a tangible medium of expression. In the case of traditional film, fixation occurs when the light causes a chemical reaction on the film. With digital cameras, the moment comes when the image is captured in the camera's digital memory and saved to a computer data storage device.

Tools and Tips: Copyright Considerations for Photographs

- Remember that it's the *photographer*, not the *subject* of the photo, who owns the copyright.
- Authors of nonfiction books are often expected to provide photos and other illustrations. Such authors should make sure that the responsibility for clearing photo permissions and making payment is clearly defined in the contract.

Plagiarism—Copying the words or ideas of another and using them as one's own is informally known as plagiarism. Plagiarism may amount to copyright infringement if original expression is appropriated, but it often may not violate any law. Plagiarism is considered unethical throughout the academic and scientific communities, and a plagiarist will usually find his or her reputation damaged and credibility shattered, regardless of whether the copying amounts to **infringement**.

Plaintiff—In a civil lawsuit, the plaintiff is the party who seeks damages against the **defendant.**

Poetry—Poetry is a type of literature, distinguished from prose, that is often pithy, lyrical, and rhythmic in quality. Poetry is subject to copyright protection and should be registered as a literary work. Because poems are often short and their words loaded with meaning and distinctive expression, direct quotations from a poem are unlikely to be considered **fair use** under copyright law.

Power of Attorney—A power of attorney is a written instrument in which one person (the principal) appoints another (the attorney in fact or agent) to perform certain specific duties on behalf of the principal. A power of attorney has the effect of permitting one person to act with legal authority on behalf of another in various financial and personal matters.

Preamble—The introductory paragraphs of a legal document are collectively known as the preamble. The preamble of a **contract** for example, typically identifies the parties, subject, date, scope, definitions used, and the purpose of a **agreement**. The preamble may also include a list of **recitals**, a series of statements often preceded by the word "whereas," that lay out the reasons the parties wish to enter a contract.

Preempt—A preempt is a bid in an auction for rights in a literary property that is designed to knock other bidders out of the competiton.

Preemption—Preemption is a legal doctrine that recognizes that federal law will take precedence over state law in certain matters. Preemption ensures a uniform national standard in applying and enforcing laws and prevents states from passing laws that are inconsistent with federal law.

Since January 1, 1978, federal copyright law has preempted the patchwork of state copyright laws offering varying levels of protection across the country. While states may offer additional protections to authors and artists, they cannot pass legislation that conflicts with federal copyright protection. For example, **VARA** Visual Artists Rights Act provides certain moral rights to artists whose work qualifies as fine art and expressly states that it preempts state law. However, some states, like New York, recognize different and additional moral rights, such as the improper display of a work, that are not included in the federal law. Courts have not been consistent in applying the preemption doctrine in the area of copyright law, and many cases include state law claims that are distinguishable from the federal copyright claims.

Prequel—A story that employs the same characters in a sequence of events taking place prior in time to that of an earlier work, rather than later in time, as a **sequel**.

Press Pass/Press Privileges/Press Credentials—Members of the working press often need some sort of credentials, such as press passes, to gain admittance to events they are covering. Press credentials can be issued by courts, police agencies, government agencies, organizations holding newsworthy events, publishers, and organizations of journalists. Press credentials serve to identify members of the working press and attest to a certain level of professionalism. A writer, author, or reporter doesn't need credentials to enjoy freedom of the press and freedom of speech, but the possession of credentials can be helpful in gaining access to officials and events.

Press Pen—When officials find it necessary to put up barricades to keep the public at a reasonable distance from such newsworthy locations as crime scenes or press conferences, the press is often provided with closer access in a special area. These special areas are sometimes called press pens.

Press Shield—A privilege, sometimes granted by law and sometimes by tradition, used by a reporter to protect a source. Many states have press shield laws granting a certain level of privilege to the news media, but some do not and the state laws vary. Such laws are designed to encourage freedom of the press by prohibiting prosecutors from forcing reporters to reveal the identities of confidential news sources in investigations or court proceedings.

Tales from the Trenches: Bad Facts or Bad Law? The Story of Vanessa Leggett

Vanessa Leggett, a freelance journalist, was held in contempt of court for not revealing a confidential source of information in response to a grand jury subpoena regarding a murder investigation in Texas. For four years, she conducted interviews for a book on the subject. When the FBI learned that she was writing a book about the case, it tried to recruit her as a paid informant and, when that failed, served her with the first in a series of grand jury subpoenas in order to learn what information she had obtained. The FBI instructed her to turn over all of her notes, and copies of the notes, regarding the case. Noting that the Fifth Circuit Court of Appeals does not recognize a qualified privilege for journalists to protect sources in criminal cases, the district court ordered her to comply with a series of questions and held her in

---

contempt when she continued to exercise her constitutional rights. Leggett was taken into custody where she was held for 168 days, longer than any other reporter in U.S. history for refusing to reveal information from confidential sources. Her appeal to the Fifth Circuit Court of Appeals was denied, and the U.S. Supreme Court denied certiorari, in *Leggett v. United States*, 535 U.S. 1011 (2002).

The Fifth Circuit is one of the few circuit courts that does not recognize a qualified privilege for journalists to protect their confidential sources in the context of a criminal case. In most circuits, the Constitutionally protected freedom of the press is balanced against the obligation of all citizens to provide information relevant to a crime. Leggett's long ordeal leaves the circuit courts divided on this issue.

Primary Rights—The core rights granted by a writer to a publisher are often called primary rights, with ancillary rights sometimes designated as **subsidiary** rights (sub rights) or secondary rights. The distinctions between these categories of rights can vary according to circumstances. Primary rights are almost always exclusive, meaning that only the publisher may exploit them. Subsidiary rights are sometimes exclusive, but may be **nonexclusive**, meaning that either the publisher or the author may exploit them.

Prior Restraint—Censorship imposed before publication is called prior restraint. Courts are generally reluctant to impose prior restraint because, except in rare circumstances like national security, censorship of the press is seen to conflict with the **First Amendment.**

Print-on-Demand—Publishing technology now permits the digitization of entire books and has created sophisticated presses capable of printing a single book at a time. This print-on-demand (POD) technology has changed the traditional publishing model by making very small print runs practical and eliminating certain storage, shipping, and distribution problems. While POD has created economical self-publishing opportunities for many authors, it has also created opportunities for thinly disguised **vanity publishers** to take advantage of gullible would-be writers. POD has also made it possible for traditional publishers to digitize a book and keep it in print literally forever, because books can be printed whenever ordered, without the need to maintain inventory.

Privacy—*See* **invasion of privacy**

Privilege—A privilege is a particular benefit or advantage bestowed on certain individuals or groups that others do not share. Legal privileges protect some relationships. Certain privileges have been recognized to protect confidential information from becoming public. A privilege can prevent one party from testifying in court and can also prevent the release of documents and other materials during the discovery phase of a lawsuit. For instance, an attorney may not testify against his client because private communications between them are privileged. The attorney client privilege encourages full and accurate disclosure by the client to the attorney, allowing the attorney to better represent the client's interests. All citizens are entitled to the privilege against self-incrimination under the Fifth Amendment. This means that in a criminal case, you do not have to provide information that could be used to convict you, or that could lead to information that could be used to convict you. Sometimes journalists enjoy a qualified privilege from disclosing their confidential sources in many jurisdictions.

A privilege, such as the privilege against self-incrimination, may be established by law, but others are created when parties agree that their communications will remain confidential. While the agreement may be communicated orally or in writing, a written agreement provides more assurance that the privilege will be recognized in court. A privilege is not automatic; it must be pleaded as an **affirmative defense** by the defendant. *See* **press shield, libel.**

Pro Se—A pro se litigant represents herself. Under the Constitution, any individual is entitled to represent herself in court without the assistance of a lawyer. Some courts, such as small claims courts, are specifically designed by law to encourage pro se litigation.

Ask Author Law:

Q: I have discovered that a commercial Web site has several of my articles online. Can I sue this Web site in small claims court for the value of the use of my articles?

A: Unfortunately, you can't use a small claims court in this situation. Because copyright is based on a federal statute (federal question jurisdiction) you must use the federal courts for a copyright infringement lawsuit. You can represent yourself (pro se) in federal court and you can bring the suit in the federal court closest to where you live. Procedures in the federal courts are quite straightforward and many federal courts have a pro se clerk who can provide information on how to file your own suit. Although court clerks can help you with the correct procedure to follow, they can't give legal advice. You will have to budget for the filing fee (about $150) and service of process and other expenses. Sometimes the filing of an infringement suit brings a settlement offer, so it's possible that an investment of fees and time could be worthwhile. You could also be investing in a major headache. There are no guarantees, you still must have registered your copyright, and you could face a lot of frustration.

There is another remedy available under the **Digital Millennium Copyright Act (DMCA)** called **notice and takedown.** The DMCA was enacted in part to facilitate access to the Internet by giving access providers a safe harbor from charges of infringement for the actions of their subscribers. Providers are shielded from infringement charges if

---

they file the name and contact information of an individual to be notified in the event of infringement with the Copyright Office in the Library of Congress and promptly take down any infringing material upon receiving good faith notice of the infringement by the copyright owner. So, if you have been infringed on the Internet, but you don't want the expense and hassle of filing a lawsuit, you can get the infringing matter taken down by sending a written notice to the ISP/host of the Web site that has posted your work without permission. Invoking the notice and takedown provisions of the DMCA does not compromise your right to sue the primary infringer in any way. See Digital Millenium Copyright Act for detailed instructions on the Notice and takedown process.

Proposal—A book proposal is a package for submission to an agent and/or publisher consisting of a synopsis or outline of a book, a marketing analysis, biographical information about the author, and one or more sample chapters. Many nonfiction books are sold on the basis of a proposal, but publishers of fiction usually like to see a complete manuscript. a proposal for a magazine article is called a **query**.

Pseudonym—*See* **pen name**.

Publication—Since 1909, federal copyright law has recognized that publication is the distribution of copies of a work to the public on an unrestricted basis. Publication can also be established by offering to distribute copies to a group of people for purposes of further distribution, public performance, or public display.

Prior to 1978, the publication of a work, with the required copyright **notice**, was a significant event because federal copyright protection was available *only* for published works. Since 1978, federal copyright protection is available from the time a work is created so the act of publication has lost much of its importance. Publication is still a meaningful act, though. A copyright must be registered within five years of publication to establish prima facie evidence of the validity of a copyright. If a copyright notice is displayed on the work, it must contain the first year of publication, and the duration of copyright protection for an anonymous or pseudonymous work or a **work made for hire** is measured from the date of first publication. The date of first publication may also be important for works seeking protection under an international treaty such as the **Berne Convention**.

Tips and Tools: What Constitutes Publication for Copyright Purposes?

Federal copyright law basically requires the distribution of copies of a work to the public in order for publication to occur. It does not matter if the copies are sold, leased, rented, or otherwise transferred, but the distribution must be authorized by either the copyright owner or someone appointed by the copyright owner. The public performance or display of a work does not constitute publication for copyright purposes. Furthermore, since the law requires that "copies" be distributed, the sale of one original book or work of art would not amount to publication. Under the current law, the distribution or dissemination of copies to a limited group, for a limited purpose, is also not likely to constitute publication.

It is often difficult to determine the publication status of works that are published on the **Internet**. While many Web sites are publicly available, it primarily depends on the intent of the copyright owner. The Copyright Office leaves it to the copyright owner to decide whether an online work is published or unpublished for purposes of copyright registration.

Publication Date—The publication date of a work is the date the work was first published in the United States, and this date is important in determining the timeliness of a copyright registration with the **Copyright Office**.

Public Domain—This is the status of a creative work, symbol, or invention that is not protected by a copyright, trademark, or patent. Material in the public domain may be freely used or copied. The existence of the public domain serves an important **public policy** by ensuring the free flow of information and public access to creative works and inventions. The U.S. Supreme Court upheld the extension of the copyright term under the **Sonny Bono Copyright Term Extension Act** of 1998, limiting public domain somewhat. The federal government is constitutionally prohibited from owning copyrights, so most federal publications are in the public domain. This is *not* true for state and local governmental publications, however.

Tips and Tools: How to Determine When a Work Is in the Public Domain

A work in the public domain may be freely copied. Thus, it is important to be able to determine whether the use of a work is limited by an intellectual property right. In recent years there have been several amendments to federal copyright law that have affected the duration of copyright protection, including the **Berne Convention Implementation Act** of 1988, the Copyright Renewal Act of 1992, and the **Sonny Bono Copyright Term Extension Act** of 1998. Since a work does not need to be registered in order to receive copyright protection under current law, it is wise to assume that any work created since January 1, 1978, is protected by copyright.

The first thing to do is to check the work itself for evidence of copyright registration. A work will often contain a copyright notice, the date and place of publication, and the name of the author and publisher.

It may also be necessary to conduct a search of the records of the **Copyright Office.** Copyrights registered since 1978 can be found online in the databases that can be accessed on the Copyright Office's Web site: www.copyright.gov. For older works, the *Catalog of Copyright Entries*, which was published by the Copyright Office from 1891 to 1978, is available at many libraries around the country. A search of the

Copyright Office's records can also be made at its offices in the Library of Congress. Another option is to have a Copyright Office staff member perform the search for you at a rate of $75 per hour. A private search firm that specializes in copyright searches can also be hired for a fee.

It is important to note that a copyright search can be inconclusive. For example, unpublished works created prior to 1978 were entitled to protection under common law without the need for registration. Changes to the copyright law in recent years have complicated matters by extending the duration of copyright protection and making renewal registrations for works registered between January 1, 1964, and December 31, 1977, optional. For works under copyright protection on or after January 1, 1978, registration is not required for copyright protection to attach since protection is automatic upon the creation of the work. In addition, the search may be incomplete if the work was registered under a different title or as part of a larger work. Furthermore, although a work may appear to be in the public domain in the United States, it may still be fully protected under the copyright laws of another country and therefore cannot be freely used in that country.

Public Figure—A public figure is a person who is famous or infamous for something he or she has done and is, therefore, more difficult to **libel**.

Public Performance—A public performance occurs when a work is performed or displayed at a place open to the public or at a nonpublic place where a substantial number of people outside the usual circle of family members and friends are gathered. A public performance also includes the transmission of a performance to a public place, or to the public, by means of any device or process, regardless of whether the individual members of the public view the performance in the same place and at the same time. Airing a television program, for example, constitutes a public performance even though viewers may be watching television alone in their homes. A public performance does not necessarily constitute a **publication** of a work if it is not recorded in some manner in order to be fixed in a tangible medium as required by federal copyright law.

Public Policy—The core principles underlying the foundation of law are called public policy. Public policy is created to support a particular ideology or to serve a public need. It encompasses a broad range of issues, including the public's interest in free enterprise and free expression. Copyright law satisfies many public policy needs such as fostering the progress of art and science for the benefit of the public. Furthermore, the fact that a copyright is granted for only a limited period of time satisfies the public's need for access to creative works by permitting them to fall into the **public domain**. Matters of public policy are taken so seriously by courts that contracts can be held to be unenforceable on public policy grounds.

Publicity, Right of—The individual right of publicity varies between jurisdictions. It is your right not to have your name or image used for commercial purposes without your consent—the right of publicity prohibits using a person for an advertisement, product endorsement, or in a commercial contest without consent. It's important to note, however, that editorial use of a person's name or image does not violate her right to publicity. Editorial use is not commercial use, even if a writer or publication earns money in the editorial process.

Publish on Demand—*See* **print on demand**.

Punitive Damages—*See* **damages**.

Q

Query—A query is a **proposal** for a magazine article, generally in the form of a letter that describes the proposed subject, treatment, and qualifications of the writer. Sometimes a query is also sent to an agent or book publisher asking for permission to send a manuscript or **proposal**.

R

Recitals—The factual statements at the beginning of a contract, often beginning with the word "whereas," are called recitals. Recitals are common in older contracts but are considered archaic by many modern lawyers. Most recently drafted publishing contracts don't use them. It can make sense, though, to identify the facts behind each party's position at the beginning of a contract, so recitals, even if they sound old-fashioned, can be useful.

Recording Industry Association of America—The RIAA was established to represent the United States recording industry. Its stated purpose is to foster a business and legal climate that supports and promotes the creative and financial vitality of its members. As part of its mission, the organization protects the **intellectual property** rights of its members and the **First Amendment** rights of recording artists. RIAA members are recording companies that manufacture or distribute approximately 90 percent of the sound recordings produced nationwide. The organization is involved in an aggressive campaign against music piracy. You can learn more about RIAA on its Web site: www.riaa.org.

Recording of Interviews—Many writers record the interviews they conduct. The law of recording varies from state to state. In some states it is illegal to record a conversation unless all parties to the conversation know about and consent to the recording. In other states it's legal to record a conversation provided that at least one party (presumably the person doing the recording) knows about it.

Ask Author Law

Q: I host a local radio show and I'm wondering if the interviews I do of guests on my shows are owned by me and I can reproduce them or do I need to get permission when I want to use part of that interview in a written piece?

A: Just like you own a copyright in your own words from the moment they are "fixed in a tangible medium of expression" your guests own the copyright in their words when the show is recorded, which constitutes fixation. So the answer to your question is that the guests' comments are owned by them, not by you, and the normal permission requirements would apply.

A good practice would be to get every guest to sign a consent form before the show, giving you permission to reproduce copies of the broadcast and to use the interviews for other projects. (It's even possible that your station already has consent forms signed by guests.) If you use phone interviews, obtaining written consent is less practical but you could make it a practice to ask for consent and record it prior to the interview. Verbal consent is a defense to copyright infringement, but the problem is proving that you had the consent. A recording where you explain your intended uses of the material and get consent would provide the necessary proof.

When you want to use material from your archive and you don't have proof of consent, then you should follow the same procedures for use of the material that you would if you wanted to use someone else's written material. Some of your proposed uses could be brief quotations that might constitute fair use. Or you might paraphrase and attribute as an indirect quote. Other uses would require consent. If so, you should contact the interviewee and ask for permission. If you get verbal permission, be sure to make notes of your conversation or record it. See **Copyright**.

You may be wondering why you didn't need to get consent for the original interview. That is because by participating in the interview the guest is giving you implied consent to broadcast and record the interview. That implied consent would probably also apply to rebroadcasts and other radio uses of the interview but wouldn't cover use in written pieces.

Redline—*See* **blackline** and **markup**.

Reprints—A reprint is a second or subsequent printing of an article. Many writers retain reprint rights and sell the same article again and again in different markets. Reprint rights are valuable so writers should protect them. See **electronic rights.**

Register of Copyrights—The Register of Copyrights provides advice to Congress, drafts legislation, prepares technical studies, administers the copyright law, and acts as associate librarian of Congress for copyright services. The Register of Copyrights also administers the compulsory license arbitration process. The Register of Copyright is assisted by the copyright general counsel, the associate register for policy and international affairs, the associate register for national copyright programs, and the chief operating officer. *See* **Copyright Office.**

Registered Trademarks—These are trademarks that have been registered with the U.S. Patent and Trademark Office or with the proper state authorities, usually a state's secretary of state. A trademark that has been registered with the patent and trademark office is designated by the use of the symbol ® following the mark. Use of the TM and SM symbols to indicate trademark or service mark status is not regulated by federal law, but may be subject to state or foreign laws.

Rejection—Rejection occurs when a publisher finds a manuscript unacceptable and declines to publish it. When writing an article or book under contract, it is important that the contract clearly spell out a basis for rejection. *See* **acceptable manuscript**.

Remainder—The practice of selling off the overstock or excess inventory of a book by a publisher is called remaindering. Writers should try to get contractual provisions that call for a reversion of rights when a book goes out of print or is remaindered.

Remedy—When someone files a lawsuit seeking redress for a legal wrong committed against him he must ask for a remedy that is provided for under law. Examples of remedies include **damages, declaratory relief, injunction,** and **seizure**.

Renewal of Copyright—Prior to 1978 copyright was limited to a term of twenty-eight years and could be renewed for one additional term. Since the current copyright law took effect, copyright is extended for a single term (currently the life of the author plus seventy years) and does not need to be renewed. *See* **Sonny Bono Copyright Term Extension Act**.

Reporters Committee for Freedom of the Press—Created in 1970 at a time when the nation's news media faced a wave of government subpoenas asking reporters to name confidential sources, this organization provides legal help to journalists and works to ensure a free press in a variety of ways, including the operation of a toll-free legal defense hot line (800-336-4243) and a resource-filled Web site (www.rcfp.org). The address is 1101 Wilson Blvd., Suite 1100, Arlington, VA 22209.

Representations—Factual statements made by one party to another party in a contract are representations. In a publishing contract, an author may represent to the publisher that he or she is authorized to grant the rights at issue, and that the final product is the original work of the author. *See* **warranties** and **indemnities**.

Reproduction Rights—The right to make copies or reproductions of a work is one of the exclusive rights given to the copyright owner.

Rescission—The formal cancellation of a **contract**.

Reservation of Rights—This clause in a publishing contract specifies that all rights not granted to the publisher are retained by the author. It's essential for both author and publisher to know and understand exactly what rights are being granted. A reservation of rights clause helps achieve that clarity. *See* **book publishing contract**.

Reserve Against Returns—When a publisher holds back some accrued royalties to offset returns of unsold books. A modest reserve against returns is fair. It should be limited to the first one or two royalty periods and should be reasonably related to the prospective number of returns. *See* **book publishing contract**.

Returns—The practice of permitting booksellers to return copies of unsold books to the publisher for full credit is unique to publishing and is viewed as highly problematic by most in the publishing community except for bookstores.

Revision—A revision is a fairly substantial rewriting or updating of a literary work. An extensive revision may be a derivative work. A **book publishing contract** should spell out the terms of any proposed revisions, and authors should be careful that revision clauses aren't unfair.

Ask Author Law

Q: My editor recently approached me about a doing a revision of a trade book I wrote for her several years ago. But when I found out that the "revi-

sion" involved nearly doubling the size of the book and substantially changing the tone, I declined. Now the editor has hired another writer to do the revision. The new writer is going to share the copyright with me, get a substantial advance, and then get half of my royalties when it earns out. What can I do?
A: Your question raises several issues that revolve around the revision clause of your contract. You should look at that clause to determine whether your editor's planned revision and terms of the deal with the revising writer are consistent with your publishing contract. Unfortunately, a broad revision clause is an invitation for the publisher to select a collaborator for you who will share your credit, your copyright, and your royalties.

A revision clause can dictate the amount of work that may qualify as a revision, when the revision can take place, and how the process will be handled. If revision is undefined in your contract, your editor will have some latitude in arguing that her plan is a revision. Ideally, however, your revision clause will include a definition of revision that caps the amount of new matter at no more than 25 percent. You should address this point when you negotiate the contract. If your editor is suggesting changes outside the scope of a permissible revision in your contract, you should bring this to her attention. If on the other hand, you have a broadly defined revision clause, then a major overhaul of your book is probably within her rights. If you are really unhappy about this situation you may want to enlist the help of a good publishing attorney.

Another issue is copyright ownership of the newly added material. The ownership of material added by the revision is less likely to become an issue if the amount of material added is small (i.e., a true revision). Things get more complicated when a contract has a broad enough revision clause to permit a publisher to double the size of the work. Again, start by studying the contract—new material added to the book by a revising writer will either belong to the publisher (if the revision is a work made for hire/assignment) or the reviser (no work made for hire/assignment).

Your question also raises the issue of authorship credit. Some revision clauses are silent on the issue, while others give control to either the publisher or the author. Obviously, an author would want the contractual right to sole credit for his work, even if another author is hired to do a revision. In addition, look for a provision that permits you to withdraw your name if you don't like the book.

The final issue is how you and the revising author will be paid. The revision clause will discuss (some more clearly than others) how payment will be made to a person hired to revise the work in the event that you decline to do so. Some contracts provide for sharing of royalties (on a pro rata basis or by a simple split). Others provide that the publisher will deduct the "actual cost of preparing the revision" from the royalties due to the author. In the latter case, the revising writer is paid a simple fee that will probably have to be earned out.

After looking at your contract, you'll find that either your editor's plan is within the contract or it's not. If it's not, or the clause is ambiguous on any of the substantial issues, you should contact your editor, your agent, or your attorney to attempt to resolve the matter. If nothing else, be prepared to address revision issues in your next negotiation.

Reversion of Rights—When a book goes out of print or publication otherwise ceases, the rights should revert to the author. Such reversion of rights, however, is not automatic and should be provided for in a **book publishing contract.**

Riders—Amendments to contracts are called riders. Riders are considered to be part of the entire agreement existing between the parties and the terms are therefore binding and enforceable. Riders are often used to modify or clarify the terms of the contract without rewriting and reexecuting the entire contract. A rider may also contain a schedule, which can be a list of items or a timetable, such as a manuscript delivery schedule or a royalty payment schedule, that is annexed to the original contract.

Right of First Refusal—See **option clause, first negotiation right.**

Royalties—This is a payment mechanism for books in which payment is based on sales rather than a **flat fee.** The royalty rate is usually named as a percentage of the price of a book.

Royalty Statement—A royalty statement is issued by a publisher to the author on a regular basis, usually twice a year, showing sales and payment due. See **audit.**

Royalty-Free Sales—In a **book publishing contract**, some sales of books are made without a corresponding royalty payment. Remainder sales, some deep discount sales, inventory reduction, and sales at **author discount** are examples.

S

Sampling—A sample is a digital copy of an excerpt of a **sound recording** that can be played once or "looped" to play repeatedly in a new recording. For example, it is possible to sample the drum beats or a guitar riff of a sound recording and then use that recorded sample repeatedly in a new song. A sample can also be used on its own to provide listeners with an example of a larger work such as a song or compact disc, often to encourage the purchase of the larger work. Sampling can infringe both the sound recording and the underlying **musical work**.

It is generally necessary to obtain permission from the copyright owners of both the sound recording and the musical work in order to legitimately use a sample. However, because sound recordings were not entitled to federal copyright protection until 1972, samples from sound recordings made prior to that date may be used without protection unless they are protected by state law. In a situation where the sound recording was created before 1972, it is important to research the copyright status of the sound recording and it is still essential to obtain permission from the copyright owner of the musical work.

There are instances in which the unauthorized use of a sample is not considered infringing. Because copyright protection extends only to elements of a work that are original and nontrivial, a sample of a sequence not protected cannot be infringement. The length of the sample and the qualitative or quantitative significance of the portion sampled to both works are also factors to be considered. Courts will consider whether the sample and copyrighted work are substantially similar and whether the sample consists of only a small, commonly used sequence or phrase. Use of an unauthorized sample may also be permitted if it is determined to be a fair use.

Satellite Transmissions—A satellite transmission is entitled to copyright protection under the exemption for ephemeral recordings established under federal copyright law. Satellite transmissions are considered to be digital transmissions and are thus subject to compulsory licensing fees. A satellite transmission may constitute an infringing public performance or display of a copyrighted work.

Satisfactory Manuscript—*See* **acceptable manuscript.**

Schedule C—The tax form used for reporting income and expenses to the Internal Revenue Service by a self-employed individual. Many writers and authors need to use Schedule C.

Ask Author Law: What Tax Schedule Should Writers Use?

Q: I have been told to report my book and photo royalties not as income on Schedule C, but as royalties on Schedule E. The word is that by doing so, I can skip paying the 15.3 percent self-employment tax, which consists of 2.9 percent Medicare and 12.4 percent Social Security. True?
A: The Internal Revenue Service looks unkindly on writers, photographers, artists, and other self-employeds who try to escape self-employment taxes. Perhaps we have a case of semantics here. Yes, the word "royalties" is used on Schedule E, and yes, the IRS defines royalties as "payments for intangible properties"—for example, books and artistic works, which would include photos. But the IRS is adamant that you report royalties for your creative efforts on Schedule C, making that

income subject to self-employment tax. Schedule E is for reporting royalties received by *other* people—for example, those who purchase or inherit copyrights on books, photos, and other material that they did not create. Limit your use of Schedule E for reporting royalties to listing those received from coal, oil, or gas sites.

Caution: You are playing the "audit lottery" if you report book and photo sales on Schedule E. True, your ploy might never be discovered, but should it be, expect to be hit with a hefty bill for back taxes, interest, and penalties.

—Julian Block, tax attorney

Science Fiction and Fantasy Writers of America—The SFWA, originally known as Science Fiction Writers of America, was founded in 1965. In 1992 the name was changed to Science Fiction and Fantasy Writers of America, Inc. The SWFA is a nonprofit organization with a membership of more than twelve hundred science fiction and fantasy writers, artists, editors, and allied professionals. The organization promotes science fiction and fantasy writing and assists members with publishing contracts and rights issues through its grievance committee. The SWFA annually awards a Nebula Award for the science fiction or fantasy best short story, novelette, novella, and novel of the year. The organization can be contacted at SFWA, Inc., P.O. Box 877, Chestertown, MD 21620. You can learn more about the SFWA on its Web site at www.sfwa.org.

Scientific Rendering—The scientific rendering of an **invention**, plan, or process is entitled to copyright protection as either a literary work—if it is text—or as a pictorial, graphical, or sculptural work. The subject of the rendering, however, is not entitled to protection because copyright law only protects the expression of an idea. The underlying invention, plan, or process may be eligible for protection under **patent** law.

Scholarly Writings—Scholarly writings include books, articles, and dissertations prepared by professors, academics, scholars, and researchers. Scholarly writings are generally created to communicate ideas, theories, and discoveries and to inspire debate. They are entitled to copyright protection as literary works. *See* **academic authors and publishers.**

Sculptural Works—Copyright protection extends to three-dimensional sculptural works such as carvings, ceramics, figurines, molds, and relief sculptures. The creator of a sculpture may be entitled to certain moral rights if the work is produced in limited edition and qualifies as a work of visual art under **VARA** (Visual Artists Rights Act). When registering a sculptural work with the **Copyright Office**, you may send a photograph or other form of identification. You should not submit the work itself.

Secondary Rights—Secondary rights are the same as subsidiary rights and are, generally, the rights granted in a publishing contract not included in the main **grant of rights.**

Second Serial Rights—Serial rights are the same as periodical rights. Second serial rights are exactly that, a license to a magazine or other periodical to use the work after it has been published elsewhere first.

Seizure—Sometimes money damages or an injunction aren't enough to protect a victim of copyright infringement. In cases of piracy, the copyright act permits the remedy of seizure and destruction of infringing work under extreme circumstances.

Self-Publishing—Changes in technology have made self-publishing an attractive option to writers with lots to say and difficulty with getting traditional publishers interested in helping them say it. Print-on-demand technology has made self-publishing easier than ever. Writers should be sure, though, that a print-on-demand publisher is truly that and not a vanity or subsidy publisher in disguise. Publishing consultants Tom and Marilyn Ross have written extensively about self-publishing and founded an organization for self-publishers called SPAN (Small Publishers Association of North America). Its Web site is www.spannet.org.

Semiconductor Chip Protection Act—The SCPA was enacted by Congress in 1984 to protect the structural design of semiconductor chips with a combination of copyright and patent laws. The law creates a new form of intellectual property for the semiconductor chip. The SCPA protects the **mask work**, or the series of images representing the pattern of the material located within the layers of a chip when it is fixed in a semiconductor chip product. Protection for semiconductor chips is similar to copyright, and registration is handled by the Copyright Office. The term of protection runs for ten years commencing with either registration or commercial use.

Sequel—A story written after another story that employs the same characters in a new series of events take that place after the original story. In the motion picture industry, a sequel is a movie made after another, regardless of whether the successive work is set prior to, during, or after the time period of the original. As with other derivative works, only the author of a work has the right to create or authorize a sequel.

The Courts Say: Sequel Rights Remain the Property of the Author to Dispose of as He or She Chooses

Trust Co. Bank v. MGM/UA Entertainment Co., 593 F. Supp. 580, *aff'd*, 772 F.2d 740 (11th Cir. 1985)

In an action for a declaratory judgment regarding the motion picture sequel rights to Margaret Mitchell's novel, *Gone with the Wind*, the district court held that a 1961 agreement extending motion picture rights to the book did not convey sequel rights. In 1936, Margaret Mitchell granted the motion picture rights to her novel to MGM's predecessor. The agreement did not mention sequel rights, and Mitchell steadfastly refused subsequent offers to part with them. The 1961 agreement extended the provisions of the earlier grant of rights, and included a clause that prohibited the production of a "motion picture or other production with the plot or the story or the characters of the Novel, in which the lives of the characters therein shall be carried beyond the time of the ending of the Novel." The court rejected the defendant's argument that this express restriction was actually a grant of sequel rights for other time periods. The court noted that in the movie industry, a sequel refers to a work that follows another, regardless of whether the successive work is set prior to, during, or after the time period of the original.

Serial Rights—Rights to publish a short work in a newspaper, magazine, or other periodical are called serial rights.

SESAC—Acronym for Society of European Stage Authors and Composers, but the acronym is no longer used. The company is officially known as SESAC, Inc., and is headquartered in Nashville, Tennessee. SESAC was established in 1930 and is the second-oldest nonprofit performing rights society in the United States. Other performing rights clearinghouses include **ASCAP** and **BMI**. SESAC was originally formed to provide representation for European composers not adequately represented in the United States. The organization's repertory was once limited to European and gospel music, but it now represents nearly all genres, including dance, rock, jazz, and country music. SESAC is the smallest of the three performing rights societies and prides itself on maintaining individual relationships with both songwriters and publishers.

SESAC has developed a selective affiliation process, and it solicits submissions accordingly. The organization provides music users with a "blanket license" agreement that is recognized as the most convenient and cost-effective method to obtain the required authorization to perform all of the copyrighted music in the SESAC repertory. The organization computes royalties based on several factors, including music trade publication chart activity, broadcast logs, computer database information, and state-of-the-art monitoring. Learn more at www.sesac.com.

Shrink-Wrap Agreement—A shrink-wrap agreement is a license to use software that a consumer agrees to by opening the shrink-wrap on a package containing the software. Courts have held shrink wrap licenses to be enforceable when the notice terms are clearly printed on the package and can be read through the clear shrink wrap. *See* **click-wrap agreement**.

Signature—The formal, usually handwritten, physical representation of a person's name as written by that person. A signature is placed at the end of a document to attest its validity. A contract is not valid unless it contains the signatures of the parties involved. Similarly, the valid transfer of any right included in a copyright must be in writing and must display the signature of the copyright owner. *See also* **digital signature.**

Slander—Slander is spoken defamation, as opposed to libel, which is written defamation.

Small Claims Court—*See* **pro se.**

Society of American Travel Writers (SATW)—The SATW is a nonprofit professional organization that promotes responsible journalism, offers professional support and development for its members, and encourages the conservation and preservation of historic sites and natural wonders around the world. The organization has more than thirteen hundred members including writers; photographers; editors; electronic and print journalists; film lecturers; broadcast, video, and film producers; and public relations professionals. Established in 1955, SATW is headquartered in Raleigh, North Carolina. The SATW Foundation was created in the 1980s to improve travel journalism by recognizing and rewarding excellence in the field, and it sponsors the annual SATW Foundation Lowell Thomas Travel Journalism Competition, an independent competition open to all North American journalists. SATW can be contacted at 1500 Sunday Dr., Suite 102, Raleigh, NC 27607. Phone: 919-861-5586, Web site: www.satw.org.

Society of Environmental Journalists—A nonprofit educational organization, the SEJ was established in 1990 by a small group of award-winning journalists to advance public understanding of environmental issues by improving the quality, accuracy, and visibility of environmental reporting. Headquartered in Jenkintown, Pennsylvania, the organization provides educational opportunities and vital support to journalists of all media who face the challenging responsibility of covering complex environmental issues. SEJ's current membership includes more than fourteen hundred journalists and academics working in news media in the United States and thirty-two other countries. The organization offers a mentoring program for its members which pairs established environmental reporters with less experienced ones. SEJ can be contacted at P.O. Box 2492, Jenkintown, PA 19046. Phone: 215-884-8174, Web site: www.sej.org.

Society of Professional Journalists (SPJ)—The SPJ was founded in 1909 as a Sigma Delta Chi fraternity at DePauw University in Greencastle, Indiana. Now a nonprofit professional organization with headquarters in Indianapolis, Indiana, SPJ is the nation's largest and most broad-based journalism organization. The organization's membership includes broadcast, print, and online journalists, and journalism educators and students. The organization works to promote freedom of the press and to encourage the free flow of information to the public. SPJ also works to inspire and educate the next generation of journalists and protects First Amendment guarantees of freedom of speech and press. SPJ offers its members career services and support and the option to participate in continuing education programs and conferences, as well as journalism advocacy opportunities. SPJ can be contacted at Eugene S. Pulliam National Journalism Center, 3909 N. Meridian St., Indianapolis, IN 46208. Phone: 317-927-8000, Web site: www.spj.org.

Soft Cover—*See* **paperback, trade paperback.**

Software—The **computer programs** containing the processes and instructions pertaining to the operation of a computer system are known as software. Hardware, on the other hand, consists of the physical equipment used to access, view, modify, and store software. Software is entitled to copyright protection as either a literary work or an audiovisual work.

Software and Information Industry Association—SIIA, a non-profit professional organization, was established in 1999 with the merger of the Software Publishers Association and the Information Industry Association. The resulting organization currently has a membership of nore than six hundred code and content providers. The stated mission of SIIA is threefold, (1) to demonstrate to the world that the software and digital information industry is the fastest growing industry sector and a major contributor to the global marketplace, (2) to protect the intellectual property of its member companies and advocate a legal and regulatory environment that benefits the entire industry, and (3) to empower its members with knowledge by serving as a resource for a wide range of traditional and emerging subjects that affect their businesses. The organization's antipiracy program protects the intellectual property of SIIA members and informs the public about the evils and penalties of software piracy. The program leads the industry in identifying and prosecuting software and Internet piracy cases. SIIA can be contacted at 1090 Vermont Ave., NW, Sixth Floor, Washington, DC 20005, or by telephone at 202-289-SIIA, Web site: www.siia.com.

Song Lyrics—The words to a song usually receive copyright protection along with the musical score as part of a musical copyright. Federal copyright law recognizes an exclusive right of public performance of a musical work in both the lyrics and the song itself. Some lyrics quality for protection as a literary work.

Sonny Bono Copyright Term Extension Act—Also known as the Mickey Mouse legislation because it was strongly supported by Disney in order to keep the Mickey Mouse cartoon character out of the public domain, the CTEA extends the term of a copyright for an additional twenty years. Copyright for works created by individual authors on or after January 1, 1978, now endures for the life of the author plus seventy years. For joint works, the term now extends for seventy years following the death of the last surviving author. The CTEA also lengthens copyright protection for sound recordings fixed before February 15, 1972, for an additional twenty years. Works made for hire (like Mickey Mouse), as well as anonymous and pseudonymous works, are now protected for the lesser of ninety-five years from the year of first publication or one hundred twenty years from the year of creation. The law also extends copyrights in their first term on or after January 1, 1978, for twenty-year period, changing the term from forty-seven to sixty-seven years.

In addition to extending the term of copyright, the CTEA also expands the class of successors to termination rights to include administrators, personal representatives, and trustees. It also adds an exemption from liability for libraries or archives to reproduce, distribute, display, or perform a published work during the extended copyright term for purposes of research, preservation, or scholarship. This exemption applies only where the work is not being commercially exploited and if it cannot be otherwise obtained at a reasonable price.

The CTEA as passed by Congress also includes the Fairness in Music Licensing Act of 1998, which exempts small businesses, restaurants, and similar entities from paying performance royalties on music played from a licensed radio or television broadcast, or a cable system or satellite carrier and contains provisions for the determination of reasonable licensing fees by **performing rights societies** for individual proprietors.

See also **First Amendment** for a discussion of *Eldred v. Reno,* 537 U.S. 186 (2003), upholding the constitutionality of this act.

Sound Effects—Sound effects that are part of an audiovisual work such as a motion picture are protected by the copyright of the work as a whole. Sound effects that exist on their own are entitled to copyright protection as a **sound recording** if they are recorded on a phonorecord such as a CD or cassette tape.

Sound Recordings—The copyright in a sound recording protects only the sounds as they occur on a phonorecord such as a CD or cassette tape. Federal copyright law did not extend protection to sound recordings until 1972, but some sound recordings were entitled to protection under state law. Today, a copyright protects the rights of both the performer who creates the sounds and the person who records and processes the sounds to create the final recording. Many types of sounds can be protected as a sound recording, including a musical performance, a recitation, or a naturally occurring sound. Sounds that are part of an audiovisual work, however, are protected by the copyright in the overall work. The copyright in a sound recording provides the author with the right to reproduce the work, to create derivative works, and to distribute the work. The **Digital Performance Right in Sound Recording Act of 1995** created an exclusive public performance right for certain digital transmissions of sound recordings, subject to specific exemptions and compulsory license requirements.

Sovereign Immunity—The Eleventh Amendment of the U.S. Constitution provides immunity for states from federal lawsuits by individuals. States may, however, consent to be sued in certain situations and Congress may choose to revoke this immunity in relation to specific statutes if it expressly states its intent to do so in a valid exercise of power.

The Courts Say: Copyright Remedy Clarification Act Did Not Effectively Abrogate State Immunity from Suit

Chavez v. Arte Publico Press, 204 F.3d 601 (5th Cir. 2000)

Denise Chavez sued the University of Houston's press in federal court for copyright infringement in connection with its publication of her book *The Last of the Menu Girls* and for Lanham Act trademark violations for its use of her name as the selector of plays in an anthology it published. Chavez alleged that the press continued to publish her book after she withheld her permission because errors in earlier printings were never corrected. The Copyright Remedy Clarification Act (CRCA), enacted in 1990, amended the Copyright Act to expressly abrogate state immunity in the context of copyright infringement. After years of litigation, the Fifth Circuit Court of Appeals found that the CRCA was neither a valid exercise of Congress's power under the Fourteenth Amendment's enforcement provision, despite Chavez's claim that she was deprived of her property without due process of law, nor a valid exercise of power under the privileges and immunities

---

289

clause of the Fourteenth Amendment. The court had previously ruled that Congress could not require states to waive immunity as a condition for participating in a federally regulated activity.

Special Sales—In publishing, royalty rates for sales through non-traditional channels are generally lower and listed as special sales in contracts and statements. Examples of special sales might be books sold in bulk to companies for use in promotion or books bundled with toys, sporting goods, or other consumer products. Authors whose books might lend themselves to corporate sponsorship or tie-in marketing should carefully review the special sales royalty rates in their contracts.

Specific Performance—When a contract calls for a party to perform a particular action or meet a particular obligation, the carrying out of that obligation is called specific performance. If the contract is breached one party might try to force specific performance upon the other. A court might force specific performance in the completion of a sale, but most of the time parties are limited to money damanges rather than specific performance.

Speeches—A speech is a verbal address delivered to an audience. It can be a public address, a sermon, or a college lecture. Extemporaneous speeches are not eligible for federal copyright protection unless they are original and have been fixed in a tangible medium. However, a speech that is not protected under federal law may be eligible for common law or state copyright protection.

Prior to 1978, **publication** was the key event that triggered federal copyright protection, and as a result, the public nature of the speech was an important factor in determining whether a speech was protected by copyright. Under current law, however, this factor has lost its significance and fixation of the speech is now the key event in obtaining copyright protection.

Tips and Tools: Copyright Rights to Speeches

If your speech meets the requirements for federal copyright protection—it is original and has been fixed in a tangible medium—then you are entitled to the full benefit of copyright protection that you would receive for any other copyrightable work. If you decide to have the speech published in a book, you can transfer most of your rights to the publisher but retain your right to perform the speech.

As with other copyrighted works, you are the only person who is authorized to perform your work, and you have exclusive control over its use and distribution until you assign those rights to somebody else. If you only made the speech once and did not fix it in a tangible medium by recording it or printing it out, then the speech is not entitled to federal copyright protection. The speech may, however, be entitled to protection under the common law or statutory law of your state.

Do you write speeches for others? Many people incorrectly believe that speeches are owned by the speaker, but, in fact, speeches are owned by the writer of the speech.

Spin-offs—Spin-offs are other works or products that use elements of an original work to create something new. Spin-offs are **derivative works**, so an unauthorized spin-off may constitute copyright infringement unless its creator can demonstrate **fair use**.

The Courts Say: A Trivia Quiz Book Constitutes Infringement of a Copyrighted Television Program

Castle Rock Entertainment v. Carol Publishing Group, Inc., 150 F.3d 132 (2nd Cir. 1998)

The producers of the popular television program *Seinfeld* sued the author and publisher of a trivia quiz book based on the show for copyright infringement and unfair competition. The Second Circuit affirmed the decision of the district court that the book, *The Seinfeld Aptitude Test*, infringed the copyright in the television show and the copied material did not amount to fair use. The book, which consisted of 643 trivia questions and answers about the events and characters depicted on the television show, drew all of its material from the show and even included direct quotations. The court found both qualitative and quantitative copying sufficient to establish a prima facie case of infringement. The court considered the amount copied in the aggregate and not the specific amount copied from each episode of the show. In rejecting a defense of fair use, the court found that the book did not provide criticism or commentary about the show but merely repackaged the copyrighted plots and characters in another format. The court considered the book's commercial purpose and slight transformative use, and noted it relied completely on the creative, fictional elements of the television show that were protected by copyright. The court concluded that the ultimate test of fair use is whether the copyright law's goal of promoting the progress of science and the useful arts would be better served by allowing the use or preventing it.

Split—The division of income from a literary work between various parties such as the author and publisher or among coauthors is called the split.

Statute of Anne—Enacted by the English Parliament in 1710, the Statute of Anne laid the foundation of modern copyright law. It was the first law to grant a limited monopoly in the form of a copyright to authors. The Statute of Anne granted creative rights directly to authors rather than to publishers and it established a limited period of protection, two terms of fourteen years each, after which the work would enter the public domain. Only a new work was eligible for copyright protection under the law.

Statute of Limitations—This is the period from the time a cause of action arises in which a lawsuit can be filed. A claim generally accrues when the wrongful act occurs, and not necessarily when the resulting damage is suffered. It is therefore important to act on a claim as soon as the unlawful activity is discovered. Under federal copyright law a civil lawsuit must be filed within three years and a criminal lawsuit must be filed within five years. Statutes of limitations for breach of contract are established by state law. For example, in New York State a lawsuit for breach of contract must be filed within six years.

Statutory Damages—See **damages.**

Statutory Law—The laws enacted by a state or federal legislative body. While legislative law may include laws that have been proposed but not yet enacted, statutory law includes only laws that have been formally enacted. Federal statutory law can be found in the U.S. Code. *See* **case law, common law, administrative law.**

Style—Style is the label given to a publication's way of referring to, expressing, and punctuating certain common terms.

Stylebook—A stylebook contains the publisher's preferred style rules. Most use a common reference book such as the *Associated Press Style Book and Libel Manual* and the *Chicago Manual of Style.*

Sub Rights—*See* **subsidiary rights**

Subsidiary Rights—*See* **secondary rights.**

Subsidy Publisher—A subsidy publisher charges the author to print and distribute a book. The term is a euphemism for **vanity publisher.** Many **print-on-demand** publishers are subsidy publishers under a new name.

Substantial Similarity—In order to prove copying in a **copyright infringement** action, the **plaintiff** must prove access and substantial similarity between the original elements of the two works. Substantial similarity is a flexible concept and there is no standardized test used by the courts to determine whether it exists. In general, a court will consider only the similarities of expression in the two works since ideas and concepts are not protected by copyright. In addition, a court will consider only how similar the two works are and will not look to elements of the infringing work that were not copied. In determining whether substantial similarity exists, courts may apply different standards for works of fiction and factual works, and the tests applied may differ from circuit to circuit. If you are exploring the possibility of filing a copyright infringement action, an attorney can advise you how to best meet the relevant standard in your circuit. It is important to note that a finding of copying does not necessarily lead to a verdict of infringement because the defendant may be able to establish a fair use defense.

The Courts Say: Substantial Similarity Requires More Than Simply Stirring the Memory

Warner Bros., Inc., v. American Broadcasting Companies, Inc., 720 F.2d 231 (2d Cir. 1983)

The copyright owners of various Superman products sued the creators and broadcasters of the television program *The Greatest American Hero* for copyright infringement. The Second Circuit affirmed the decision of the district court and held that Ralph Hinkley, the fictional main character on the television program, was not substantially similar to the fictional character of Superman to support a claim of copyright infringement. The court found that the Hinkley character was a bumbling, reluctant superhero who was very different from the confident, serious Superman even though they shared some of the same superhuman traits. The court determined that the references to Superman in the television show or in promotions for the show highlighted the differences between the two characters. Rejecting survey evidence from the

S

general public offered by the plaintiffs, the court found that the concept of substantial similarity in the context of copyright infringement is not familiar to the general public and the fact that some people, applying their own standards, were reminded of Superman by the Hinkley character was not relevant to the inquiry. The court stated that stirring one's memory of a character is not the same as appearing to be substantially similar to that character.

Successors and Assigns—This language, often found in contracts, refers to an individual's heirs, either at law or by assignment. The bundle of rights contained in a copyright may be transferred to another upon death, through a will or by intestate succession, and the person receiving the rights in this manner may be referred to as a successor. Similarly, a person who receives the copyright rights of another through a transfer while all parties are living may be called an assign. A publishing contract may state that it is binding on the author's successors and assigns, or vest the author's successors and assigns with certain responsibilities or duties in the event that the author dies or becomes incapacitated.

Suggested Retail Price—*See* **list price, catalog price, cover price, retail price.**

Sunshine Laws—See **Freedom of Information Act** and **Open Meeting Laws.**

Syndication—Syndication is the process of distributing the same column or article to numerous noncompeting publications. Syndication rights are valuable **reprint rights.**

T

Takedown—The **Digital Millennium Copyright Act** provides for the limited liability of Internet service provides (ISPs) for copyright infringement if they meet certain requirements, including the removal, or takedown, of infringing material upon notification from the copyright holder. The ISP must remove the material or disable access to it and then notify the subscriber who posted the material. If the subscriber responds with a counternotification, the ISP must put the material back up within ten to fourteen business days. *See* **notice and takedown, DMCA.**

Taxes—This is a subject many writers would prefer to avoid, but ignoring it would be a huge mistake. Writers need to deal with a variety of tax issues, including sales, business, and property taxes, but by far the most significant tax issue faced by writers is income tax. *See* **accountant, Schedule C, tax attorney.**

The Voice of Experience: Enrolled Agents Provide Useful Tax Guidance, Preparation

Joseph Anthony, enrolled agent
Portland, Oregan

Joseph Anthony worked as a full-time freelance journalist for fifteen years before becoming an enrolled agent in 1993. "I specialized in fi-

---

nancial writing, and eventually got to the point where I was more interested in doing it than just writing about it," Joe says with a laugh. "But EAs have the worst publicity machine in the country. Nobody knows exactly what that *is*!"

Q: So, what is an EA?
A: In most parts of the country, there are no specific qualifications for calling yourself a tax professional—anyone can hang out a shingle and say "I do taxes." The enrolled agent credential is different. It is the only federally licensed tax professional program in the country, and requires that you meet certain educational requirements and pass a two-day test. EAs typically won't do your books. We prepare returns, provide tax advice, and are authorized to represent clients before any branch of the IRS, whether or not we have prepared the tax return.

Q: What tax problems do you find writers typically encounter?
A: Writers face many of the same tax issues as any other self-employed professional. Essentially, they're a small business. And as an unincorporated small business, they're at a higher risk of audit because they're filing a Schedule C. While I don't like the phrase "red flag," Schedule C returns do tend to be audited more often. As a self-employed person, writers can deduct many more expenses than an ordinary wage earner, but they also have a more complicated tax life.

Q: Do you ever recommend that writers incorporate?
A: People often look to that step as a way to try to minimize their personal liability. I'm not a lawyer, but I do recommend that my clients who are considering incorporating talk with a lawyer about what protection you're really getting and not getting. There can be some tax benefits to some forms of incorporation, but there can also be some tax disadvantages. You have to look at the tax picture case by case. There really isn't a general rule of thumb.

Q: What makes a good tax professional—and how can writers find one?
A: A *good* tax pro isn't someone who's just doing your tax return in March. He or she should be someone you can rely on as a resource for financial and tax questions that come up all year long. I suggest that writers find someone who is familiar with the issues of self-employed

individuals and small businesses—not someone who just does individual 1040s or returns for midsize corporations. Approach the hunt as you would any research project, which is to say, interview people you're considering hiring. Nothing is more intimate in our society than talking about our financial life. And that's what you're going to be doing with your tax pro.

Q: It sounds obvious, but why should writers use a tax professional?
A: Writers, and particularly nonfiction writers, specialize in being researchers. And because they're so competent, writers assume they can figure out how to do anything themselves. That's how you get into trouble. Tax issues *are* complicated. That's why you should use tax and financial professionals who specialize in areas you don't. It is always more expensive to go back and fix a mess than to avoid that mess in the first place.

The Voice of Experience: Lawyer Advises Freelancers to Take Full Advantages of Legal Tax Strategies

Julian Block, tax attorney
Larchmont, NY

Julian Block is an attorney who has been cited by the *New York Times* as "a leading tax professional" and by the *Wall Street Journal* as an "accomplished writer on taxes." He is the author of a tax-saving guide for authors, artists, and musicians that is updated regularly and available via e-mail. Contact him at julianblock@yahoo.com.

Q: Health insurance is getting impossibly expensive. What can writers do about it, taxwise?
A: Recent tax law changes include valuable breaks for freelance writers in the area of health insurance. Starting in 2003, self-employed writers got to deduct 100 percent of their payments of medical insurance premiums for themselves and their spouses and dependents. This deduction for medical insurance payments for self-employeds is *not subject to* the 7.5 percent threshold for all other medical expenditures. This

means that the deduction is not claimed on Schedule A, where expenses are itemized, but on the *front* of Form 1040. In IRS argot, this is an "above-the-line adjustment," that is, it's one of the off-the-top subtractions applied in the section where you calculate your adjusted gross income. Thus, take this deduction the same way you claim write-offs for funds put in traditional IRAs or other retirement plans. Not only is this deduction not lumped with those sums to which the 7.5 percent limit is applied, the self-employed medical-insurance deduction is available even to someone who foregoes itemizing altogether and instead simply uses the standard deduction—the no-questions-asked amount that is authorized for someone who finds it more advantageous not to itemize. So even if you opt not to itemize, you nonetheless get an up-front deduction for 100 percent of your medical insurance premiums.

Q: *How should freelancers handle deductions for equipment such as computers and phones?*
A: There are two ways freelancers can write off their outlays for equipment purchases, such as computers and file cabinets. One is the "standard" route—recovering the cost through depreciation deductions over a period of years. Or they can opt for the often-overlooked tactic of "expensing," under tax-code section 179, and deduct the entire cost of the equipment in the year of purchase. Let's say your equipment purchases include $5,000 for computers and copiers. Instead of depreciating them over five years, they can be immediately expensed. A $5,000 write-off lowers taxes by $1,250 for an individual in the 25 percent bracket, plus applicable state taxes. There's a cap on the deduction. But the previous deduction ceiling of $25,000 was quadrupled by the 2003 tax act to a whopping $100,000 for 2003, 2004, and 2005, a change introduced to allow many more businesses to qualify under section 179.

Q: *Can writers pay their kids for doing research or clerical work?*
A: Paying your children to help out with your business is a savvy way to take care of their allowances at the expense of the IRS. This tactic keeps income in the family but shifts some of that income out of your higher bracket and into their lower one. In 2003, a child could sidestep

taxes on the first $4,750 of earnings (the figure is scheduled to increase in later years). For this business expense to stand up under IRS scrutiny, a writer's children *must* actually render services and the writer must pay them *reasonable* wages. Internal Revenue Code Section 3121(b)(3)(A) exempts the wages paid to children under the age of eighteen from Social Security taxes, provided the writer does business as (1) a sole proprietorship (IRS lingo for the lone owner of a full-time or part-time business that's not formed as a corporation or partnership) or (2) a husband-wife partnership. To put it another way: This exemption *doesn't* apply to a family business that's incorporated or a partnership with a partner other than a spouse.

Q: How long should freelancers hang on to their financial records?
A: Many taxpayers think that just because they received a refund they can forget about an audit. But that's not true. Hang on to receipts, canceled checks, and whatever else might help support income, deductions, exemptions, and other items on your return. Do that at least until the expiration of the statute of limitations for an audit or for you to file a refund claim, should you discover a mistake after filing. The statute of limitations is the limited period of time after which the Internal Revenue Service is no longer able to come knocking and you cannot recover an overpayment. In most cases, the tax collectors have only three years to audit your return after you file it. There is no time limit, however, on when the IRS can come after someone who fails to file a return or files one deemed false or fraudulent. Writers should keep copies of their actual tax returns indefinitely. They take up little space and are always helpful as guides for future returns or amending previously filed returns. Moreover, copies of tax forms might prove helpful in case the IRS claims you failed to file them.

Tape Recording—*See* **recording**.

Tape Recording Consent—A writer may need permission to tape-record an interview and an organization may need permission to tape the presentation of a speaker. Here is a form for recording a speech or presentation at an educational institution. It is designed to allow modification by the speaker as necessary.

SAMPLE CONSENT AND RELEASE FORM

I, ___(name of individual)___ , grant my permission and consent for the ___(name of institution)___ to make an audio and/or video recording of my presentation, comment, or speech delivered or made on ___(date)___ as part of a program or class given at or sponsored by name of institution.

I further grant my permission and consent for the (name of institution) to reproduce the recordings of my presentation, comments or speech and to use such tapes or reproductions for any educational or other purpose whatsoever.

Check one (initial if there are no limitations):

____ This permission is not subject to any limitations. _____

initials

____ This permission is subject to the limitations I have listed here below:

Signed: _____

Date: _____

Term of Art—A term of art is an expression or phrase that has a precise legal meaning within a particular area of law. For example, in copyright law, the terms **musical work** and **sound recording** are terms of art. Some terms of art are **legalese** in which the meaning has evolved through use.

Termination of Contract—A well-drafted contract should specify how the agreement will end. In a **book publishing contract**, for example, a contract may terminate for such reasons as failure by the author to deliver an acceptable manuscript.

Termination of Rights—*See* **reversion of rights.**

Time Is of the Essence—When a contract states that time is of the essence, one party must perform a specific duty by a specific date or within a certain time in order for the other party to perform under the contract. This language is a **term of art** used in situations where timing is so important that the failure to perform within the time period stated in the contract can result in cancellation of the **contract**. A breach of this **contract** term is probably a **material breach**.

Titles—Literary titles are not eligible for copyright protection. However, if someone copies your title, you may be able to bring an action under **trademark** and **unfair competition** law if you can prove to the court that there is a likelihood of confusion.

Tort—Tort law encompasses a broad range of civil wrongs, including personal injury, breach of contract, and product liability claims. Torts involve the violation of a legal duty owed by the **defendant** to the **plaintiff.** Torts may be intentional or negligent, and a court will usually award monetary damages to the plaintiff in the event that the defendant is found liable.

Trademark—A trademark is a word, slogan, design, sound, color, or other symbol used to distinguish a good or service. Trademarks identify a product, as well as the owner or source of the product, and signify a particular level of quality attached to the product. The distinctiveness of a mark determines the strength of the protection it will receive. A generic term or design cannot act as a trademark. Descriptive marks, geographic marks, and personal names are entitled to weak protection since the word or design has other meanings in addition to its use as a mark. An ordinary mark can, however, become distinctive over time through the public's association of the mark with the product.

This is known as acquiring secondary meaning. Suggestive marks and arbitrary and fanciful marks receive the strongest protection due to their unique nature. The strength of a mark is indicative of its economic value and the scope of legal protection it may enjoy. The stronger the mark, the easier it is to prove infringement. Trademark protection is based on use, and a trademark will not expire, as long as its commercial significance is maintained. However, trademark protection will end if the mark becomes generic.

Ask Author Law

Q: I am writing a novel and was told by an editor that I must remove the words "Ford," "Greyhound," "Chrysler," et cetera, or be prepared to fork over royalties. I've never been told this before, and don't know what to do. I've researched trade name law but can't find anything pertaining to this in particular. If I'm using, say, Ford, as simply stating what my character drives, (i.e., a Ford pickup) does this pose ligitimacy to said editor's advice? Any information you can share is most sincerely appreciated.

A: This editor is way off base. Of course you can write about trademarked products in your fiction—the First Amendment gives you that right. What the trademark protection prevents you from doing is marketing your own automobile under the brand name of another or using the trademark in commerce or advertising without identifying it as a registered trademark. Your proposed use is legally acceptable and the editor is incorrect. Which leads me to ask just how credible this editor is about publishing issues. Is this someone you plan to do business with? If so, please be careful.

Q: I'd like to know about titles and trademarks. I understand that titles cannot be copyrighted, but what about trademarks? I'd like to trademark the title of my book because it's the first of a series of self-pub books and is the theme of the motivational speaking I do. Is it possible to trademark my title? If not, can I trademark a concept belonging to me? Does that mean someone else can't use this term in his title? If so, do I need to register my trademark somewhere like you do a copyright? Can I register it myself? What if I just use a trademark symbol without the hassle of registration. I hope you can shed some light on this perplexing topic. I need to go to law school!

A: As you know, copyright protects the exact expression of ideas, but not the underlying facts or concepts. Trademark can protect underlying concepts and ideas if they identify the source of a product or service and help distinguish it from others in the minds of consumers. Trademark law really offers two kinds of protection—it protects consumers from being confused or misled about the source of products and services and it protects businesses from having the value invested in their brand and reputation from being ripped off by competitors. A good example from the field of publishing is the Hardy Boys juvenile detective series. Consumers know what to expect when they buy a Hardy Boys book, and because the concept is trademarked, the publisher has a right to keep others from stealing readers by using a title that includes the words "Hardy Boys."

Generally, you can't get trademark protection for individual titles, but you can protect the overall concept of your series of books and speaking programs because the trademark tells consumers who you are and what you offer that is different from the offerings of other speakers and authors. Trademark protection might be possible for an individual title if it develops something lawyers call "secondary meaning" by becoming so closely identified with a particular work or author that readers have come to associate the title with a particular work. *Gone with the Wind* is an example of a title that has acquired secondary meaning.

From the description of your idea for a series of books and related programs, it sounds like your concept would qualify for trademark protection. It is permissible to use the TM symbol with any mark, even if it is unregistered. The ® symbol, however, cannot be used with a mark unless the mark has been registered by the Patent and Trademark Office. While it's possible to handle trademark registration yourself, it's a much more complex process than copyright registration and there are numerous ways to get into trouble along the way. I routinely advise clients to save money by registering their own copyrights, but I almost always advise that trademark registrations be handled by an experienced intellectual property attorney.

Tips and Tools: Should You Register Your Own Trademark?

Registration of a trademark is complicated and best handled by a trademark lawyer, but that being said, it is possible for an individual to register her own trademark. Registration at either the federal level or the state level will list your mark in an official register to alert others to its existence and will provide you with additional benefits should you ever need to sue anyone for infringement. While in general, registered trademarks receive a higher level of protection than unregistered marks, not all registrations are equal. You can register your trademark at either the state or federal level, and registering it in both places can often work to your advantage.

You may register your mark with a state's secretary of state if you have used your mark locally within that state. A mark must be in use in that state before it can be registered. State laws differ, but generally state registration places your mark in the state register and in some cases, provides additional benefits such as the right to collect attorneys' fees or punitive damages. While state trademark law cannot narrow the rights provided by federal law, it may provide additional rights and benefits.

Under the Lanham Act, the federal statute pertaining to trademarks, an unregistered trademark may receive protection similar to that of a registered mark in certain circumstances if it is used in commerce. As the owner of an unregistered mark you could, for example, bring a federal claim for false designation of origin or for false advertising. However, federal registration makes it easier to prove infringement and permits recovery of injunctive relief, money damages, and treble damages.

Your application for federal registration may be based upon either the use of a mark or the intent to use a mark in interstate commerce, but registration may only be obtained once a bona fide use has occurred. Distinctive marks may be registered on the principal register, which immediately provides constructive notice of ownership and the priority date of filing; permits you to file an infringement suit in federal court; establishes prima facie evidence of the validity of the mark; and after five years of continuous use, can render the mark "incontestable." Incontestability status will prevent most challenges to the validity of your mark.

You may also apply for federal registration if your mark is not distinctive in nature but may acquire secondary meaning over time. In this case, your mark will be listed in the supplemental register, which provides few of the benefits of being listed on the principal register. A mark on the supplemental register, however, is on file with the Patent and Trademark Office and can be used to prevent a later registration of a similar mark on either register. Supplemental registration also entitles you to use the official notice of federal registration with your mark. If you are listed in the supplemental register, it is very difficult to prove infringement because your registration may be viewed as an implied admission that the mark is not inherently distinctive. You should first apply for registration on the principal register and then only apply for registration on the supplemental register if your application for the principal register is rejected.

Tips and Tools: Patent, Trademark, and Copyright Distinguished

Patents, copyrights, and trademarks all protect different elements of intellectual property. Patents provide protection for inventions, copyrights protect expression, and trademarks protect the goodwill and source identification of a product. The three forms of intellectual property can conceivably work together to provide protection for one product. For example, the product itself, an invention, can be patented while its instructions are protected by copyright and the name of the product and corporate logo are protected by trademark law.

Copyright law and patent law grant very different rights. While patent law grants an inventor a monopoly on the knowledge embodied in an invention, copyright law protects only the expression of an idea and not the idea itself. The two types of protection sometimes overlap as in the murky areas of **computer programs** and semiconductor chips. It is often difficult to discern whether a particular process constitutes an invention or a form of expression protected by copyright. While a computer program is generally accepted as copyrightable material, the underlying processes may be entitled to patent protection. On the other hand, the **Semiconductor Chip Protection Act** created a new form of intellectual property that combines elements of both patent and copyright law.

Trademark law and copyright law overlap in their protection of commercial goods. Unlike a copyright, which protects a work against copying, a trademark does not restrict the copying of a mark but instead prohibits a use that creates a likelihood of confusion and thus harms the trademark owner's goodwill against the sale of some other product as his. An artistic image protected by copyright may also be registered as a trademark if it identifies the source of a product and represents the goodwill of the owner in the marketplace. Furthermore, many instances of copyright infringement also involve actionable claims of trademark infringement and other unfair competition violations for the distribution and false identification of copyrighted goods in commerce. See **copyright**.

Trademark Office—The U.S. Patent and Trademark Office (PTO) is one of fourteen bureaus within the Department of Commerce. The PTO issues **patents**, registers **trademarks**, and administers the federal patent and trademark laws. The stated purpose of the PTO is to promote industrial and technological progress in the United States and to strengthen the national economy by administering the patent and trademark laws, and by advising the secretary of commerce, the president, and the administration on intellectual property issues.

Any member of the public can perform a free trademark search at the PTO Public Search Library, located at Madison East, 1st Floor, 600 Dulany St., Arlington, Virginia 22313. Library hours are 8:00 a.m. to 5:30 p.m. In addition, word marks may be searched at one of the seventy Patent and Trademark Depository Libraries throughout the country. Searches can also be conducted online through the Trademark Electronic Search System, available through the Patent and Trademark Office's Web site at www.uspto.gov.

Information about registering a trademark is available on the PTO's Web site. The forms may be downloaded and mailed in, or an application may be submitted through the Trademark Electronic Application System (TEAS).

The mailing address for the trademark division of the Patent and Trademark Office is: Commissioner for Trademarks, P.O. Box 1451, Arlington, Virginia 22313-1451. The telephone number for the Trademark Assistance Center is 800-786-9199 or 703-308-4357 for residents of northern Virginia. *See* **copyright office**.

Trade Books—This term refers to books published by traditional publishers and intended for the general public.

Trade Dress—Trade dress is protected by **trademark** law and it refers to the way in which a product or service is packaged. It includes all aspects of presentation when combined into an overall design or image of an item or the shape and appearance of a product and its container. Because the distinctiveness of a product lies at the crux of trade dress, courts will consider whether there is a likelihood of confusion between one product and an allegedly infringing product.

Trade Secrets—A trade secret is a type of intellectual property that consists of business information that a company wants to keep secret in order to obtain an advantage over its competitors. A trade secret can be a process, formula, pattern, or even a list of customers. The formula for Coca-Cola, for instance, is a trade secret. Trade secrets are protected by state law, and a business must generally make reasonable efforts to preserve the confidentiality of the information in order to secure a valid trade secret property right in the information. A trade secret will be protected from misappropriation by an infringer who obtains the information through improper methods or a breach of confidentiality. Infringement of a trade secret is a tort, and a court will consider whether the information is valuable and secret, and whether it was obtained in an improper manner. There are, however, several legal methods of discovering a trade secret, including independent discovery and reverse engineering.

Translations—Translations of a copyright-protected work are independently protectable by copyright as **derivative works,** provided the creator of the derivative work has the necessary permission.

Treaties—Formal multinational agreements that govern relations between countries are called treaties. The **Berne Convention** is an example of a major treaty governing copyright law at an international level. Treaties that have been ratified by the U.S. Senate have the same force and effect as a federal statute.

Trespass for Reporters—Despite the first amendment and freedom of the press, reporters are not exempt from most laws. They must respect the property rights and privacy of others and are subject to liability for breaking laws such as the laws against trespass.

The Courts Say: Undercover Investigative Reporters May Be Liable for Trespass

Food Lion, Inc. v. Capital Cities/ABC, Inc., 194 F.3d 505 (4th Cir. 1999)

The Food Lion grocery store chain, which was the subject of an undercover investigation of its food handling practices by ABC's *Prime Time Live* television program, sued the network, its corporate parent, and the two network reporters who conducted the investigation for fraud, breach of duty of loyalty, and trespass. The two reporters had been

---

hired by Food Lion, on the basis of false job applications, and secretly recorded the activities and conversations they witnessed during the few weeks they worked there. The fourth circuit affirmed the district court's ruling that the reporters were liable for trespass. The court applied the laws of North Carolina and South Carolina where the activities occurred and noted that in both states it is considered trespass to enter upon another's land without consent. Although the reporters had Food Lion's consent to enter the store as employees even though they had obtained that consent through misrepresentations on their job applications, that consent could not serve a defense to trespass because they committed wrongful acts in excess of their authority as employees.

The court concluded that the reporters trespassed because they exceeded their authority as employees when they breached their duty of loyalty owed to Food Lion as their employer by using hidden cameras to capture activities in the nonpublic areas of the store. In response to the defendants' claims that the reporters were engaged in news gathering and thus Food Lion's claims should have been subject to heightened scrutiny under the First Amendment, the court concluded that the press does not enjoy special immunity from generally applicable laws.

U

U.S. Government Publications—Publications of the U.S. government are not eligible for copyright protection and are part of the public domain. In general, documents created by federal government employees within the scope of their official duties are not eligible for copyright protection.

There are, however, some significant exemptions to the general rule. The federal government can enforce any copyright assigned or otherwise transferred to it. It is also possible for the U.S. government to hold a copyright in a work prepared by a third party under a government commission or grant. Whether or not copyright protection extends to a particular work prepared by a third party is determined by the particular situation and a balance of public policy interests. In addition, copyright protection extends to postage stamp designs and other works of the U.S. Postal Service. When copying a government work, it is always a good idea to check with the particular agency to confirm the copyright status of the particular document you intend to use. Publications created by foreign, state, or local governments are generally eligible for copyright protection and should not be assumed to be in the public domain.

Unbound Sheets—Unbound sheets are printed sets of book pages that are left loose and stored for future use. Often un-

bound sheets are sold to book clubs, foreign publishers, or custom publishers as part of a **subsidiary rights** deal. Sometimes
unbound sheets are used for trade paperbacks or special deluxe
editions.

Unfair Competition—Unfair competition is a legal principle that
generally refers to fraudulent competition in trade or commerce,
usually by misleading the public as to the origin of a product or
service. Unfair competition frequently involves the imitation of
the distinctive details of a product or its packaging to confuse the
consumer into believing that there is a connection between that
product and another product or company. The dishonest activity
does not need to rise to the level of trademark infringement, and
the product does not need to be a counterfeit of the original.

The Federal Trade Commission enforces consumer protection
laws designed to protect the public from unfair competition and
other deceptive trade practices. Federal protection from unfair
competition is contained in the Lanham Act and other federal
legislation. While the Lanham Act generally deals with trademarks, it establishes broader causes of action for unfair competition, including false designation of origin and false descriptions
and representations of fact. Most states provide protection to the
public from various forms of unfair competition through specific
legislation as well as the state's common law, although a state law
may be preempted by a federal law that confers similar benefits.

Universal Copyright Convention—The UCC is one of the two
major international treaties the United States is a member of, the
other being the **Berne Convention**. The UCC was signed in Geneva in 1952 and revised in Paris in 1971. The UCC requires
that member states extend the same copyright protection to the
published and unpublished works of authors of the other member countries that they extend to their own authors. The United
States became a member of the convention in 1955 and is still a

member today, although it also has become a member of the more important Berne Convention.

University Presses—Many universities have established presses to publish academic and professional books and journals. The primary goal of a university press is to promote scholarly research and intellectual discourse. These presses often specialize in specific disciplines, such as philosophy, science, or management, and therefore appeal to niche markets. They may, however, also publish small numbers of trade books for a wider audience. University presses are nonprofit organizations and may offer lower royalties and less unfavorable terms compared to traditional trade publishers. *See* **academic authors**.

Unjust Enrichment—One theory for proving **damages** in a **copyright infringement** case is to show that the infringing party profited somehow from the infringement and was unjustly enriched as a result.

Unpublished Works—An unpublished work has not been distributed to the public by sale or other transfer of ownership, or by rental, lease, or lending. Copyright vests in a work at the time it is created, whether or not it is published. Unpublished works, therefore, are entitled to copyright protection just as published works are, and like published works, they can be registered with the U.S. Copyright Office.

Registration of a copyright in an unpublished work consists of the application along with the appropriate fee and one copy of the work.

Prior to January 1, 1978, unpublished works were eligible for a common law or state law copyright until the work was published or registered with the Copyright Office, at which point federal copyright protection would begin. This common law copyright was not subject to any limitation on duration as long as the work remained unpublished and unregistered. Common law copyright in the United States was generally abolished by the Copyright Act of 1976, which became effective on January 1, 1978.

Tools and Tips: When Should You Register Your Copyright in Unpublished Works?

Unpublished works are entitled to copyright protection even without the formality of registration. However, there are some specific considerations to bear in mind when deciding whether to register your copyright in your unpublished manuscript or other work. Registration of your copyright will provide you with many benefits that are not available to unregistered works regardless of publication.

Registration of your copyright prior to publication provides significant added protection from infringement, especially if you will be shopping your manuscript around to various publishers and agents in an effort to secure publication. Registration provides a public record of your work, and once the manuscript is no longer in your control, the possibility of infringement increases.

It is necessary to register any work created in the United States, whether it is published or not, prior to filing a lawsuit for copyright infringement. If you register your work prior to publication, or within five years after publication, you will establish prima facie evidence of the validity of the copyright, a valuable tool in court. Furthermore, if the unpublished work is registered prior to its infringement, statutory damages and attorneys' fees will be available to you in a court action. Otherwise, you will only be able to recover actual damages and profits, and with an unpublished work, calculating these figures will be a difficult task.

Registration of your unpublished work will also relieve you of the task of registering it upon publication. If you register your unpublished work and the published form is not substantially different, it is not necessary to reregister the work once it has been published. See **copyright**.

Uruguay Round—In September 1986, the Uruguay Round, the largest international trade negotiation in history, was launched in Punta del Este, Uruguay. The 125 participating governments dealt with all aspects of global trade, including intellectual property, and many agreements were not finalized until December 1993, more than seven years later. The Uruguay Round created the **World Trade Organization (WTO)** and resulted in the development of a series of agreements collectively known as the Uruguay Round Agreements. In 1994, the United States passed the Uruguay Round Agreements Act, which implemented the Uruguay Round Agreements, including the **Agreement on Trade-Related Aspects of Intellectual Property Rights (TRIPS)**.

V

VARA—Under the Visual Artists Rights Act of 1990 (VARA), artists enjoy the rights of integrity and attribution with respect to their works of **visual art**. VARA amended U.S. copyright law to protect an artist's right to be credited as the author of a work and to prevent the alteration or destruction of the work without the artist's permission. An artist additionally has the right to protect his or her honor and reputation by choosing not to be credited as the author of any distortion or modification of the work or the author of a work she did not create. These rights are commonly referred to as **moral rights**. VARA was enacted to bring the United States into compliance with the **Berne Convention** and international legal standards. The rights created by VARA are rights conferred on the artist rather than on the work of art itself, and exist independently of the artist's copyright in the work. These rights cannot be transferred. However, they may be waived by an express written statement by the artist. VARA protects the rights of the artist during his lifetime, and in the case of joint authors, during the lifetime of the last surviving artist. **Work made for hire** is not protected under VARA. VARA, as a federal law, generally **preempts** state laws that confer similar rights. However, some states, including California and New York, have enacted statutes that provide broader protection to visual artists. Rights conferred by state law, that fall outside the limited scope of VARA, provide additional legal protection to artists in those states. Because VARA is narrow in scope, offering protection only to artists for works meeting the limited definition of a work of visual art, writers seeking similar protection for their works must negotiate these rights in their publishing contracts.

Vanity Publisher—A vanity publisher generates income from the writer rather than the purchaser of a book. Vanity publishers require the writer to cover the costs of editing, producing, printing, and binding the book, and do not usually make affective efforts to market or distribute the book. Then when the books do not sell, the publisher urges the writer to pay more money to buy the books to save them from destruction. If the writer has assigned any copyright rights to the publisher, the publisher may try to sell those back to the writer.

While the practice of charging a writer to publish her book is not illegal, it is questionable. Some vanity publishers offer high royalty rates and promises of recouping up-front charges, but there is little chance of this happening. The vanity publisher typically publishes few copies of the book, makes no effort to get the book reviewed, and spends little or no effort in marketing or promoting the book. Furthermore, most book buyers and booksellers will not do business with vanity publishers.

Since vanity publishing has a dubious reputation, many vanity publishers will try to market themselves to would-be authors as a subsidy or joint-venture publisher. Whatever the terminology, look for the proof. Beware of contracts that do not firmly establish the number of books that will be printed at an established price and have an unusually high royalty rate or complex, ambiguous royalty clause. Also make sure that you understand what the financial commitment of the publisher is before signing a contract. If the publisher does not have a financial commitment to the book, you can be sure there will be no marketing or promotion of your work. Some vanity publishers do not even have a marketing department.

While there may be a very good reason for you to consider paying for the publication of your book, you should make certain that such an agreement is on your terms and does not require you to invest more than you can afford or are willing to spend. A few legitimate publishers will work with you to co-publish your book, but they usually provide specific services such as editing or printing and binding. They will not use the slick sales tactics that are the hallmark of a vanity publisher, and will not pressure you to sign a contract without giving you the opportunity to research the company and review the contract with an attorney. If you cannot go with a mainstream publisher, you may want to consider **self-publishing**, which allows you to outsource specific elements of the publishing process and thus remain in control of the costs involved in producing and marketing your book. *See also* **subsidy publisher**.

Venue—The term venue can refer either to the place where an incident leading to legal action occurred, or to the place where the trial will take place. These are often, but not always, the same place. A publishing contract may specify that the venue of any legal action arising from the contractual relationship will be the appropriate state or federal court in the state where the contract was signed or where the publishing company is located. Venue may also be waived in a contract, so it is important to make sure that the venue provision of any contract you sign does not interfere with your right to sue. Venue should not be confused with **jurisdiction**, which refers to the power of a court to decide a case.

Vetting—An author or publisher may choose to have a manuscript vetted, or thoroughly reviewed by an attorney, to guard against problems with libel, invasion of privacy, copyright ownership, or other legal pitfalls. In addition, manuscripts are routinely vetted by editors who may question facts and review for accuracy.

Video Displays—Video displays, including computer screen displays and **video game displays**, are entitled to copyright protection. It is generally not necessary to file a separate registration with the Copyright Office for the screen display and the underlying computer program or video game. The Copyright Office does not require a specific reference to the screen display in an application for a video game or computer program because it is considered to be a part of the entire work. However, a separate claim for the screen display may be made on an application for a video game or computer program, and the application would then need to include identifying material for those displays. If a sample of the video display is deposited, it should consist of a printout, photograph, or drawing of the screen. The Copyright Office will accept a $^1/_2$-inch VHS videotape for predominantly audiovisual works such as video games. In determining whether a video display is entitled to copyright protection, the Copyright Office will examine all of the identifying material submitted. *See* **copyright**.

Video Game Displays—Video games may be protected by copyright as audiovisual works because even though the idea of the game itself cannot be protected, the particular shapes, sizes, colors, sequences, arrangements, and sounds that add to the idea in the form of a video game display can be protected.

The Courts Say: Copyright Protection of a Video Game Depends on the Total Sequence of Images as the Game Is Being Played

Atari Games Corp. v. Oman 888 F.2d 878 (D.C. Cir. 1989)

The U.S. Court of Appeals for the District of Columbia reversed the decision of a district court and held that video games are entitled to copyright protection as audiovisual works. The lower court deter-

---

mined that the design and configuration of the video display of Break-out, the video game at issue, did not meet the minimum standard of artistic expression required by copyright law. The district court found that the game was a typical paddle-and-ball game and that the display, which consisted of a rectangular paddle directing a ball into colored rectangular bricks, as well as audio signals indicating when the ball collided with other characters, did not contain any artistic elements of expression that could be separated from the idea of the game itself. The district court upheld the determination of the Copyright Office that the game did not constitute a "work of authorship" under copyright law.

The court of appeals, however, concluded that in deciding whether a video game is entitled to copyright protection, consideration should be given to the total sequence of images displayed as the game is being played and not on the isolated images that appear on the screen. The court noted that simple shapes arranged in a distinctive manner are entitled to copyright protection, and artistic expression could be demonstrated in elements such as the colors and shapes used, the tone and duration of the sounds, and the speed and direction of the ball. See **copyright**.

Visual Art—The visual arts include painting, sculpture, photography, and other arts that are visual in nature and generally exist in a fixed form. Works of visual art are eligible for copyright protection.

Void/Voidable—In contract law, if an agreement is void, it is considered to be invalid and therefore has no legal force. On the other hand, a voidable contract is valid and enforceable. A voidable contract has the potential to become void at the option of one of the parties. These terms are sometimes incorrectly used interchangeably and it is important to ensure that any contract you enter into uses "void" only to signify something that is of no legal consequence and thus completely unenforceable.

Volunteer Lawyers for the Arts—Established in 1969, VLA is a nonprofit organization dedicated to providing pro bono legal services to creative professionals in the New York City area. The organization also provides educational programs on legal matters to lawyers and artists. VLA is made up of highly skilled volunteer lawyers who represent low-income artists and nonprofit arts organizations. The organization also maintains a free legal hot line, the Art Law Line, which is staffed by law students and volunteer lawyers who can answer art-related legal questions. The number is 212-319-ARTS, extension 1. Volunteer Lawyers for the Arts can be contacted at 1 East 53rd St, 6th floor, New York, NY 10022-4201. You can learn more about VLA at www.vlany.org. There are VLA organizations in some other cities. To find them check with your local Bar association or pro bono legal services programs. *See also* **pro bono.**

W

Waiver—A waiver is the intentional surrender of a legal right. A publishing contract may expressly state that no provision within the agreement may be waived, altered, or modified without written permission from the publisher. Contracts also sometimes specify that the parties waive their right to sue in favor of arbitration. Any clause waiving your right to sue should be carefully considered and negotiated.

Warranties and Indemnities—In terms of contract law, a warranty is an assurance by one party that a fact may be relied upon by another party. In a publishing contract, a writer may warrant to a publisher that he or she has the authority to enter into the contract and that the work at issue does not infringe any copyright or other proprietary right, or contain defamatory or otherwise unlawful material. An indemnity is a promise by the writer.

Tools and Tips: How to Deal with Indemnification Clauses

A position paper from the contracts committee of the American Society of Journalists and Authors—reprinted with permission

Warranty and indemnity (aka indemnification) clauses can be among the most onerous of contract provisions that writers today may encounter. Exact language may vary, but typically these zingers involve some variation on the theme "you will indemnify and hold harmless the publisher against any and all claims or actions arising out of a breach or alleged breach of the foregoing warranties." What do warranty and indemnification mean and how should you deal with such clauses?

In legalese, when you warrant something, you are making a representation that the other party can rely on as being true. Warranty clauses in publishing contracts often start out with fairly reasonable representations: that the work has not been previously published and you are not plagiarizing someone else's writing, for example. No problem there. But keep reading. They often go on to say that you warrant the work "contains no defamatory, libelous, or unlawful matter and Publisher's exploitation of its rights shall not violate or infringe any copyright rights, rights of privacy and/or publicity, or *any other* statutory, common law, or other rights of any party," or words to that effect. Hmmm. Can you really represent that no portion of your article violates *any* provision of law in fifty states or any country? Or that your writing or the publisher's use "will not violate or infringe upon" such a wide range of possible "rights"? Of course not.

Yet that indemnity clause puts serious financial teeth behind just such a warranty—and the bank account they bite will be your own!! By "indemnifying and holding harmless" your publisher (and also, depending on how broadly written the provision is, the publisher's officers, directors, employees, agents, licensees, and others), you are agreeing to pick up the tab for warranty-related claims. The bottom line, of course, could include not only lawyers (at hundreds of dollars an hour) but also court costs and ultimately damage awards. Worse yet, under many of these clauses, you are agreeing to be liable for such costs on "all claims," a catch-all phrase that includes *even completely frivolous claims!*

A HISTORICAL PERSPECTIVE

Some say indemnity clauses first appeared in book publishing contracts (where, because of the dollar amounts potentially involved, they may make more financial sense) and were later imported by overeager counsel into magazine publishing. Recent reports suggest that many mainstream magazines are no longer routinely inserting indemnity clauses in their standard magazine publishing contracts. Whether this reflects these publishers' even more onerous predilection for all-rights contracts or a more reasonable assessment of the parties' respective rights and obligations remains to be seen.

YOUR POSITION AND POSSIBLE RESPONSES

Short of actual misconduct on your part (for which of course you *should* be held accountable), it is obviously unfair to ask a writer to underwrite defensive litigation. This is a sad cost of doing business for the publisher.

As you negotiate, remember that (unless you are John Grisham) the publisher probably does not *really expect* to look to your assets to bankroll defensive litigation. And you can point out that most publishers these days already carry libel and other forms of insurance to cover precisely such business contingencies. If you are presented with a publishing contract that includes a broad indemnity clause, the experience of ASJA members suggests a variety of possible responses:

1. Suggest that the clause be deleted. That's right—ask to strike the offending paragraph in its entirety. Point out that many major magazine publishers no longer insist on including such dreadful language. Highlight the respective financial abilities of the parties to defend potential suits. Inquire about whether the publisher already carries libel and other business liability insurance. Ask whether the publisher actually expects it would *get* anything if it pursued a writer's assets. Question whether the magazine really wants impartial reporting—and point out the "chilling effect" these clauses can have on honest (or even mildly negative) reporting where controversial issues are involved.

2. Limit your warranties to a "best of your knowledge" standard. To that onerous representation that no portion of your article violates *any* provision of law, or that your writing or the publisher's use "will not violate or infringe upon any rights of privacy and/or publicity or *any* other rights of any party," add six magic

324

words as a qualifier: to the best of Writer's knowledge. ASJAers report that many magazines routinely accept such a change to their boilerplate contract, perhaps because it makes such obvious sense.

3. Limit your obligation to final judgments. Emphasize that you do not intend to pick up the cost of defense for every frivolous lawsuit that comes down the pike. One more set of magic words: *provided that such liability is finally established by a court of competent jurisdiction, and that such judgment is sustained after all appeals have been exhausted.* Translation: you refuse to bear responsibility for the modern-day business reality of frivolous lawsuits. You will pick up the tab *only* if there is a judgment saying you screwed up—and provided the appeals courts ultimately agree. (Note: If you lose at the trial level, you may need to be prepared to *pay* for those appeals. And see the note below about settlements.)

4. Consider purchasing professional liability insurance. Particularly if you write in high lawsuit-prone areas (such as true crime), you may want to consider obtaining your *own* insurance. Sure, it is annoying to have to pay to cover a risk that arguably belongs to the publisher. But if it helps you sleep at night, it is a bargain. Plan B: find out if it is possible to tailgate on the publisher's liability insurance policy by having you named as an "additional insured."

5. Limit your warranties to what you yourself (and not your editor) wrote. Here is language one ASJA member inserted in his book contracts: "The parties agree that the foregoing warranties do not and will not apply to modifications of or additions to the text or illustrations made by the Publisher without the Author's knowledge or over the Author's objection." You might even just put a period after "Publisher."

6. Limit your potential liability to the contract price. This same ASJAer adds the following clause: "provided that the Author's liability hereunder is limited to the total sums payable to the Author under the terms of this Agreement" and, in the case of a book, "for the edition or printing of the Work in which the breach is alleged to have occurred." On a $1,000 magazine arti-

cle, that means your potential liability could be $1,000—not the roof over your head. A side note here: if the publisher does agree to such a limitation, make sure subsequent paragraphs do not undo that protection with broader, conflicting language.

CONCLUSION

The proliferation of indemnity clauses, especially in the magazine world, appears to be another case of lawyerly overkill. Do not get caught without a flak jacket. Insist on modifying the contract terms until you feel the risk you are assuming is acceptable.

A NOTE ABOUT SETTLEMENT

Worried that a publisher might decide to settle in an effort to keep costs down—and that that might reflect badly on you? Sad fact of life: the publisher will typically be a separate party in any lawsuit, so its decision to settle (or not) will not be yours to make. Often, the publisher's deeper pockets are a more appealing target—and give the publisher more inclination to settle. But settlement may be in your best interest as well. The vast majority of cases *are* settled before trial, often for purely financial reasons. And most settlement agreements stipulate that even if money is paid, it is "not an admission of any guilt or wrongdoing but solely in an effort to resolve a disputed claim."

Now the bad news: if a publisher settles *and* you have signed an indemnity agreement, you may be sent a bill for the settlement amount. Sure, you can try to fight it—by continuing your part of the lawsuit in hopes of proving at trial or on appeal that you were not at fault, for example, or by arguing that your agreement with the publisher is unenforceable. But it can be a costly battle.

Web (World Wide Web)—The World Wide Web is a popular way to display and view material on the **Internet**. While the Internet has been in existence since the late 1960s, the World Wide Web was created in the early 1990s. The terms are often used interchangeably, although the World Wide Web generally refers to information or Web pages viewed in a graphical browser interface such as Microsoft's Internet Explorer or Netscape's Navigator. Data is presented in a browser using HyperText Markup Language (HTML) and transmitted over the Internet using the HyperText Transport Protocol (HTTP).

Webcasting—A webcast is the digital performance of a **sound recording** on the **World Wide Web**, and is subject to the compulsory licensing requirements of the **Digital Millennium Copyright Act of 1998**. The statutory license is available for eligible certain noninteractive, non-broadcast, non-subscription transmissions. Webcasting does not include transmissions from terrestrial radio and television broadcast stations because they are subject to the licensing rates and regulations of the Federal Communications Commission (FCC).

Webcasting involves several, often complex, layers of copyright ownership. In the case of a **musical work**, licenses must be obtained from both the copyright owner of the musical composition and the copyright owner of the sound recording. Licenses can be obtained from **performing rights societies** or directly from the copyright owners. The copyright law allows webcasters to make one ephemeral recording in order to transmit the webcast from a server if certain requirements are met. However, a separate ephemeral recording license must be obtained if more than one copy will be made, and these licenses are generally negotiated directly with the copyright owners.

Web Page—A Web page is a document that exists on the **World Wide Web**. Each Web page can be identified and accessed with a unique universal resource locator (URL), or address. A basic Web page consists of text and code, often HTML, and sometimes graphic materials or dynamically generated content from a database. A collection of related, interlinked Web pages is called a **Web site**.

Web Publishing—The process of making a coded **Web page** file available for viewing on the **World Wide Web** is often referred to as publishing the page. This definition, however, is not recognized for purposes of the U.S. Copyright Office. There are currently no regulations defining the publication of an online work, and therefore it is up to you to tell the Copyright Office whether you consider your work to be published or unpublished for copyright registration purposes.

Web Rights—The rights and remedies available to the authors and users of online material are evolving. Many laws currently in effect were drafted before digital technology revolutionized popular culture, academia, the business world, and the publishing industry. New laws have been passed to attempt to rectify the situation, but this legislation has been largely reactive rather than proactive.

In general, copyright law provides the same rights and protections to works available in a fixed, digital format on the **Internet** as it does to works available in hard copy. Due to rapid advances in technology, however, it is more difficult to actually protect works available online. Copying is easier, and while a photocopy of a page from a hard copy book looks obviously like a copy, material online can be downloaded, printed, cut-and-pasted, or linked with virtually no distinction between the original and the copy.

Web Site—A Web site is a collection of **Web pages** on the **World Wide Web**. Each Web site consists of a home page, and may contain other static or database-generated pages that link to each other. Web sites may be owned and managed privately or by a corporation or organization. The **domain name** of a Web site is not protected by copyright law.

Creating and maintaining a Web site is a good way for writers and publishers to gain public exposure. A Web site can be used to solicit business or to make your ideas and creations available to others. However, it is important to be aware of the risks involved in posting your work on a Web site because it is very easy to download material and copy material from one Web site to another. While there are many copyright protection systems available, such as digital watermarking, effective enforcement measures for the protection of copyrighted materials online are still in their infancy.

Original material posted on each Web page belonging to a Web site is subject to copyright protection just as a hard copy would be. The original material, including text, photographs, artwork, audiovisual items, and music or sound recordings, contained on a Web site can be registered with the U.S. Copyright Office. Because there are currently no regulations in place to handle the registration of online material, the registration procedure is the same as that for hard copies. Material appearing on a Web site may be deposited with the Copyright Office in one of two ways. First a clearly labeled computer disk containing the entire work can be submitted, along with representative portions of the work in a format that can be examined by the Copyright Office, such as a printout or videotape. Alternatively, you may submit a reproduction of the entire work, regardless of length, in an appropriate format. Material on a Web site that also is distributed in hard copy, such as a book or video, need only fulfill the deposit requirement for the hard copy. **Computer programs**, **databases**, and works fixed in CD-ROM format that are transmitted online are subject to different registration rules.

Web sites are often revised to present updated information or a new version of a work. The **Copyright Office** requires a separate application and filing fee for each new revision that constitutes copyrightable authorship. In other words, minor changes would not require a new copyright application.

Wholesale—Publishers frequently offer writers a set number of copies of their published work at wholesale prices, often 30 percent to 50 percent off the retail price. This is generally a negotiable clause in the contract. A writer may request more books or a deeper discount. Many writers use these copies to resell at speaking engagements and conferences or to send to those who assisted in the preparation of the work.

Wills, Trusts, and Estates—Copyright is a form of property and may be owned, sold, assigned, or inherited. Like other property, the disposition of a copyright upon the death of the owner may be established by will. A will is a basic legal instrument that states a person's wishes regarding the distribution of his or her property at death. This is a state-specific area of law, and an attorney should *always* be consulted. In addition to your copyrights, your personal property at death will include your manuscripts, unpublished papers, publishing contracts, royalties, and any other related materials. You may make separate provisions for your copyrights and the works they protect. Depending on your individual situation, you may want to consider naming a literary executor in your will to handle these matters.

If you have literary assets such as continuing royalties, a trust can be created to ensure that the assets benefit your chosen heirs. A trust is a legal entity created by a grantor, and managed by a trustee, for the benefit of designated beneficiaries. There are many different types of trusts, and an attorney or accountant in your state can assist you in finding one to suit your circumstances. You may want to appoint a literary trustee who can maintain the publishing contracts and copyrights that provide the source of income for the trust.

Copyrights, manuscripts, unpublished papers, publishing contracts, and related interests are considered part of your estate. If your estate is large enough, it may be subject to an estate tax. Proactive estate planning, in consultation with an attorney and an accountant in your state, can ensure that your beneficiaries reap the benefits of your hard work.

Tools and Tips: What Is a Literary Executor and Do You Need One?

A literary executor can be named in a will for the limited purposes of managing and distributing the literary property of an estate. The executor of an estate is often a family member or close friend who may have no specialized knowledge of copyrights and publishing matters. A literary executor, on the other hand, should be someone who understands the publishing industry and who can negotiate contracts and assert your rights on behalf of your beneficiaries. The literary executor can be appointed as an advisor to the executor of the estate or can be vested with broad authority to make all decisions regarding your literary property. If you decide to appoint a literary executor, it is important that you clearly define the responsibilities and duties of the position, and any compensation, in your will.

A literary executor can handle any or all of the following matters:

- Copyright maintenance. This may include the sale, transfer, or license of any rights provided by copyright, the termination of copyright licenses, copyright registration, and the authority to bring suit for copyright infringement.
- Distribution of your personal papers and unpublished works in whatever manner you choose. You may choose, for instance, to have your manuscripts archived at a university, your unpublished books and poems published, and your personal letters destroyed.
- Contract negotiation. This includes negotiation with literary agents, publishers, and other interested parties; the authority to establish royalty rates; and the ability to issue payment as required.
- Royalty management. The literary executor may also be the literary trustee of a trust.

Work Made for Hire—Work made for hire is a concept that confuses even the most sophisticated of copyright experts. That's because under copyright law there are two distinct definitions, one or the other of which, but not both, will apply. Section 101 of the Copyright Act says that a work made for hire is (1) a work prepared by an employee within the scope of his or her employment, *or* (2) a work specially ordered or commissioned as a contribution to a collective work, as a part of a motion picture or other audiovisual work, as a translation, as a supplementary work, as a compilation, as an instructional text, as a test, as answer material for a test, or as an atlas, if the parties expressly agree in a written instrument signed by them that the work shall be considered a work made for hire.

The employer or party for whom the work was prepared is considered the author of the WMFH, unless the contract between the parties expressly states otherwise. The employer or commissioning party owns *all* the rights included in the copyright, and the writer who signs a valid WMFH agreement has *no* further rights in the work.

The designation of a work as a WMFH carries with it other significant consequences. For example, a work made for hire is protected by copyright for a term of ninety-five years from the date of publication or one hundred and twenty years from the date of creation, whichever expires first. The term of copyright for other works is the author's life plus seventy years. In addition, a WMFH designation affects the owners' renewal rights, termination rights regarding transfers and licenses, and the right to import or publicly distribute certain goods bearing the copyright.

In situations where it is not clear whether a work has been made for hire, the status of the work is determined by the relationship between the parties: is the writer an employee or an independent contractor? The common law of agency is used to determine whether a writer is an employee or an independent contractor. Because the copyright act is a federal law, courts will not use definitions created by individual states.

The Courts Say: There Are Several Factors to Consider in Determining Whether an Employer-Employee Relationship Exists

Community for Creative Non-Violence v. Reid 490 U.S. 730 (U.S. 1989)

The U.S. Supreme Court has held that a key issue in determining if a work is a WMFH is if the work was prepared by an employee or an independent contractor. If the work was created by an employee, as defined in the common law of agency, then it is a WMFH. In determining that the artist hired by a nonprofit organization to design a particular sculpture was an independent contractor and therefore the author of the work and the owner of the copyright, the Court listed several factors that must be considered in determining the nature of the employment relationship. These factors include the skill required, the source of instrumentalities and tools used in the creation of the work, the location of the work, the duration of the relationship between the parties, the hiring party's right to assign additional projects to the hired party, the extent of the hired party's discretion over when and how long to work, the method of payment, the hired party's role in hiring and paying assistants, the regular business of the hiring party, whether employee benefits have been provided to the hiring party, and the tax treatment of the hired party.

The Court determined that the artist was not an employee of the organization because the artist supplied his own tools, worked in his own studio in another city, was retained for less than two months, had absolute freedom to decide when and how long to work, was paid a sum dependent on the completion of a specific job, and had discretion in hiring and paying any assistants. The Court also noted that the organization was in the business of combating homelessness, not sculpting; did not pay payroll or social security taxes for the artist; and did not provide him with any employee benefits.

Tools and Tips: Work Made for Hire Myths and Misconceptions

Many misconceptions have grown up around the concept of WMFH.

Myth: If I'm an independent contractor it can't be a work made for hire.
Fact: The copyright law has a specific provision that permits specially commissioned works to be works made for hire *if* the work falls into one of the qualifying categories *and* the parties have agreed ahead of time in writing signed by both of them that it's a WMFH. When the commissioning party and the publisher agree ahead of time that a qualifying work by an independent contractor is to be a work made for hire and that agreement is signed by the independent contractor, then the contracting publisher will be deemed the legal author and copyright owner.

Myth: I get royalty payments for a book I was commissioned to write, so that means it can't be a work made for hire.
Fact: Work made for hire and the method of payment are two independent concepts. The parties to a work made for hire agreement can provide for a royalty payment plan. Conversely, a publisher might pay a flat fee to exclusively license a work from an author who retains the copyright.

Myth: Any literary work can be a work made for hire.
Fact: There are only nine categories of works made for hire. If the type of work isn't one of them, then it will not be deemed a work for hire *despite* a written agreement. In all cases where there might be doubt as to the WMFH status and corresponding copyright ownership, the written agreement between the parties should also contain language *assigning* copyright ownership to the commissioning party. Absent a specific assignment of the copyright, the author rather than the commissioning party will be the owner of the copyright.

The Courts Say: Can You Lose Your Copyright Through a Check Endorsement?

Playboy Enterprises, Inc., v. Dumas 53 F.3d 549 (2d Cir. 1995)

Playboy sued the widow of artist Patrick Nagel, seeking a declaration from the court that it was the sole owner of the copyrights in the artist's paintings that had appeared in the magazine from 1974 to 1984. The only evidence of a written agreement signed by both parties was a series of endorsed checks, rendering payment for each painting, which included a legend stating, in some cases, that the work was made for hire and language designed to transfer various rights in the work to the publisher. Three separate check legends were used over time. The Second Circuit Court of Appeals held that the legend on the back of a check indicating that the payee assigned "all right, title and interest" in a painting was not sufficient to transfer copyright in the work to the publisher. The court found that a check endorsement may constitute a valid writing for the purposes of federal copyright law if the legend on the check confirms an agreement, either explicit or implicit, made prior to the creation of the work. Considering each of the three different versions of the check legend, the court determined that only the legends that expressly addressed a work made for hire relationship were valid on that topic. Where a valid work made for hire agreement existed, the publisher became the copyright owner. The court found that by continuing to endorse the checks, it could be assumed that the artist consented to the work-for-hire relationship even though there was no evidence of a prior agreement. The court concluded that where the check legend was ambiguous and did not expressly mention that the work was made for hire or that the entire copyright transferred to the publisher, the copyright remained with the artist.

The district court, to which the case was remanded, concluded that only the artist himself, not one of his agents, was able to authorize a work made for hire relationship by means of a check endorsement.

Sample Work Made for Hire Agreement

This is a contract for a commercial booklet written for a drug manufacturer on a WMFH basis. The WMFH language is appropriate (although draconian) for purposes of securing the copyright in the publisher's name. Note that the trade-off for this particular writer is that the publisher ("Buyer") assumes all liability— something that was very important to the writer. The writer didn't insist on having the copyright because this was a strictly commercial piece. The payment terms also favored the publisher somewhat, but the writer found them typical and acceptable.

WORK MADE FOR HIRE AGREEMENT

This is a work made for hire agreement between Author Name ("Author") whose address is Complete Address and Buyer Name ("Buyer") whose address is Complete Address. The parties agree that:

I. Author Name has written a specially commissioned work made for hire of approximately _____ words tentatively entitled "Title of Work" ("the Work") for which Buyer Name has agreed to pay a total of $5,400.00 (five thousand four hundred dollars) payable as follows: $400.00 (four hundred dollars) upon signing of this agreement; and the balance of $5,000.00 (five thousand dollars) upon publication of Work.

The Copyright Act requires that specific language in order for a work to qualify as a work made for hire. It isn't entirely clear that the "Work" falls into one of the categories of a work made for hire. The language in Paragraph I above, for example, would not suit a non-fiction book, which is not eligible for WMFH status. Paragraph I is also somewhat atypical in that it covers payment terms in the first paragraph. This agreement would be fairer to the writer if it were to specify that copyright doesn't transfer until full payment has been made, an important protection against giving up the copyright and then not getting paid.

2. For the good and valuable consideration described in Paragraph I above, Author Name hereby conveys ownership of all rights in the Work, including copyright, to Buyer Name and agrees that, to the extent required by applicable law in the event that the Work is ever determined not to be a work made for hire, he/she will and hereby does assign, free of any liens or encumbrances, all of her worldwide right, title, and interest in said Work to Buyer Name, including, without limitation, any and all copyrights and all physical elements of said Work, to have and to hold unto his successors and assigns, and this document shall be proper evidence thereof.

Paragraph 2 makes up for any language deficiency in the WMFH provision of Paragraph I by including "belt and suspenders" language that makes it clear that copyright is being assigned to the Buyer with unambiguous terminology. If this were a contract for a nonfiction book, this additional assignment language would be necessary to secure the copyright for the buyer.

3. In exchange for full ownership of all rights in said Work, Buyer Name agrees to indemnify Author Name and hold him harmless from any claims, suits, action, losses, or damages incurred or sustained by him in connection with or resulting from any claim, suit, action or proceeding arising out of or relating to Buyer Name's use, adaptation, distribution or publication of the Work.

In exchange for turning over the copyright, this agreement provides for a full indemnification in the event of any claims against the writer. This is only fair. If a writer must give up all rights, he should also be released from liability.

IN WITNESS WHEREOFF the parties hereto have duly executed this agreement as of the day and year written below.

Date: _____   By: _____

                                          Buyer Name

Date: _____   By: _____

                                          Author Name

Work Product—Work product generally consists of notes, documents, memoranda, and other materials prepared in preparation of another document, story, or case. The confidentiality of certain types of work product, such as that of attorneys or reporters, may be protected under federal or state law.

Attorney Work Product. The work product of an attorney consists of any materials prepared by an attorney or other representative in anticipation of litigation or for trial. Most states have laws or court rules protecting the confidentiality of attorney work product. A party may apply to the court for access to the work product of another attorney if he can demonstrate a substantial need for the material. However, an attorney's mental impressions, conclusions, opinions, or legal theories are always protected from disclosure. Of course a party does not need to apply to a court for access to the work product of his attorney.

Reporter's Notes. The confidential information and sources of information of a reporter are protected from disclosure during legal proceedings in most states. These laws are known as **press shield** laws and usually require that the privileged information be obtained in the course of the reporter's professional duties.

World Intellectual Property Organization—The WIPO, based in Geneva, Switzerland, was established in 1970 when the United

International Bureaux for the Protection of Intellectual Property became the World Intellectual Property Organization. In 1974, the WIPO became a specialized agency of the United Nations. The organization promotes intellectual property protection on a global level and oversees various international conventions, including the **Berne Convention**. The organization currently comprises 182 member states and has been instrumental in shaping international law to protect the rights of intellectual property owners around the world.

Part of the WIPO's mission is to ensure that international laws and standards encompass new technologies and address current issues in the field of intellectual property. In 1996, for example, the organization implemented the WIPO Copyright Treaty to bring computer programs and other new media within the scope of the Berne Convention. The treaty addresses the rights of distribution, rental, and communication to the public, and mandates that signatories of the treaty provide adequate legal protections and remedies against the circumvention of effective technological measures used by authors to protect their work. The United States signed the treaty on March 6, 2002.

In 1996, the WIPO entered into a cooperation agreement with the **World Trade Organization** (WTO), and the two organizations have since participated in joint programs to provide developing countries with technical assistance to enact and enforce intellectual property laws and to modernize their intellectual property systems in order to comply with the requirements of the WTO's **Agreement on Trade-Related Aspects of Intellectual Property Rights (TRIPS)**. WIPO's Web site: www.wipo.int.

World Rights—World rights are often negotiable in a publishing contract. In magazine publishing, it is common to negotiate **First North American Serial Rights**, leaving the writer free to negotiate world rights at another time, or with another publisher. World rights may be granted in full, or may be negotiated on a per-country or per-language basis.

World Trade Organization—The World Trade Organization (WTO), headquartered in Geneva, Switzerland, is an international organization that deals with the rules of trade between nations. The WTO was established on January 1, 1995, as a result of the **Uruguay Round** negotiations and currently consists of 148 member countries, including the United States. WTO agreements are negotiated, signed, and ratified by these member countries. One of the organization's main goals is to ensure the free flow of international trade. The organization provides a forum for trade negotiations and for settling trade disputes.

Prior to the creation of the WTO, the **GATT Treaty** (General Agreement on Tariffs and Trade) governed international commerce. From its inception in 1948, GATT provided both trade rules and tariff concessions. The acronym GATT not only refers to the treaty but also to the organization that was established to support it. The organization was replaced by the WTO, but an updated version of the GATT treaty is still in effect. The general principles of the original GATT treaty relating to intellectual property have been incorporated into the **Agreement on Trade-Related Aspects of Intellectual Property Rights (TRIPS)**, administered by the World Trade Organization, which establishes ground rules for the global protection of copyrights and other forms of intellectual property used in international trade.

The WTO has entered into a cooperation agreement with the **World Intellectual Property Organization** (WIPO) to facilitate implementation of TRIPS. The two organizations have participated in joint programs to provide developing countries with technical assistance to enact and enforce intellectual property laws and to modernize their intellectual property systems in order to comply with the requirements of TRIPS. WTO's Web site is www.wto.org.

Writers Guild of America—The WGA protects and promotes the interests of writers in radio, television, video, motion pictures, and related industries. The guild provides representation for its members in resolving disputes and participates in the negotiation and ratification of collective bargaining agreements. The guild also actively lobbies for improved domestic and foreign copyright legislation. Prospective members living west of the Mississippi can contact the Writers Guild of America, West at 7000 West Third Street, Los Angeles, CA 90048. The Web site is www.wga.org. The Writers Guild of America, East can be contacted at 555 West 57th St., Suite 1230 New York, NY 10019. The Web site is www.wgae.org.

Writers' Rights—Helping writers, particularly freelancers, protect the rights in their work has become increasingly important in the digital era. Many of the writers' organizations listed in this book are actively involved in rights advocacy. One of the best ways for individual writers to learn about their individual rights and responsibilities as authors is to join and become active in the writers' organizations for which they qualify.

Tales from the Trenches: Writers Emerge Victorious in Electronic Rights Fight

A recent class action settlement of more than $18 million marks a victory in a twelve year battle waged by freelance writers over electronic rights. See *In re Literary Works in Electronic Databases Copyright Litigation*, MDL No. 1379 (S.D.N.Y. March 31, 2005) (preliminary settlement) page 148.

The fight raged through the federal courts for eight years until the Supreme Court handed a win to writers in 2001. In *New York Times Co. v. Tasini*, 533 U.S. 483 (2001) (see page 183), the court held that publication of writers' works in digital databases without explicit consent constitutes infringement of their copyrights. In the wake of the *Tasini* decision, three separate class action suits were quickly filed by twenty-one individual writers and three writers' organizations. Those cases were consolidated into a single action that extended the battle over electonic rights for four more years.

In addition to money, writers organizations won the right to participate in and/or manage the process of notification and claim administration normally handled by firms specializing in class action administration. Sources familiar with the tortured negotiations reported many twists and turns along the way, some of them quite startling.

"Class action administration is big business," one source said. "I couldn't believe it when I heard about a proposed notice plan submitted by one of the folks in the class action biz. It was a 'standard' plan that included, among other expenses, a huge budget for ads in major newspapers. If that had gone through some of the publishers would actually have earned more in advertising than they had to pay for the infringements." Such absurdities galvanized the writers to press for, and get, some interesting concessions, including a role in notifying writers and handling claims, agreement from many of the publishers to include notices in their own publications at cost. The writers' organizations established a Web site (www.freelancerights.com) to help manage the notification claims process.

Nick Taylor, Authors Guild president, called the settlement substantial enough to vindicate freelancers who "deserve compensation and control of their work in the electronic marketplace." Statements of defendants were polite but less enthusiastic. *The New York Times* called the settlement "fair to all the parties involved" and one of the databases said it was pleased that authors and publishers had "come together for a settlement regarding the electronic use of copyrighted materials."

When asked if this settlement ends the e-rights war, sources said that it releases only the databases and the publishers who were directly named. Publishers not named in the suit would still be liable for infringements. Likewise, writers included in the class are barred from suing once the claims have been paid. Another source suggested that writers not included in the class could probably find a basis to seek damages. "I think it's fair to say the war may not be completely over, but the major battles are behind us now," the source observed.

Others foresee major battles to come. A seasoned veteran suggests that the rights wars should have been waged on two fronts, but the freelance community focused on the past and neglected the future. The lawsuits triggered a corresponding "rights grab" by many publishers; so, although the class action was a good thing to do, and the settlement was a validation, the legal approach by itself wasn't enough to insure important future rights, the veteran said. "With very few exceptions, if you want to write for magazines or newspapers today, you pretty much have to give up the underlying rights that made the settlement payments possible."

X

X-Rated—An X rating indicates that the material contained in a film is intended for adults only. In 1990 the Motion Picture Association of America (MPAA) replaced its X rating with an NC-17 rating (no children under seventeen admitted). The substitution was meant to mitigate the stigma attached to x-rated material. Erotica is often considered x-rated material, and writers of erotica may find their work subject to various forms of censorship. Erotic literature is sometimes considered pornography, although the latter term most often applies to visual material. There have been attempts by national, state, and local governments to regulate sex-related or otherwise "offensive" content on the **World Wide Web**. *See* **obscenity**.

X-Ray—An X-ray is an example of copyrightable subject matter that is often overlooked when thinking about copyright law. An X-ray is subject to copyright protection as a photographic image fixed in a tangible medium of expression. However, if the individual taking the X-ray is an employee, the X-ray is a **work made for hire** and the employer is considered the author of the X-ray for copyright purposes. X-rays are part of a person's medical record, and the confidentiality of this type of health information is protected by various federal and state privacy laws. There are times, however, when X-rays are the subject of copyright disputes. One photographer/artist, for example created side-by-side photographs and X-rays of seashells as distinctive works of art.

Y

Young Adult Books—"Young adult" is an age classification that publishers, librarians, and educators have designated for midgrade and middle school readers. Young adult books, often called "YA," can be of any genre, including science fiction, mystery, romance, or biography. These books often deal with issues faced by teenagers, and the coming-of-age story is a popular theme.

Z

Zapruder Film—On November 22, 1963, Abraham Zapruder was among the people lined up along a parade route in Dallas to see President John F. Kennedy go by. As the presidential motorcade approached, he focused his 8 mm movie camera and ended up capturing the assassination of President Kennedy on home movie film. The Zapruder film became a key piece of evidence in the inquiry following the assassination. Mr. Zapruder then sold his film and his copyright interest in it to *Life* magazine, a division of Time, Inc.

However, in *Time, Inc., v. Bernard Geis Associates*, 293 F. Supp. 130 (S.D.N.Y. 1968), the U.S. District Court for the Southern District of New York held that the defendant's publication of various frames of the Zapruder film in a book about the assassination was **fair use**. When *Life* refused to grant the defendant permission to reprint the frames, the defendant commissioned sketches of the frames to be used in place of the actual images. The court determined that the sketches were in fact identical copies. Concluding that the defendant's use of the film was a fair use, the court found that there is a public interest in having the fullest information available concerning the assassination, and that there was little injury to *Life* from the defendant's use of the frames. The court noted that there was no competition between the plaintiff and defendant and reasoned that the frames used in the defendant's book were merely supportive of the defendant's theory and were not the main subject of the book.

About the Authors

Stacy Davis is a lawyer, editor, and author. Admitted to the courts of New York, she has practiced in the areas of publishing and immigration law. She has worked as a staff editor for a major legal publisher and as a freelance editor for several clients.

Karen Dustman received her *Juris Doctor* degree from U.C.L.A., where she served on two law reviews and worked as an extern for a Federal District Court judge. Admitted in the courts of California and Nevada, she combines the practice of law with a successful freelance writing career as the author of three books and more than a hundred articles.

Anthony Elia is litigator with a New York firm. He is admitted to practice in New York courts and before the United States Patent and Trademark Office as a registered patent attorney. His work in the field of intellectual property law includes counsel, litigation, and negotiation on behalf of authors and writers' organizations.

Sallie Randolph is a practicing attorney and writer. Admitted to practice in New York and in the federal district court in Washington, D.C., she concentrates her law practice on the representation of individual authors, usually by consulting with or serving as co-counsel to other attorneys on publishing and copyright matters.

Her authorship credits include six books; dozens of magazine, newspaper, and legal articles; speeches; scripts; presentations; newsletters; editorial projects; instructional materials; commissioned works; and collaboration on the legal chapter of *The ASJA Guide to Freelance Writing: A Professional Guide to the Business, for Nonfiction Writers of All Experience Levels*, edited by Timothy Harper (St. Martin's Griffin, 2003).

A frequent speaker at programs for writers and lawyers, she has also taught writing, journalism, and law in a variety of educational settings. Her teaching experience includes a clinical professorship for several semesters at State University of New York at Buffalo School of Law, where she developed a copyright compliance program, instructed and supervised law student interns, taught courses in author law and legal ethics, and directed a publishing and copyright clinic.